BOUNDARIES
IN MARRIAGE

Resources by Henry Cloud and John Townsend

Books

Boundaries (and workbook)
Boundaries in Dating (and workbook)
Boundaries in Marriage (and workbook)
Boundaries with Kids (and workbook)
Boundaries with Teens (Townsend)
Changes That Heal (and workbook) (Cloud)
Hiding from Love (Townsend)
How People Grow (and workbook)
How to Have That Difficult Conversation You've Been Avoiding
Making Small Groups Work
The Mom Factor (and workbook)
Raising Great Kids
Raising Great Kids Workbook for Parents of Preschoolers
Raising Great Kids Workbook for Parents of School-Age Children
Raising Great Kids Workbook for Parents of Teenagers
Safe People (and workbook)
12 "Christian" Beliefs That Can Drive You Crazy

Video Curriculum

Boundaries
Boundaries in Dating
Boundaries in Marriage
Boundaries with Kids
Raising Great Kids for Parents of Preschoolers
ReGroup (with Bill Donahue)

Audio

Boundaries
Boundaries in Dating
Boundaries in Marriage
Boundaries with Kids
Boundaries with Teens (Townsend)
Changes That Heal (Cloud)
How People Grow
How to Have That Difficult Conversation You've Been Avoiding
Making Small Groups Work
The Mom Factor
Raising Great Kids

BOUNDARIES IN MARRIAGE

UNDERSTANDING
THE CHOICES
THAT MAKE OR BREAK
LOVING RELATIONSHIPS

DR. HENRY CLOUD & DR. JOHN TOWNSEND

ZONDERVAN®

ZONDERVAN.com/
AUTHORTRACKER
follow your favorite authors

*To all the couples who, with courage, work
out their boundaries in the service of love.*

We want to hear from you. Please send your comments about this
book to us in care of zreview@zondervan.com. Thank you.

ZONDERVAN

Boundaries in Marriage
Copyright © 1999 by Henry Cloud and John Townsend

Requests for information should be addressed to:

Zondervan, *Grand Rapids, Michigan 49530*

Library of Congress Cataloging-in-Publication Data

Cloud, Henry.
 Boundaries in marriage : understanding the choices that make or break loving
relationships / Henry Cloud and John Townsend.
  p. cm.
 ISBN 978-0-310-24314-4 (softcover)
 1. Marriage. 2. Marriage—Religious aspects—Christianity. 3. Married people—psychology.
4. Married people—conduct of life. I. Townsend, John Sims, 1952- . II. Title.
HQ734.C5926 1999
306.81—dc21   99-31469

Published in association with Yates & Yates, www.yates2.com.

Printed in the United States of America

09 10 11 12 13 14 • 46 45 44 43 42 41 40 39 38 37 36 35 34 33 32 31 30 29 28 27 26

Contents

Part 4: Misunderstanding Boundaries in Marriage

A Tale of Two Couples

*R*ecently, I (Dr. Townsend) had two separate dinners with two married couples who are friends of mine. These two couples are in their later years, and each of the couples has been married for more than four decades. They are in what we call the "Golden Years," the period of marriage in which all the love and work over the years culminate, we hope, in a deep and satisfying connection. However, I was struck by the huge difference between the two couples.

With Harold and Sarah, I enjoyed a buffet dinner where you get a ticket for various parts of the meal and you have to leave the table with your ticket and go get your item. The dinner was winding down; we were ready for dessert. Harold reached into his shirt pocket and pulled out his dessert ticket. Tossing it in front of Sarah, he said casually, "Sarah. Dessert." Not "Please, Sarah, will you get my dessert for me?" And certainly not "Can I get your dessert, honey?" Harold was assuming Sarah would obediently comply with his two-word command.

I didn't know what to say, so I sat there and watched. Sarah was clearly embarrassed by Harold's public display of control. She sat there for a couple of seconds, apparently deciding what to do. Then she seemed to gather up her courage and quietly but forcefully said, "Why don't you get your own dessert?"

Harold looked surprised. Evidently he wasn't used to her refusing to obey his commands. However, he recovered, made a weak joke about uppity women, and left the table to redeem his ticket. While he was gone, Sarah said to me, "Sorry, I just couldn't let it go this time, with my friends here." I felt so sad for Sarah, realizing that her reaction to her husband tonight was the exception rather than the rule. I also realized that, on a deeper level, while Harold and Sarah were legally connected, they were emotionally disconnected. Their hearts were not knit together.

Frank and Julia were different. I was traveling, and they were hosting me. We went to their home after dinner. After a while, it was time for me to return to my hotel, and I needed a ride. Julia, a counselor like me, was primarily responsible for my trip and had been chauffeuring me to various speaking engagements and meetings. So clearly she was the person to take me back.

However, Frank looked at his wife and said, "You look tired, honey. I'll take John back to his hotel." I could see the conflict in Julia's face between her duty to me and her need for rest. Finally, she said, "Okay, thanks." And Frank drove me to the hotel.

The next day, at the conference, I talked to Julia. I remarked on Frank's kindness in offering the ride and on her struggle with taking the offer. She said, "It wasn't always that way. In our twenties, he wouldn't have offered, and I wouldn't have taken the offer. But we worked on this issue a lot during those days. I had to put my foot down on some issues, and we almost divorced. It was a difficult period, but it has paid off. We can't imagine not being each other's soul mates." During my time with them, I had observed that Frank's and Julia's hearts were knit together, that they were emotionally connected.

Though both couples had many years of marriage experience, each couple's love and relationship had taken very different turns. Harold and Sarah were unable to love deeply and relate to each other, because Harold controlled Sarah and Sarah allowed him to control her. They had what are called major boundary conflicts, in which one person crosses the lines of responsibility and respect with another. When one person is in control of another, love cannot grow deeply and fully, as there is no freedom.

Frank and Julia could have very likely ended up the same way. From what I could tell, they started off similarly in their early married years. Frank dominated, and Julia complied. However, she confronted the problem, she set limits and established consequences, and their marriage grew. Clearly, both couples were reaping the results of how they had conducted themselves in the earlier seasons of marriage. The first couple harvested a sad result; the other, a joyous one.

Your Life Begins Today

If you are reading this book, most likely marriage is important to you. You may be happy in your marriage and want it to keep growing. You may be struggling and dealing with major or minor problems. You may be single and want to prepare for marriage. You may be divorced and want to prevent the pain you went through if you remarry.

Most of us have no greater desire and prayer than a lifetime of love and commitment to one person with whom we can share life. Marriage is one of God's greatest gifts to humanity. It is the mystery of living as one flesh with another human being (Ephesians 5:31–32).

> *When two people are free to disagree, they are free to love. When they are not free, they live in fear, and love dies.*

Marriage is first and foremost about love. It is bound together by the care, need, companionship, and values of two people, which can overcome hurt, immaturity, and selfishness to form something better than what each person alone can produce. Love is at the heart of marriage, as it is at the heart of God himself (1 John 4:16).

Yet, love is not enough. The marriage relationship needs other ingredients to grow and thrive. Those ingredients are *freedom* and *responsibility*. When two people are free to disagree, they are free to love. When they are not free, they live in fear, and love dies: "Perfect love drives out fear" (1 John 4:18). And when two people together take responsibility to do what is best for the marriage, love can grow. When they do not, one takes on too much responsibility and resents it; the other does not take on enough and becomes self-centered or controlling. Freedom and responsibility problems in a marriage will cause love to struggle. Like a plant without good soil, the marriage relationship will struggle in an unfriendly environment.

Boundaries in Marriage is fundamentally about love. It is about promoting it, growing it, developing it, and repairing it.

We want to help you develop love through providing a better environment for it: one of freedom and responsibility. This is where boundaries, or personal property lines, come in. They promote love by protecting individuals.

We wrote *Boundaries: When to Say Yes, When to Say No, To Take Control of Your Life* several years ago because we saw that many people's personal and spiritual conflicts had to do with a lack of structure and boundaries. They couldn't say no to controlling or irresponsible people, and so they were always controlled by others' demands on them. However, many people have asked us since then, "Why don't you write a book on setting limits in one's marriage, so that we can solve problems before they start?" We thought that was a good idea, and this book is the result.

> *Today is the day to work on your own boundaries in marriage.*

As you will see, character is key here. When people grow in character, they grow in the ability to set and receive boundaries in their marriages, and they mature. When they resist hearing the word *no*, they remain immature.

Many people believe that as we humans grow up physically, we automatically grow up emotionally as well, but that's simply not true. Age is a necessary but insufficient requirement for growing up. There are immature old people, and there are appropriately mature young people. Harold and Sarah are still dealing immaturely with old, old boundary issues. Frank and Julia have resolved them and have gone to much deeper stages of love and maturity. The point we are trying to make here is that today is the day to work on your own boundaries in marriage. As the Bible teaches, make the most of today, for the days are evil (Ephesians 5:16). What you take initiative to deal with today will affect the rest of your married life. And what you ignore or are afraid to address will do the same. You're headed toward either a Harold and Sarah marriage, or a Frank and Julia one, and you are doing that right now.

You may both be open to the concept of setting and receiving truth and boundaries with each other. This openness will make the process much easier, as you will be on the same page with regard to both values and personal growth. Or you may have a spouse who is against boundaries. This close-mindedness can be dealt with also.

An Overview

We have structured the book into several parts. Part I, "Understanding Boundaries," introduces you to the idea of (or gives you a refresher course on) boundaries and how to set them in your marriage and with yourself. Part II, "Building Boundaries in Marriage," deals with the necessity of two separate lives becoming united, with the fundamental beliefs that undergird a marriage of boundaries, and with how to set boundaries against outside people and influences. Part

> *B*oundaries in Marriage *is not about fixing, changing, or punishing your mate.*

III, "Resolving Conflict in Marriage," describes six types of conflict and how to set limits with a spouse who accepts boundaries and with one who resists boundaries. Part IV, "Misunderstanding Boundaries in Marriage," looks at some of the ways boundaries can be misused.

These sections provide practical information, examples, tables, and suggestions to help you apply boundaries concepts to your marriage.

Clarifying a Misconception

We need to make clear, however, that *Boundaries in Marriage* is not about fixing, changing, or punishing your mate. If you aren't in control of yourself, the solution is not learning to control someone else. The solution is learning self-control, one of the nine fruits of the Spirit (Galatians 5:23). So don't look at this book as a way to make someone else grow up. It is more about taking ownership of your own life so that you are protected and you can love and protect your spouse without enabling or rescuing him or her.

So welcome to *Boundaries in Marriage!* We hope this is a helpful resource for you, whatever condition your marriage is in. We pray that as you learn to make the word *no* a good word in your marriage, responsibility and freedom will then help love take deep roots in both of your hearts. God bless you.

HENRY CLOUD, PH.D.
JOHN TOWNSEND, PH.D.
NEWPORT BEACH, CALIFORNIA
1999

Part One

Understanding Boundaries

—— *Chapter 1* ——

What's a Boundary, Anyway?

Stephanie sat in front of the fireplace drinking her cup of herbal tea and reflecting upon the evening. Her husband, Steve, had gone to bed an hour earlier, but the gnawing feeling in her stomach prevented her from joining him. In fact, the feeling was propelling her away from him. She was relieved when he had said that he was tired, for she didn't know what she would have done if he had wanted to make love to her. The feeling of relief scared her. She knew that it was not a good sign for their relationship.

As she thought about the night, she found herself connecting her feelings not only with what had happened this evening, but with what had gone on in their relationship in the last few years. She was pulling away from Steve more and more. She knew that she loved him and always would love him. She just didn't know how to get past the lack of attraction to him. She had a negative feeling about their relationship that she could not shake.

"Get specific. What is it?" she could hear her friend Jill asking her. Jill was much better at sorting out thoughts and feelings than Stephanie.

As she sorted through answers to Jill's question in her mind, the answer came surprisingly quickly in a movie-like collage of memories. Times and conversations she and Steve had had passed through her mind as though she were a detached observer. First, she recalled this evening, when he had ignored her wishes for where they would go to dinner. And several times during the meal he had ignored what she was saying. It was as if he did not really hear her.

Then there was their vacation. She had wanted a nice quiet mountain setting where they could be alone together. He had wanted a big city with "lots of action." As usual, they had followed his wishes.

Then there was her desire to go back to school and finish her degree. They had agreed on that when she had dropped out of college her senior year to put him through law school. But every time she brought it up, he explained why it was not a good time right now for them. Stephanie had a hard time understanding that. What he really was saying was that it was not a good time *for him.*

Many other scenes came to her mind, but that phrase—"for him"—seemed to encapsulate all of them: Their relationship was more "for him" than it was "for them," or even "for her." As she thought about it, her detachment gave way to anger and contempt. Quickly, she retreated from such a negative feeling.

Get a grip, she told herself. *Love is filled with sacrifice.* But, as much as she tried to see herself sacrificing for love, she felt as if she were sacrificing a lot, yet experiencing very little love.

With that thought, she stared into the fire awhile longer, gulped her last sip of tea, and headed for bed, hoping Steve would be asleep.

The Importance of Boundaries

How had Stephanie, after several years of marriage, found herself in such a state? What had gone wrong? She and Steve had begun so strong. He was everything she had always wanted. Kind, strong, successful, and spiritual, Steve seemed to embody it all. But as time went on, their relationship lacked depth and intimacy. She could not understand how she could love someone so much and experience such little love along the way.

The issues are different for many couples, but the perplexity is often the same. One spouse feels something is missing, but she can't figure out what it is. She tries to do the right things. She gives, sacrifices, honors the commitment, and believes the best. And yet she doesn't achieve intimacy, or worse than that, she doesn't avoid pain.

In some cases, the confusion hides itself behind the simplistic explanations that problems such as addiction, irresponsibility, control, or abuse provide. "If he just weren't so controlling." Or, "If she just would stop spending." Partners think that they can explain why their relationship lacks intimacy by the presence of "the problem." They are surprised to find that even when the "problem" goes away, the person with whom they can't connect or find love remains.

In other cases, there may be no "problems," but the marriage does not live up to the promise that one or both of the partners had in the beginning. Commitment may be strong, but love, intimacy, and deep sharing are not present. Why does this happen with two people who are so committed to the relationship?

In our work with couples over the years, we have observed that, while many dynamics go into producing and maintaining love, over and over again one issue is at the top of the list: boundaries. When boundaries are not established in the beginning of a marriage, or when they break down, marriages break down as well. Or such marriages don't grow past the initial attraction and transform into real intimacy. They never reach the true "knowing" of each other and the ongoing ability to abide in love and to grow as individuals and as a couple—the long-term fulfillment that was God's design. For this intimacy to develop and grow, there must be boundaries.

So, with that in mind, in this chapter we are going to take a big-picture look at what boundaries are. We will give an introductory course for those of you who have never read our book *Boundaries* and a refresher course for those of you who have.

What *is* a boundary? In the simplest sense, a boundary is a property line. It denotes the beginning and end of something. If, for example, you go down to the county courthouse and look up your address, you can probably get a plot map showing your property lines. You can see where your property begins and your neighbor's ends—a prerequisite for being good neighbors to each other.

Ownership

If you know where the property lines are, you can look up who *owns* the land. In physical property, we say that Sam or Susie "owns" the land and the things on the land.

In relationships, ownership is also very important. If I know where the boundaries are in our relationship, I know who "*owns*" things such as feelings, attitudes, and behaviors as well. I know to whom they "belong." And if there is a problem with one of those, I know to whom the problem belongs as well. A relationship like marriage requires each partner to have a sense of ownership of himself or herself.

I (Dr. Cloud) witnessed this lack of ownership in a couple recently. Caroline and Joe came in for marriage counseling saying that they could not stop arguing with one another. When I asked her what the arguments were about, Caroline replied, "He is just so angry all the time. He gets so mad at me that it really hurts; he is so mean sometimes."

I turned to Joe and asked, "Why do you get so mad?"

Without having to think for a second, he replied, "Because she always tries to control me and my life."

Sensing that this could become a game of Ping-Pong, I looked to the other side of the table and asked Caroline, "Why do you try to control him?"

Again, in a millisecond, she replied, "Because he is so into his own things that I can't get his time or attention." Each of them blamed their own behavior on the other person.

Sensing that they might see the humor in what they were doing if I continued, I asked, "Why do you not pay attention to her?"

"Because she is so nagging and controlling—I just have to get away from her," he instantly shot back.

Trying one last time to have someone take ownership for his or her own behavior, I asked her why she nags. Without missing a beat, she answered, "Because he won't do anything I want."

I wanted them to see my head moving back and forth whenever I asked the question "Why do you . . . ?" The answer given was always something about the other person. The ball of ownership was hit back over the net each time it landed in one of their courts. Neither one ever took personal ownership of his or her behavior. In their minds, their behavior was literally "caused" by the other person.

I longed for Joe to say, for example, "I get angry at her because I'm too immature to respond to her more helpfully. I'm deeply sorry for that and need some help. I want to be able to love her correctly no matter what her behavior is. Can you help me?" This response would be music to a counselor's ears. But, with this couple, we were a long way from the symphony.

I felt as if I were in the bleachers in the Garden of Eden when God confronted Adam after he had sinned (see Genesis 3:1–13). Adam had chosen to disobey God's command not to eat of the tree of knowledge of good and evil. There was no doubt about it, Adam had done it. When God asked what had happened, he got the same lack of ownership we saw with Caroline and Joe.

> *The ball of ownership was hit back over the net each time it landed in one of their courts. Neither one ever took personal ownership of his or her behavior.*

"Who told you that you were naked?" God asked. "Have you eaten from the tree I commanded you not to eat from?"

"The woman you put here with me—she gave me some fruit from the tree," Adam said, "and I ate it." Adam blamed his behavior on his wife. Just like Joe; just like all of us. "I did _____ *because* of you." And God ran into the same problem with Eve. When he asked her about her behavior, look what happened:

"What is this you have done?" God asked.

"The serpent deceived me, and I ate," Eve replied. Eve's behavior and disobedience get explained away on account of the serpent. "If it weren't for the serpent...."

In essence, Caroline and Joe, like Adam and Eve, and like you and me, were saying, "If it were not for you, I would be a more loving, responsible person."

So the first way in which clarifying boundaries helps us is to know where one person ends and the other begins. What is the problem, and where is it? Is it in you, or is it in me? Once we know the boundaries, we know who should be owning whichever problem we are wrestling with. For example, Joe was not taking ownership of his feelings, and Caroline, of her behavior. This issue of "ownership" is vital to any relationship, especially marriage.

Responsibility

Boundaries help us to determine who is responsible for what. If we understand who owns what, we then know who must take responsibility for it. If I could get Joe to see that his reactions were his problem and not Caroline's, then I could help him to take responsibility for changing his reactions. As long as he blamed Caroline for his reactions, then she had to change for his reactions to change. In his mind, if she were not so controlling, for example, he would not be so angry.

> *If we can see that the problem is our problem and that we are responsible for it, then we are in the driver's seat of change. For the first time, we are empowered.*

If we can discover who is responsible for what, we have an opportunity for change. If we can see that the problem is our problem and that we are responsible for it, then we are in the driver's seat of change. For the first time, we are empowered. When Caroline got a sense that she was responsible for the misery she thought Joe was causing, she was empowered to change that helpless, powerless feeling of misery, *no matter what Joe was doing.* Once she began to take responsibility for her reactions to Joe, she could work on changing them. For example, she learned not to let his anger affect her and to respond to him more directly. She also learned to stop nagging him to do things, and instead to ask him to do something and give him choices.

Responsibility also involves action. If something is going to happen, it's going to happen because we take action. We need to change some attitudes, or behaviors, or reactions, or choices. We must actively participate in the resolution of whatever relational problem we might have, even if it is not our fault.

Once Joe saw that his anger was his problem and not Caroline's, he took responsibility for it. He learned he was not going to be "not angry" because Caroline changed. He was going to be "not angry" because he grew and responded differently to what she did. He learned what Proverbs teaches

> *We must actively participate in the resolution of whatever relational problem we might have, even if it is not our fault.*

us—that a lack of boundaries and anger go hand in hand: "Like a city that is broken into and without walls is a man who has no control over his spirit" (Proverbs 25:28 NASB). He learned not to react, but to think through his choices, to find where his anger and feelings of being threatened by her were coming from. Many other new things became part of his growth, but they all began with boundaries, with clarifying what he had to take responsibility for.

Each spouse must take responsibility for the following things:

- Feelings
- Attitudes
- Behaviors
- Choices
- Limits
- Desires
- Thoughts
- Values
- Talents
- Love

Responsibility tells us we are the ones who must work through our feelings and learn how to feel differently. *Our* attitudes—not those of our spouse—cause us to feel distressed and powerless. How we behave and react is part of the problem, and we have to change these patterns. We allow ourselves to get pushed beyond certain limits and then become resentful or powerless. We do not turn desires into accomplished goals, or we do not deal with our sick desires.

Responsibility empowers us to have a good life. To give Adam and Eve the responsibility God gave them was to empower them to have the life all of us desire—one filled with love, wonderful surroundings, and lots of opportunities to use our abilities and talents. He gave them the ability and the opportunity to make the life they chose. When they did not choose in a life-giving way, they also bore the responsibility for that choice as well, just as we do.

> *We are not at the mercy of our spouse's behavior or problems.*

But the good news of boundaries is that God's plan of responsibility has not changed. We are not at the mercy of our spouse's behavior or problems. Each spouse can act both to avoid being a victim of the other spouse's problems and, better yet, *to change the marriage relationship itself.* Later in this book we will show you how to change your marriage for the better, even if your spouse is not interested in changing. But the process always begins with taking responsibility for your own part in the problem.

Freedom

"His irresponsibility is making my life miserable," Jen began. She then went on to tell me a terrible story of how her husband had successfully avoided adulthood for many years at her expense. She had suffered greatly at the hands of his behavior, both financially and sexually.

As I listened, though, I could see that her deep sense of hopelessness kept her in prison. I could see countless ways she could be free from her husband's patterns of behavior. She could make numerous choices to help both herself and the relationship. But the sad thing was that she could not see the same choices that were so clear to me.

"Why don't you stop paying for his mistakes and bailing him out? Why do you keep rescuing him from the messes he gets himself into?" I asked.

"What are you talking about?" Jen asked, alternating between muffled sobs and a scornful expression. "There's nothing I can do. This is the way he is, and I just have to live with it."

I could not tell if she was sad about what she perceived as a hopeless case or angry with me for suggesting she had choices.

As we talked further, I discovered an underlying problem that kept Jen from making such choices. *She did not experience herself as a free agent.* It never occurred to her that she had the freedom to respond, to make choices, to limit the ways his behavior affected her. She felt that she was a victim of whatever he did or did not do.

This was the same problem troubling Joe and causing him to react so severely to Caroline. She would attempt to control him, and he would experience her attempts as *actually* controlling him. In reality, Caroline had no control over Joe whatsoever, and had he understood that, he would not have been so reactive to her. He did not see himself as a free agent.

> *She did not experience herself as a free agent. It never occurred to her that she had the freedom to respond, to make choices, to limit the ways his behavior affected her.*

God designed the entire creation for freedom. We were not meant to be enslaved by each other; we were meant to love each other freely. God designed us to have freedom of choice as we responded to life, to other people, to God, and to ourselves. But when we turned from God, we lost our freedom. We became enslaved to sin, to self-centeredness, to other people, to guilt, and to a whole host of other dynamics.

Boundaries help us to realize our freedom once again. Listen to the way that Paul tells the Galatians to set boundaries against any type of control and become free: "It was for freedom that Christ set us free; therefore keep standing firm and do not be subject again to a yoke of slavery" (Galatians 5:1 NASB). Jen felt herself enslaved by her husband's patterns of behavior and did not see the choices available to her. Joe saw himself as subject to Caroline's nagging attempts to control him. But God tells us to not be subject to any kind of enslaving control at all.

> *Just as your next-door neighbor can't force you to paint your house purple, neither can any other human being make you do anything.*

When someone realizes the freedom he or she has from a spouse or anyone else, many options open up. Boundaries help us to know just where someone's control begins and ends. As with the property lines above, so it is with relationships. Just as your next-door neighbor can't force you to paint your house purple, neither can any other human being make you do anything. It violates the basic law of freedom God established in the universe. For love to work, each spouse has to realize his or her freedom. And boundaries help define the freedom we have and the freedom we do not have.

Marriage is not slavery. It is based on a love relationship deeply rooted in freedom. Each partner is free *from* the other and therefore free *to love* the other. Where there is control, or perception of control, there is not love. Love only exists where there is freedom.

The Triangle of Boundaries

Three realities have existed since the beginning of time:

1. Freedom
2. Responsibility
3. Love

God created us free. He gave us responsibility for our freedom. And as responsible free agents, we are told to love him and each other. This emphasis runs throughout the whole Bible. When we do these three things—live free, take responsibility for our own freedom, and love God and each other—then life, including marriage, can be an Eden experience.

Something incredible happens as these three ingredients of relationship work together. As love grows, spouses become more free from the things that enslave: self-centeredness, sinful patterns, past hurts, and other self-imposed limitations. Then, they gain a greater and greater sense of self-control and responsibility. As they act more responsibly, they become more loving. And then the cycle begins all over again. As love grows, so does freedom, leading to more responsibility, and to more love.

This is why a couple who has been married for fifty or more years can say that the marriage gets better and better as time goes on. They become more free to be themselves as a result of being loved, and the love relationship deepens.

One woman said it this way: "Before I married Tom, I was so caught up in my own insecurities and fears to really even know who I was. I have been so blessed by the way he loved me. When I was afraid or irresponsible in the early years, he was patient, not reactive. He was strong

> *Love only exists where there is freedom.*

enough to love me and require more of me at the same time. He did not let me get away with being like I was, but he never punished me for how I was, either. I had to begin to take responsibility for working through my barriers to love. I could not blame him for my faults. As he loved me more and more, I was able to change and let go of the ways that I was."

The really neat thing was that as I talked to this woman's husband, he said basically the same thing. Both had become a catalyst for growth for the other and for the relationship as well.

In this description we can see the three legs of the triangle. The spouses were free to not react to the other, they each took responsibility for their own issues, and they loved the other person even when he or she did not deserve it. She worked on her insecurities and changed them. And as they were both free from the other, they gave love to each other freely. And that love continued to transform and produce growth.

Remember, where there is no freedom, there is slavery, and where there is slavery, there will be rebellion. Also, where there is no responsibility, there is bondage. Where we do not take ownership and do what we are supposed to do with our own stuff, we will be stuck at a certain level of relationship, and we will not be able to go deeper.

Love can only exist where freedom and responsibility are operating. Love creates more freedom that leads to more responsibility, which leads to more and more ability to love.

Protection

The last aspect of boundaries that makes love grow is protection. Think of your house for a moment. You probably have some protection around your property somewhere. Some of you have a fence with a locked gate, for example, to protect your property from trespassers. Some people, if they were able, would come in and steal things that matter to you. As Jesus said, "Do not give dogs what is sacred; do not throw your pearls to pigs. If you do, they may trample them under their feet, and then turn and tear you to pieces" (Matthew 7:6). You need to be careful and to protect yourself from evil.

Some of you do not have a fence, but you lock your doors instead. However you do it, you have a protective boundary available when needed to keep "bad guys" out. But your locked gate or door is not a wall, either. You need to be able to be open the gate or door when you want to invite "good guys" onto your property or into the house. In other words, boundaries need to be permeable. They need to keep the bad out and allow the good in.

As it is with your house, so it is with your soul. You need protective boundaries that you can put up when evil is present and can let down when the danger is over.

Regina had had enough. Married to Lee for nineteen years, she had tried to be loving until it had almost killed her emotionally. Lee had a long-standing problem with alcohol and also with anger. Sometimes the two problems would come together and make life unbearable for her. In addition, he would pick at her in an emotionally devastating way with biting, sarcastic remarks. "Nice dress—didn't they have it in your size?" was the kind of thing he would say. He would not help her with the kids either, seeing it as the "wife's job."

She was an adapting, loving person who had always tried to avoid conflict and to win people over with love. When people were mean, she would become nicer and try to love them more. The problem with Lee was that her love only gave him more and more permission to be unloving himself. His drinking and other behaviors continued to get more and more pronounced, and she finally could not take it anymore.

She discovered that it was not good to be the silent sufferer. Some people at her church encouraged her to speak up to Lee about how his problems affected her. She took some courses on assertiveness and began to confront him.

Sadly, Lee did not listen. Sometimes he ignored her confrontations, at other times he apologized without changing, and at still other times he grew angry and defensive. But at no time did he take her words to heart, see how he was hurting her, and change.

Regina finally gave Lee a choice to own his problem and take responsibility for it, or to move out. She would no longer allow his drinking and anger to affect her and the children. She would take protective steps to "guard the good" and not let evil destroy it.

At first he did not believe her, but she stood her ground. Finally, he moved out. Had he not done so, she might have moved out herself or gone to court. But, seeing for the first time that his behavior had consequences, Lee took his problem seriously. He obtained some help and turned his life around. He and Regina were reconciled a year and a half later, and their marriage was saved.

Regina was happy that they were back together and that the marriage was doing well. This was a fruit of the protective stance she had so painfully taken. She had set some limits and boundaries to protect herself, her children, and ultimately her marriage from a destructive cycle.

Self-Control

There is a lot of misunderstanding about boundaries. Some people are against boundaries because they see them as selfish; other people actually use them to be selfish. Both are wrong. Boundaries are basically about self-control.

A client once said to me, "I set some boundaries *on my husband.* I told him that he could not talk to me that way anymore. And it did not work. What do I do now?"

"What you have done is not boundaries at all," I replied.

"What do you mean?"

"It was your feeble attempt at controlling your husband, and that never works." I went on to explain that boundaries are not something you "set on" another person. Boundaries are about yourself.

My client could not say to her husband, "You can't speak to me that way." This demand is unenforceable. But she could say what she would or would not do if he spoke to her that way again. She could set a boundary "on herself." She could say, "If you speak to me that way, I will walk out of the room." This threat is totally enforceable because it has to do with *her.* She would be setting a boundary with the only person she could control: herself.

> *Boundaries are not something you "set on" another person. Boundaries are about yourself.*

When you build a fence around your yard, you do not build it to figure out the boundaries of your neighbor's yard so that you can dictate to him how he is to behave. You build it around your own yard so that you can maintain control of what happens to your own property. Personal boundaries do the same. If someone trespasses your personal boundaries in some way, you can take control of yourself and not allow yourself to be controlled, or hurt, anymore. This is self-control.

And ultimately, self-control serves love, not selfishness. We hope that when you take control of yourself, you will love better and more purposefully and intentionally so that you and your spouse can have the intimacy you desire.

Examples of Boundaries

In the physical world, many boundaries define property and protect it. Fences surround homes. Homes are built in gated communities. Most homes have doors and locks. In the old days, people even had moats with alligators.

In the immaterial world of souls and relationships, boundaries are different. You would look funny with a moat around your heart, and the alligators would require a lot of maintenance. So God has equipped us with special boundaries for the interpersonal realm. Let's look at some.

Words

The most basic boundary is language. Your words help define you. They tell the other person who you are, what you believe, what you want, and what you don't. Here are some examples of words being used as boundaries:

- No, I don't want to do that.
- No, I won't participate in that.
- Yes, I want to do that.
- I will.
- I like that.
- I don't like that.

Your words, or lack of them, define you to another person. Remember Stephanie, the wife in the opening illustration of this chapter who was pulling away from her husband, Steve? Stephanie slowly lost ground on her property by not saying what she wanted and what she did and did not like about how Steve was acting. Her silence was like a trampled-down fence.

Truth

Truth is another important boundary. God's truth and principles provide the boundaries of our existence, and as we live within this truth, we are safe. Here are some truths that help define the structure of how we are to relate:

- Do not lie.
- Do not commit adultery.
- Do not covet.
- Give to others.
- Love one another.
- Be compassionate.
- Forgive.

As we structure our relationships around God's eternal truths, our relationships succeed and thrive. When we cross these boundaries, we lose the security that truth provides.

In addition, being honest and truthful about ourselves and what is going on in a relationship provides boundaries. Not being truthful to one another gives a false impression of where we are, as well as who we are. For example, when Regina was adapting to Lee's hurtful behavior, she wasn't being honest with him about what was really going on inside of her. She was acting happy and loving, but in reality she was miserable inside and hurting deeply.

As Paul says, "Each of you must put off falsehood and speak truthfully to his neighbor, for we are all members of one body" (Ephesians 4:25). If we are not being truthful with each other, our real relationship goes into hiding. Then, instead of one real relationship, we have two relationships: the outside relationship, which is false; and the inside, hidden relationship, which is true. Intimacy is lost, and so is love. Love and truth must exist together.

Consequences

When Regina had had "enough," she finally set the boundary of consequences. She said she would no longer live with Lee while he drank. This consequence defined the boundary of what she would allow herself to be exposed to. Where her words failed to communicate, her actions did. She kicked him out.

God has given us the Law of Sowing and Reaping (see chapter 2 for a fuller explanation of this law) to communicate what is acceptable and what is not. If we just use words, others sometimes do not "get the message." In fact, people in denial are deaf to words of truth. They only respond to pain and loss. Consequences show where our boundary line is.

> *People in denial are deaf to words of truth. They only respond to pain and loss.*

Some spouses need severe consequences like separation. Others need less severe ones, like the following, to define important boundaries:

- Canceling a credit card
- Leaving for the party alone when the perpetually late partner doesn't come home by the agreed upon departure time
- Going ahead and eating dinner when a spouse is late for the thousandth time
- Ending an abusive conversation
- Refusing to bail someone out of a jam because of perpetual irresponsibility, like overspending or not completing work on time.

Emotional Distance

Sometimes one of the partners in a hurtful relationship is not willing to change. The partner continues to do hurtful things. Or, sometimes a spouse may have betrayed a trust or had an affair, and even though he has repented, not enough time has passed for the spouse to prove himself trustworthy.

In these situations, trust may not be wise. But it is prudent to continue to interact in the relationship and to work the problem out. In such instances, one partner might have to follow the advice of Proverbs to avoid further injury: "Above all else, guard your heart, for it is the wellspring of life" (Proverbs 4:23). Guarding one's heart might include saying the following:

- I love you, but I don't trust you. I can't be that close until we work this out.
- When you can be kind, we can be close again.
- When you show you are serious about getting some help, I will feel safe enough to open up to you again.
- I can't share deep feelings if you are going to punish me for them.

In these instances, the couple has a commitment to work on things along with the wisdom to guard the heart with some emotional distance until it is safe and prudent to move closer. This prevents further hurt and deterioration of the relationship.

We caution you, however, that you must take this stance only with a pure heart. Impure hearts use boundaries to act out feelings such as revenge and anger. Because none of us is pure, we have to search our motives for establishing boundaries to make sure that they serve love and not our impure motives. Using distance or withdrawal of love, for example, to punish the other is a sign that we are setting boundaries not to resolve the conflict, but to get revenge.

> *Impure hearts use boundaries to act out feelings such as revenge and anger.*

Physical Distance

Sometimes, when all else fails, people must get away from each other until the hurt can stop. Distance can provide time to protect, time to think, time to heal, and time to learn new things. In severe cases, protective separation prevents actual danger. Physical distance can be minimal, or more significant:

- Removing oneself from an argument or heated situation
- Taking some time away from one another to sort things out

- Moving out to get treatment for an addiction
- Separating from physical abuse or substance abuse
- Moving into a shelter to protect children

These boundaries protect the marriage and the spouse from further harm. As Proverbs tells us, "The prudent see danger and take refuge, but the simple keep going and suffer for it" (Proverbs 27:12). Physical distance at times provides space for healing as well as safety to preserve partners and the marriage itself. Although usually a last resort, it is sometimes the thing that saves.

Other People

Sandy could not stand up to Jerry alone. Every time she tried to set boundaries with him, she folded in the heat of conflict. She did not yet have the spine she needed. He was always able to overpower her.

I suggested that she talk about certain issues with him only while I was present. At first she saw that as a cop-out and would not give herself permission to do it. But after a few more failures, she agreed that she was just unable.

Sandy limited herself to discussing the difficult topics only in their counseling sessions. Slowly she was able to depend upon me to monitor and intervene when Jerry got out of hand. As that happened, the boundaries I provided in structuring the sessions gave the marriage a new path. He began to respond.

Later, she went to her support group for the rest of the structure she needed to gain her own boundaries. Other people were the "spine" she did not have in the beginning. Slowly she internalized their care, support, teaching, and modeling. God has always provided help from his family to those who need it. Here are some ways:

- Use a third party to help you resolve conflict.
- Use a third party to help you protect and support yourself.
- Use a group for healing and strengthening.
- Use others to teach you boundaries.

- Use counselors, friends, or pastors to provide the safe place to work on difficult issues.
- Use shelters in extreme situations.

Take care, however, that other people are helping and not hurting. Other people may be unhelpful if they help you hide from conflict instead of trying to resolve it. We will cover this point in chapter 11 on protecting your marriage from intruders.

Time

Time is another boundary that structures difficulties in relationships. Some people need time to work out a conflict or to limit the conflict itself:

- Give yourself an allotted time to talk about certain things: "We will discuss our budget for one hour, and then we will leave it alone until next week."
- Set a certain time to work on a particular issue instead of discussing it in the heat of the moment.
- Establish seasons for certain goals: "This summer we will work on our communication, and in the fall work on our sexual difficulties."

Just as the physical world has different kinds of boundaries, the interpersonal world has different ones as well. Just as sometimes a fence is appropriate and a door is not, sometimes confrontation and truth are important and physical distance is not. Later in this book, in Part III, we will guide you through how to know when to do what.

Stephanie

Stephanie, with whom we opened this chapter, was not experiencing the more serious problems with Steve that some of our other couples have revealed. She was suffering, however, from the emotional distance that being on the wrong end of a one-sided relationship creates. In some ways her story is more revealing of the need for good boundaries in a marriage. She was unhappy in the face of no overt problems. This can sometimes be the worst kind of misery.

Her story has a good ending. And it incorporates all the principles we have looked at in this chapter.

Stephanie first figured out where she ended and where Steve began. When she did, she found that there was really very little of her at all in the marriage. She had adapted to him and had complied with his wishes so much that she barely existed at all. She could no longer even remember what it felt like to be herself. Her desires for school and some meaningful work of her own were long forgotten as he pressured her to continue to go on as they were. And she had given in over and over until she lost herself. When she thought about what

> *The passive spouse decides she wants to have "a life of her own." And she leaves. She may even call this move "getting some boundaries." Nothing could be further from the truth.*

was hers and what was his, she realized that she could not blame him for her loss of herself. She was the one who had complied with his wishes. She was the one who was afraid of conflict and so chose to adapt to what he wanted. She had to take ownership of her passivity.

At this point in her journey Stephanie made a mature decision. She took responsibility for her own misery and began to *work on it in the relationship.* Instead of doing what many compliant people do when they wake up and find themselves lost, she didn't leave the relationship "to find herself." Many times a marriage will break up as the passive spouse decides she wants to have "a life of her own." And she leaves. Sometimes she may even call this move "getting some boundaries." Nothing could be further from the truth.

Boundaries are only built and established in the context of relationship. To run from a relationship as the first step of boundaries is not to have boundaries at all. It is a defense against developing boundaries with another person. The only place boundaries are real is within relationship.

Stephanie did not run. She took ownership of all of her feelings, attitudes, desires, and choices, and then she took them to Steve. And they had lots of conflict at first. But in the end, he grew as well. Steve found out that life was not about just him and that, if he continued to live that way, he was going to lose some things very important to him, like closeness with Stephanie. As she took responsibility for her life, he was forced to take responsibility for his own, and the marriage improved.

They both owned their sides of the equation. Stephanie saw that she was free from Steve and that the slavery she had always felt was coming from inside of her. She expressed her feelings and opinions more. She would not just give in to Steve's desires immediately. When he did not hear her, she let him know. And Steve learned to love her freedom and relish it. He began to feel attracted to her independence instead of threatened by it. As they did these things, love grew. And they grew as individuals as well.

But it had all started with Stephanie doing some serious boundary work: defining herself, taking ownership and responsibility for what was hers, realizing her freedom, making some choices, doing the hard work of change in the relationship and not away from it, and learning to love instead of comply.

Stephanie's relationship with Steve grew more and more intimate. They learned how to be separate people who were free to love each another. The missing ingredient all along had been a deep sense of intimacy, something the Bible refers to as "knowing" someone. But without clear boundaries, they could not know each other, and without knowing each other, they could not truly love each other.

As they each became more defined, they became two people who could love and be loved. They began to know and enjoy one another. They began to grow.

This is what we would like for you and your spouse. In this book we will help you become better defined, more free and responsible, and more in a position to love and be loved. This is the high calling God created marriage to be.

──────── *Chapter 2* ────────

Applying the Ten Laws of Boundaries to Marriage

───────────────

*W*hen we speak at seminars on boundary issues, the most often-asked questions go something like this: "How do I handle my husband's lack of intimacy?" or "What should I say to my wife when she overspends?" Many couples struggle with these important issues.

However, we find it difficult to answer these questions because we don't know each couple's particular situation. A husband who isn't intimate may be distant because he has trust issues. Or he may be self-absorbed. Or he may be normal, and his wife may have unrealistic expectations. A wife who overspends may have problems structuring herself. Or she may be in denial of the financial problem. Or she may have a controlling husband. Boundary issues in marriage always require an understanding of the situation. For us to say, "Well, tell your husband or wife this and this," without a grasp of the marriage may sound helpful, but it could also prove to be useless advice.

Though we give practical suggestions throughout the book, in the long run, learning principles helps more than learning techniques. We have, therefore, included this section on the laws of boundaries, not as practical strategies, but as principles by which to structure your marriage. These laws, which we have also explained in other contexts in *Boundaries* and *Boundaries with Kids*, take you beyond the problem-solving level of boundaries. They will help you to understand how boundaries work and may be able to help you solve problems before they start.

These laws of boundaries are not about marriage as it should be. They are about marriage *as it really is.* As with the laws of science, such as the law of gravity and the law of electromagnetism, the laws of boundaries are always in force, whether or not we are aware of them. We may jump as high as we want off the ground. We may say, "I deny the existence of gravity! I refuse to believe in it!" But we still won't get very far off the planet. The laws are more powerful than we are.

The laws of boundaries lay the foundation of how responsibility works in life. You may read them and think, *So that's why we've struggled in our marriage!* Or you may think, *So that's why this part of our relationship works well.* Either way, you will benefit by becoming familiar with these ten laws.

Law #1: The Law of Sowing and Reaping

Amy and Randall had been married for eight years, and they loved each other. However, when he was angry or upset, Randall became moody and would withdraw from Amy and the kids, except for occasional outbursts of anger. When his manufacturing business was struggling, he would sit silently through dinner. Once, during this period, the children were arguing at the dinner table. Out of the blue, Randall said, "Amy, can't you keep these children in line? I can't even have a moment's peace in my own home!" And with that, he stormed out of the kitchen into his home office, turned on the computer, and stayed there until the kids went to bed.

> *These laws of boundaries are not about marriage as it should be. They are about marriage* as it really is.

Amy was hurt and confused. But she had a pattern of "handling" Randall's moods. She would try to cheer him up by being positive, encouraging, and compliant. *He has a hard job,* Amy would think. *Nurturance is what he needs.* And for the next few hours, and sometimes days, she would center the family's existence around Dad's mood. Everyone would walk on eggshells around him. No one was to complain or be negative about any subject, for fear of setting him off again. And Amy would constantly try to draw him out, affirm him, and make him happy. All her emotional energy went into helping Randall feel better.

Amy was trying her best to solve the problem of her husband's moods. But they were just getting worse. His moods became blacker and more severe, and they lasted for longer periods of time. What was worse, Randall seemed to be unaware of his moods. "You're just overreacting," he would tell her. And sometimes he would even blame her for his moods. "If you were more supportive, this wouldn't happen," he would say. Amy felt terrible. What was going wrong?

Playing and Not Paying

Amy and Randall's struggle illustrates the importance of the first law of boundaries: the Law of Sowing and Reaping. Simply put, this principle means that *our actions have consequences*. When we do loving, responsible things, people draw close to us. When we are unloving or irresponsible, people withdraw from us by emotionally shutting down, or avoiding us, or eventually leaving the relationship.

In their marriage, Randall was sowing anger, selfishness, and withdrawal of love. These hurt Amy's feelings and disrupted the family. Yet Randall was not paying any consequences for what he was sowing. He could have his tantrum, get over it, and go about his business as if nothing had happened. Amy, however, had a problem. She was bearing the entire burden of his moodiness. She stopped what she was doing to take on the project of changing her moody husband into a happy man. Randall was "playing," and Amy was "paying." And because of this, he was not changing his ways. Randall had no incentive to change, as Amy, not he, was dealing with his problem.

> *When we do loving, responsible things, people draw close to us. When we are unloving or irresponsible, people withdraw from us.*

What consequence should Randall have been experiencing? Amy could have said to him, "Honey, I know you're under stress, and I want to support any way I can. But your withdrawal and rage hurt me and the children. They are unacceptable. I want you to talk more respectfully to us when you're in a bad mood. The next time you yell at us like that, we'll need some emotional distance from you for a while. We may leave the house and go to a movie or see some friends." Then Randall would have to deal with the result of his actions: loneliness and isolation. When you sow mistreatment of people, you should reap people's not wanting to be around you. It is to be hoped that the pain of this loneliness would help Randall take steps to deal with his feelings.

Consequences Grow Spouses Up

God designed marriage to be a place not only of love, but of growth. One pathway to growth is learning that actions have consequences. Since marriage is such a close, long-term relationship, spouses deeply affect each other with their actions. The old saying "You always hurt the one you love" is true. And this is why understanding and applying the Law of Sowing and Reaping are so important, not only for the spouse who is taking on the problems of her partner, but also for the spouse who is shirking responsibility. It is an act of love to allow our spouse to reap the effects of his selfishness or irresponsibility—unless, of course, we are acting out of revenge or a desire to see our spouse suffer.

Boundaries are the key to obeying this Law of Sowing and Reaping. When we set and keep limits with our spouse, we are saying to him, "I may love you, but I'm not paying for your problems." Refusing to rescue your spouse—such as by refusing to cheer him up when he is pouting, sacrificing to pay off his credit card bill, calling in sick for him when he has been out partying the night before—helps keep the problem with him.

Relational and Functional Reaping

This first law is played out in the two main areas of marriage: relationship and function. The *relational* part of marriage involves the emotional tie two people have to each other, such as how deeply connected they are and how they feel about each other, both positively and negatively. The *functional* part of marriage has to do with the "doing" aspects of the relationship, such as paying bills, managing time, cooking meals, keeping house, and rearing children.

In the relational aspect of marriage, sowing and reaping has to do with how spouses affect and impact each other's heart. Amy and Randall had a problem in relational sowing and reaping. He was being hurtful and difficult, yet Amy took the consequences of his behavior for him. Another example of relational sowing and reaping is the demanding wife who insists that every second of her husband's attention and time be spent on or with her. She sows self-centeredness and bondage, and he reaps resentment, guilt, and a loss of freedom.

In the functional aspect, sowing and reaping is more easily identifiable, because tasks are more concrete. For example, a husband may sow overspending, while his wife reaps the result by having to get a job, or by scrimping on food and other necessities to meet the family budget. Or a wife may sow careless housekeeping, while her husband reaps discomfort in his own home and embarrassment when company comes over.

In either aspect, the problem is the same: *The one who has the problem isn't facing the effects of the problem.* And things don't change in a marriage until the spouse who is taking responsibility for a problem that is not hers decides to say or do something about it. This can range from mentioning how her spouse's behavior hurts her feelings, all the way to setting a limit on the behavior. This helps place both the sowing and the reaping with the same person and begins to solve the boundary violation.

Law #2: The Law of Responsibility

A proper view of responsibility is necessary to set limits in marriage. On the one hand, when you marry, you take on the burden of loving your spouse deeply and caring for him or her as for no other. You care about how you affect your spouse; you care about your spouse's welfare and feelings. If one spouse feels no sense of responsibility to the other, this spouse is, in effect, trying to live married life as a single person. On the other hand, you can't cross the line of responsibility. You need to avoid taking ownership for your mate's life.

The Law of Responsibility is this: We are responsible *to* each other, but not *for* each other. The Bible teaches it this way: "Carry each other's burdens, and in this way you will fulfill the law of Christ" and "each one should carry his own load" (Galatians 6:2, 5). The word *burden* (verse 2) indicates a back-breaking boulder, such as a financial, health, or emotional crisis. Spouses actively support each other when one is carrying an overwhelming burden. The term *load* (verse 5), however, indicates one's daily responsibilities of life. This includes one's feelings, attitudes, values, and handling of life's everyday difficulties. Spouses may help each other out with loads, but ultimately, each person must take care of his own daily responsibilities.

> *You need to avoid taking ownership for your mate's life.*

Two extremes occur in marriage when the Law of Responsibility is not obeyed. On the one hand, a husband will neglect his responsibility to love his wife. He may become selfish, inconsiderate, or hurtful. He will not consider how his actions affect and influence his mate. He is not following Jesus' law of how to treat one another: "So in everything, do to others what you would have them do to you" (Matthew 7:12). This is being irresponsible to a spouse.

On the other hand, a husband may take on responsibility his wife should be bearing. For example, his wife may be unhappy, and he may feel responsible for her happiness. Perhaps he feels that he isn't making enough money, showing enough interest in her activities, or helping enough around the house. So he tries and tries to make an unhappy person happy. This is an impossible project. While a husband should be sympathetic toward his unhappy wife and take responsibility for his own hurtful behavior, he shouldn't take responsibility for her feelings. They are hers, and she must handle them herself.

Finally, the Law of Responsibility also means that spouses refuse to rescue or enable the sinful or immature behavior of their partners. Couples have a duty to set limits on each spouse's destructive acts or attitudes. For example, if a husband has a gambling problem, his wife needs to set appropriate limits, such as canceling his credit cards, separating their joint accounts, or insisting that he get professional help, to force him to take responsibility for his problem.

Law #3: The Law of Power

If any law fetches more questions than any other, the Law of Power is probably the one. Couples struggle with understanding what they have the power to change in their marriages. More often than not, they are concerned with changing not their own behavior, but their spouse's. Human nature lends itself to trying to change and fix others so that we can be more comfortable.

At our *Boundaries* seminars, one of the most common questions starts this way: "How can I get my spouse to ... ?" When we hear that, we know we have a power problem. Spouses often try to use boundaries to assert power over a mate, and it doesn't work. Mates have their own choices. Think how you feel when someone tries to make you change: Resentful? Rebellious? Resistant? These are not the attitudes of a person who is eager to change.

The Law of Power clarifies what we do and don't have power over. First, let's talk about what we don't have power over. We have no power over the attitudes and actions of other people. We can't make our spouse grow up. We can't stop our spouse from exhibiting a troublesome habit or character flaw. We can't force our spouse to come home on time for dinner, to refrain from yelling at us, or to initiate conversations with us. The fruit of the Spirit is self-control, not other-control (Galatians 5:23). God himself does not exercise such power over us, even though he could (2 Peter 3:9).

> *Spouses often try to use boundaries to assert power over a mate, and it doesn't work.*

We don't have the power to make our spouse into the person we would like him or her to be, but we don't have the power to be the person we would like to be, either. In and of ourselves, we are powerless to change such things as our short temper or our eating problem. To some extent, we all do what we hate to do (Romans 7:15). It's helpful to be aware of this powerlessness in our marriage, so we can be more understanding of our spouse's struggle. Also, being aware of our powerlessness over ourselves can help us realize how long it may take to learn to set appropriate limits in our marriage.

Thus, if for years you have been a codependent spouse (one who takes responsibility for the actions of another), don't expect to be able to have mature boundaries overnight.

If you don't have power to change your spouse, what *do* you have power over? You have the power to confess, submit, and repent of your own hurtful ways in your marriage. You can identify these hurtful ways, ask God for his help to overcome them, and be willing to change. Whatever your spouse does that bothers you, it's certain that you do things that bother him also. If you want your spouse to listen to your boundaries, ask him where you may be violating his. When you are hurt or upset, you may try to control everything, or you may withdraw into silence. Nothing is more conducive to a spouse's growth than a mate who sincerely wants to change.

> *We don't have the power to change someone else, but we can influence them.*

You have the power to grow through the unhelpful ways you are dealing with your marriage problems. Few marriage problems are the result of one hundred percent one spouse and zero percent the other. Each contributes to the problem. You may be the disciplinarian in the family and feel that your wife is too lax. You might resent getting pegged as the bad guy with the kids. However, your contribution to the problem may be that you step in when she should. Or you may nag her. Or you may not let her know that you feel powerless. You have the power to start identifying ways you are actively or passively contributing to the problem, and you have the power to change over time. Jesus called this process taking the plank out of our eye first (Matthew 7:1–5).

We don't have the power to change someone else, but we can influence them. Influence means having sway over someone. What you do can affect your spouse. For example, you don't have the power to make your spouse understand your feelings when you have had a bad day and are stressed out. But you can let her know that you would like her to empathize with your emotions. You

> *Mature adults desire the freedom of others as much as their own.*

can model the behavior by responding empathetically to her. You can attend a support group for couples working on these issues. You can set limits on her inattentiveness. Influence has its own power.

Law #4: The Law of Respect

Some people think the Law of Respect is the "bad guy" of the ten, because it doesn't teach us about setting boundaries but, rather, submitting to the boundaries of others. The Law of Respect states that if we wish for others to respect our boundaries, we need to respect theirs. There is no such thing as a free lunch. We can't expect others to cherish our limits if we don't cherish theirs.

We all get excited about finally being able to say no, set limits, and become free to choose, but we don't feel as excited about hearing no. If this is how you feel, you're in good company. Children feel this way, too! They demand freedom, but don't want others to be free to disappoint them. Mature adults desire the freedom of others as much as their own.

The Law of Respect fosters love. Loving your mate means desiring and protecting her freedom of choice. It means dying to your wish for her to see things your way and appreciating that she has her own mind, values, and feelings. Think about how you felt the last time you said no to a friend, who then said something like, "Oh, and I thought you cared." You may have felt guilty and caved in. Or you may have stuck to your boundary, but felt resentful. Either way, your closeness to this friend was damaged. This is how your mate feels when you can't hear her no.

Marriage makes the Law of Respect difficult. When two people marry, two lives blur together to make a new one, two become one. The blurring of expectations and feelings can become an issue. Many times a spouse will automatically expect that the love in the marriage means that her spouse will always see things her way. She may feel unloved when her otherwise-loving mate says, "No, I'd rather not take a walk. I'm sleepy." Sometimes this happens during the "honeymoon period," when both parties tend to see eye-to-eye on everything. But when the reality of two different wills, needs, and perspectives comes in, the honeymoon is over. This is when the Law of Respect must be applied.

I was getting a haircut the other day, and my hairdresser asked me what I had been doing lately. I told her about the book I was writing. She was very interested in our *Boundaries* book, and when she heard about *Boundaries with Kids,* she went wild and said, "I have got to have that book to help me with my kids today!"

But when I told her about this book—*Boundaries in Marriage*—she smiled anxiously and said, "Hmmm, I'm the one who gets away with everything in my marriage. I don't want my husband to get hold of that one!" She was sheepishly admitting what we all feel at some level: I want my freedom, and I don't like others' freedom to curtail mine.

A couple with whom my wife and I are close, Nick and Colleen, mentioned the same problem at dinner one night. Nick said, "Sometimes Colleen withdraws from me for no reason at all."

"There is a reason," Colleen replied. "When I try to say no to you and you try to control me, I withdraw."

Nick said, "I don't try to control you when you say no."

Colleen let it go and said, "I guess we have a difference of opinion."

The conversation drifted to other subjects. Later that evening, Nick invited me to a ball game a couple of weeks from then. I checked my schedule and said, "Sorry, I can't."

Nick threw up his arms in mock exasperation and said, "Oh, come on, you can go! Just rearrange things a little. That's what friends do."

Colleen had been watching, and she yelled, "There it is! There it is! That's how he controls my no!"

Nick looked surprised and said, "I do what?"

"She's right, Nick," I said. "I felt the pressure of not being able to say no."

The light went on for Nick as he saw how his desire for good things sometimes crossed the line of respect.

Apply the Law of Respect in your marriage. Don't storm into the living room with a list of "how things are going to change around this house." Tell your spouse you want your boundaries respected, and ask him if he feels his are being respected also. Let him know that you value and desire him to be free to say no, even if you don't like the answer. Ask him some of the following questions:

- How might I be crossing your boundaries?
- Do you feel I respect your right to say no to me?
- Do I give you guilt messages, withdraw, or attack you when you set a limit?
- Will you let me know the next time I don't respect your freedom?

These humbling and uncomfortable questions show you are concerned for your spouse more than for your own convenience. They arise out of self-sacrifice, and they show your generosity of spirit and love. And they can bind your marriage together.

If your spouse is trustworthy, it is easier to ask these questions. If your spouse is untrustworthy, you may feel you are putting yourself in the hands of someone who might use your respect for him against you. However, even untrustworthy people need to have their legitimate needs and boundaries respected. This doesn't mean, though, allowing yourself to be harmed if the

> *No one can actually love another if he feels he doesn't have a choice not to.*

spouse is unsafe. Respect his boundaries and still set limits on his untrustworthiness. An example of this balance is how a wife might approach her rageaholic husband. She should not dictate to him that he can't be angry; she should respect his freedom to protest what he does not like. At the same time, however, she might tell him, "Your raging way of being angry is not acceptable to me. If you don't find other ways of being angry with me, I will have to distance from you."

Respecting and valuing your mate's boundaries is the key to being close and loving. Your spouse experiences the gift of freedom from you and sees the love you are extending in giving this freedom. When you respect your spouse's boundaries, you are paving the way to having yours respected.

Law #5: The Law of Motivation

Larry loved sports—all kinds. His wife, Jen, loved Larry but hated sports. One of their big conflicts was when he would press her to go to a professional hockey game with him. "Come on, it will be fun!" Larry would plead. "And we'll be together."

Though she didn't like hockey at all, Jen would think to herself, *God wants me to be loving. And I don't want Larry mad at me.* Then, grudgingly, she would accompany him to the game. But without being aware of it, Jen would make sure Larry felt her displeasure. She would do the following:

- Dawdle at home so that they would leave late
- Show no interest in the game
- Be in a bad mood the whole time
- Withdraw from Larry emotionally
- Remind him for days about how miserable a time she had had

Finally, Larry grew tired of taking his unenthusiastic wife to the hockey games. "I'd rather you not go than go and not really be there," he said. Jen felt hurt that Larry hadn't appreciated her sacrifice for him. She didn't understand that her motives for saying yes to Larry's desire weren't healthy and that, because of this, neither spouse was getting what he or she needed.

The Law of Motivation states that we must be free to say no before we can wholeheartedly say yes. No one can actually love another if he feels he doesn't have a choice not to. Giving your time, love, or vulnerability to your spouse requires that you make your own choice based on your values, not out of fear.

Having to do anything is a sign that someone is afraid. The following fears prevent a spouse from setting boundaries in marriage:

- Fear of losing love
- Fear of a spouse's anger
- Fear of being alone
- Fear of being a bad person
- Fear of one's guilty feelings
- Fear of not reciprocating the love someone has given (thus hurting his or her feelings)
- Fear of losing the approval of others
- Fear of hurting one's spouse because of overidentifying with his or her pain

Fear always works against love. The "have to" destroys the "choose to." Conversely, love drives out fear (1 John 4:18). When we are freely choosing to love, we are no longer driven by the above fears. We are driven by affection. If you struggle with any of these fears, work on maturing through them, so that they do not control you and rob you of your boundaries. For example, if you fear losing love, find safe people who will stick with you, and take risks with them, such as being honest. As they stay in relationship with you, you will begin to have less fear of losing love.

In Jen's case, she was afraid of two things: not being perceived as a caring person, and losing Larry's love. Her fear negated her freedom to make a choice. She felt she "had to" go to the hockey game, almost as if Larry had a gun to her head. And the result was that she felt resentful, angry, and cut off from her husband. Jen blamed Larry; he was the bad guy who had taken away her choices.

Learning to pay attention to your motives does not mean saying yes only when you feel like it or want to do something. This is selfishness. Many times we make uncomfortable and painful choices to sacrifice for our mates. However, these choices are based on motives of love and responsibility, not fear of loss. For example, I know a couple in which the husband had an affair. The experience was devastating to his wife. She had every right to leave the marriage, and no one would have faulted her. Yet she stayed in it and suffered greatly as she worked through the betrayal with him. It was neither comfortable nor what she felt like doing at times.

At the same time, however, she wasn't staying in the marriage out of fear of isolation, financial security, or anything else. She knew she was free to leave. Yet she loved her husband and God, and she wanted to do the right thing.

> *No spouse in his right mind really wants a mate who complies with his wishes out of fear.*

To the extent that you are free to say no, you are free to say yes to something your spouse wants. This is why sometimes in marriage it is a good growth practice to say, "I can't wholeheartedly say yes to this, so I'll have to say no at this time." This gives you time and space to work out what the best option truly is. It also saves your spouse from a resentful, withdrawn mate. No spouse in his right mind really wants a mate who complies with his wishes out of fear. He does not experience love, openness, or freedom from her. She may be there in body, but not in soul. The Law of Motivation helps keep fear out of the picture.

Law #6: The Law of Evaluation

Trent was at his wit's end. His wife, Megan, had once again run the credit card up over the limit. Whenever she had a problem or felt down, shopping seemed to lift her spirits. Even though they were struggling financially, Megan didn't see her spending as a problem. "We'll pay it off someday," she rationalized. "It's just a loan." Trent, however, feared their dire financial state. Yet he always tried to work harder to provide more money, hoping this would solve the problem.

When I asked Trent if he had considered canceling the credit card, he reacted quickly. "I couldn't do that," he said. "You don't know how hard her life is. Everybody needs an outlet. And you should see her face when she comes home—she's just beaming!"

"What would she feel if the card were cancelled?" I asked.

Tears welled up in Trent's eyes. "She would be really hurt," he said. "She never had anything as a little girl, grew up dirt poor. Taking away the little she has now would devastate her. I just can't do that to someone I love."

Trent struggled in his evaluation of Megan's pain. He knew how impoverished her life had been, and he felt deeply for her. He wanted to bring her some relief. Yet, though his permissiveness helped her feel better, it was ruining their financial status.

Trent confused two very different ideas: *pain* and *injury.* Megan felt no pain when she shopped extravagantly. Yet the marriage was being injured by her impulsiveness and Trent's passivity. She wasn't feeling hurt, but a great deal of harm was being done.

When Trent set limits on the credit card, the converse was true. Megan felt a lot of pain, but no great harm was being done. Trent reduced the spending limit and asked Megan to agree to not use the card for a month every time she went over the limit. Megan was angry and resentful toward Trent, but she didn't fall apart as he had feared. In fact, she began to grow. Megan's spending had kept her anesthetized from negative aspects of her life, such as loss, failure, and stress. Without her credit card cushion, Megan had to deal with these issues, and she began maturing. She was in pain, but she was not being injured. In fact, she was healing.

Just because someone is in pain doesn't necessarily mean something bad is happening. Something good might be going on, such as a spouse learning to grow up. And this is the essence of the Law of Evaluation: We need to evaluate the pain our boundaries cause others. Do they cause pain that leads to injury? Or do they cause pain that leads to growth?

> *Just because some-one is in pain doesn't necessarily mean something bad is happening.*

It is unloving to set limits with a spouse to harm him. This is revenge, which is in God's hands, not ours (Romans 12:19). But it can be just as unloving to avoid setting a limit with your spouse because you don't want him to be uncomfortable. Sometimes discomfort is an opportunity for growth. You may need to confront your spouse, give him a warning, or set a consequence. Do not neglect setting limits in your marriage because of a fear of causing pain. Pain can be the best friend your relationship has ever had.

Law #7: The Law of Proactivity

Eric and Judy had been married for eleven years, and they felt their marriage was solid. However, Eric, on the one hand, was sarcastic with Judy when they disagreed. He would lash out in semi-humorous ways to win his point or to show his anger with her. Judy, on the other hand, was quiet and compliant. When Eric was sarcastic and hurtful, she would take it silently, attempting not to sink down to her husband's level. But the feelings didn't go away, and they built up for years.

> *Pain can be the best friend your relation-ship has ever had.*

One night they argued, and Eric needled Judy as usual. Out of the blue, she exploded in anger. "Stop it, stop it, stop it! I'm sick and tired of your immature hatefulness, and I'm not going to put up with it anymore!" She yelled for a while and then stopped. They were both in shock, as neither Eric nor Judy had seen this part of her before. Judy felt horrible, as though she were a bad person.

Judy had been keeping away from some truths she needed to express—protests against Eric's hurtfulness. These truths finally bubbled over in an intense reaction. Judy's boundaries were reactive boundaries. Had Judy been less compliant, long ago she would have sat down with her husband and said, "Honey, you have a mean side, and it makes me distance myself from you. I love you, but I won't subject myself to this treatment. I want you to work on this issue with me so that it doesn't happen again." This approach is *proactive* rather than *reactive*.

> *Proactive people solve problems without having to blow up.*

The Law of Proactivity is taking action to solve problems based on your values, wants, and needs. Proactive people solve problems without having to blow up. They "are" their boundaries, so they don't have to "do" a boundary as often as reactive folks do.

The Law of Proactivity has three facets: *(1) Reactive boundaries are a necessary part of growth and marriage.* Many people who have been victimized or powerless need the freedom that comes from strenuously protesting some evil or bad thing. At the same time, *(2) reactive boundaries are not sufficient for growth.* Impulsive screaming matches aren't adult behaviors. Love can be lost, and a lot of damage can be done when a spouse doesn't grow out of her "victim" role of constant protest. That is why *(3) proactive boundaries maintain love, freedom, and reality in relationships.* Proactive people keep their freedom, and they disagree and confront issues all the time in marriage. But they are able to hold on to the love they have for their spouse, and they do not get caught up in an emotional storm. They have worked through their reactive stage.

This law applies to different people at different points of their growth. You may have yet to experience your first tantrum. You may have a season of reactive boundaries ahead of you. Find some caring, safe people to help you navigate through it! Your spouse may not be the person for this.

Or you may be stuck in protest, constantly griping and challenging things you don't like. You are defined by what you hate more than what you love. You may need to accept some sad realities, grieve, and get in touch with things important to you, so that you can integrate positive values along with your protests.

Work on setting proactive boundaries in your marriage, deliberate boundaries built on love and based on your values.

Law #8: The Law of Envy

The most powerful obstacle to setting boundaries in marriage is envy. The Law of Envy states that we will never get what we want if we focus outside of our boundaries on what others have. Envy is devaluing what we have, thinking it's not enough. We then focus on what others have, all the while resenting them for having good things we don't possess. Adam and Eve felt envy when they ate of the only tree in the garden forbidden to them. They had everything else but this one fruit, and they weren't satisfied until they had it.

> *The most powerful obstacle to setting boundaries in marriage is envy.*

Envy is miserable because we're dissatisfied with our state, yet powerless to change it. This is why it is such a powerful obstacle: The envious person doesn't set limits because he is not looking at himself long enough to figure out what choices he has. Instead, his envious eye is keeping him focused upon the happiness of others.

> *Envy is miserable because we're dissatisfied with our state, yet powerless to change it.*

Do not confuse envy with desire. Desire involves wanting something, and it motivates us to take action to possess it. God wants to give us our desires (Psalm 37:4). Desire doesn't focus on our emptiness, nor how lucky others seem to be. Desire preserves the goodness and value of what we have and of those we are in relationship with.

In marriage, envy can lie at the heart of many boundary problems. For example, Bev, a friend of mine, was talking about her husband, Jim. "He's always been so decisive and take-charge, while I don't have a lot of power. And that makes it harder for me to say no to him."

"Why is that?" I asked.

"Because he'll overwhelm me and control me like he does people at work. I don't appreciate being treated like that. What's more, I don't want to be like he is, either, so I can't become the decisive person he is."

Bev was guaranteeing that she would never be able to set limits with Jim. She saw herself as powerless and Jim as controlling. To set boundaries with him would mean that she might have to own some of the aggressiveness she resented in him. It was less threatening to cry foul about Jim and avoid developing her own limits. You can't set limits in marriage until you are looking at yourself as part of the problem and as a great deal of the solution. Work through envy, own your problems, and take action.

Law #9: The Law of Activity

The Law of Activity states that we need to take the initiative to solve our problems rather than being passive. Have you ever noticed how some couples are divided into the "active" spouse and the "passive" one? One spouse takes more initiative, sets goals, and confronts problems. The other waits for his spouse to make a move first, then responds.

All things being equal, active spouses have an edge in boundary setting. Taking initiative increases one's chances to learn from mistakes. Active people make lots of mistakes, and wise ones grow from them (Hebrews 5:14). They try something, experience a limit, and adapt. They experience the depth of God's forgiveness because | *Active spouses have an edge in boundary setting.* |

they do things for which they need to be forgiven. Passive people have trouble learning because they are afraid to take risks. Because of this, they also have a harder time taking charge of their lives and boundaries. God is not pleased with those who "shrink back" in passivity (Hebrews 10:38). He wants his people to participate in life with him, not wait on the sidelines.

People are passive for different reasons. Some fear losing love. Others don't see their lives as their problem. Still others fear

> *Doing nothing, or being passive, stunts boundary development and growth in marriage.*

making mistakes. And some can simply be lazy. But the result is always the same: Their problems get worse. Evil thrives when no one sets limits on it. That is why friends and families stage interventions for alcoholics in denial. The problem doesn't go away without action. According to British statesman and orator Edmund Burke, "All that is needed for evil to triumph is for good men to do nothing." Doing nothing, or being passive, stunts boundary development and growth in marriage.

When one spouse is active and the other passive, several problems can occur:

- The active spouse may dominate the passive one.
- The active spouse may feel abandoned by the passive one.
- The passive spouse may become too dependent on the active one's initiative.
- The passive spouse may resent the power of the active one.
- The passive spouse may be too intimidated by the active one to say no.

When both spouses are active in boundary setting, when they both speak the truth, solve problems, and set goals, they will both grow. They can also rest in the security that if they don't address a problem, their mate can be depended on to do it. Their love grows and deepens, as they are always moving toward each other. One is not constantly waiting for the other to take the first step. Don't wait for your spouse to take the first step. Assume the first move is always yours. If you tend to be the passive spouse, let your mate know how risky it is for you to take initiative, and ask her to help you become more active. You're in good company. This is how God does it. Even when he didn't cause a problem (our sinfulness), he took the initiative to solve it (the Cross).

You may be wondering just how the Law of Proactivity differs from the Law of Activity. The difference is that the Law of Proactivity has to do with taking action based on deliberate, thought-out values versus emotional reactions. The Law of Activity has to do with taking the initiative versus being passive and waiting for someone else to make the first move.

Law #10: The Law of Exposure

You may think that you don't have boundaries in your marriage, but that may not be true. You may indeed have limits, definitions, feelings, and opinions, but you may not be communicating these to your spouse. A boundary that is not communicated is a boundary that is not working. It has the same net effect in the marriage as if there were no boundary.

The Law of Exposure states that we need to communicate our boundaries to each other. God designed boundaries to promote love and truth. Spouses need to make clear what they do or don't

> *Don't wait for your spouse to take the first step. Assume the first move is always yours.*

want. They need to work on understanding what their spouse is saying about their boundaries. When boundaries are "exposed," two souls can be connected in the marriage. But when boundaries are unexposed, spouses are less emotionally present in the marriage, and love struggles.

Take, for example, the husband who withdraws when his wife's self-centeredness wounds him. He might say, "I am having a hard time with the demands of my job." Her response might be, "Do you think I have it easy with the kids?" He feels negated and unloved. And she may not even be aware that she has ignored his feelings or viewpoint. Then, as the dance continues, the husband isolates and hides his feel-

> *A boundary that is not communicated is a boundary that is not working.*

ings from her. He thinks, *What's the use? She'll only put me down and talk about herself again anyway.* She loses the connection with him and doesn't know why. And she is cheated out of an opportunity to respond to the truth and thereby start maturing in her character.

Far better for the husband to let his wife know, "Honey, when I tell you my negative feelings, it hurts me that you become critical of me and focus the issue on yourself. This makes me withdraw from you. I want and need to be close to you, and I will work toward this. But if you continue to negate me instead of hear me, I may need to distance somewhat and take those deeper feelings to friends who will try to understand me."

When we expose our boundaries to the light of relationship, we can be fully connected to our spouses. We can resolve problems, and we can take a stand to actively love our spouses by risking conflict for the sake of the relationship. Exposure is the only way for healing and growth to take place.

Apply these laws to your marriage (see sidebar), and see how they change the way you relate to each other. Remember, you can't break laws forever without consequences. We all have to either live in accord with them and succeed, or continually defy them and pay the consequences. These laws will help your marriage adapt to God's principles of relationship.

THE TEN LAWS OF BOUNDARIES

1. The Law of Sowing and Reaping: Our actions have consequences.

2. The Law of Responsibility: We are responsible *to* each other, but not *for* each other.

3. The Law of Power: We have power over some things; we don't have power over others (including changing people).

4. The Law of Respect: If we wish for others to respect our boundaries, we need to respect theirs.

5. The Law of Motivation: We must be free to say no before we can whole-heartedly say yes.

6. The Law of Evaluation: We need to evaluate the pain our boundaries cause others.

7. The Law of Proactivity: We take action to solve problems based on our values, wants, and needs.

8. The Law of Envy: We will never get what we want if we focus outside our boundaries onto what others have.

9. The Law of Activity: We need to take the initiative in setting limits rather than be passive.

10. The Law of Exposure: We need to communicate our boundaries to each other.

───── *Chapter 3* ─────

Setting Boundaries with Yourself

Becoming More Lovable

───────────────

*L*ynn was weary of Tom's chronic lateness in coming home from work. Because he owned his own business, he was often delayed at work. It seemed like such a little thing, but as time passed, Tom's tardiness became a big problem. Lynn would arrange her day to have dinner and the kids ready on time, and she wanted Tom to be home on time as well.

Reminding, nagging, and cajoling Tom had been ineffective. Tom would either defend himself by saying, "You don't appreciate the work I have to do to put food on the table," or he would simply deny the problem altogether by saying, "It doesn't happen that often; you're overreacting." Lynn ran out of strategies.

Finally, after thinking through the problem with some wise women friends, Lynn came up with a two-point plan. One night, as the couple climbed into bed, she told Tom her plan. "Sweetheart," she said, "I want to apologize to you for my crummy attitude about dinnertime."

Tom almost fell out of bed. He was eager to hear her apology.

"I've been a complaining griper whenever you get home," Lynn continued. "You probably feel you have to toss a few pounds of raw meat in the front door before it's safe to enter. No wonder you're late. Who would want to put up with that?"

"You're right. I really don't look forward to your resentment," Tom responded, "and I'm sure it makes me avoid you. The other day, I was going to be ten minutes late. When I thought about facing your wrath, I figured I might as well make it thirty minutes, since I knew you'd be angry anyway. So I dropped by the drugstore to pick up some film."

Lynn nodded. "I'm going to try to be less angry, and more caring and approachable, even when you're late. I may not do it well, and I'll need your help here, but I really don't want to be a shrew. Also, it's not just my attitude that I'll be changing. My actions will be changing, too. I love you, and I want you to be with me and the kids for dinner, but if you can't get here on time, I will have your dinner put away in the fridge. You can reheat it yourself whenever you get in."

Tom didn't like this last part. "Lynn, you know I hate to make my own dinner! After a ten-hour day, I want to sit down to a prepared meal."

"I know you do, and I want that for you, too. But it won't happen until you can rearrange things to get here when the rest of us eat."

The next few days Tom ate a lot of microwaved dinners from Tupperware containers. Finally, he structured the end of his day to get home on time, and Lynn's important family time became a reality. When Lynn asked Tom why he had changed, he said, "I guess it was your two-point plan. First, you were a lot nicer to me. I felt more like coming home. And second, I just hate reheating dinner."

Whose Problem Is It, Anyway?

Lynn solved a small but chronic marriage problem by making an important shift in her attitude. She stopped trying to change Tom, and she started making changes in herself. Lynn moved from seeing the problem as Tom's lateness to seeing it as her unhappiness with Tom's lateness. This opened the door to things she could control. When you cease to blame your spouse and own the problem as yours, you are then empowered to make changes to solve *your* problem.

To do this, Lynn set a couple of limits on herself. First, she reined in her impulse to attack Tom for his tardiness. This was not easy, as she was clearly right and he was clearly wrong. She would have been justified in confronting him at every infraction.

But she placed a boundary on her anger, since it wasn't solving the problem. Second, Lynn set a limit on her enabling of Tom. She realized that she was making it easier for him to be irresponsible, so she said no to her desire to protect him from his dreaded dinner reheating. These two changes made a difference for both partners.

The Chapter No One Wants to Read

If you browsed through the table of contents of this book, chances are this was not the first chapter you turned to. Nobody wants to read this chapter. We all want to find ways to say no to our spouses rather than to ourselves. Yet the ideas in this chapter may be the only hope for your marriage to develop a healthy set of boundaries. *Boundaries in Marriage* is not the same as *Boundaries on Your Spouse*. This book is not about changing, fixing, or making your spouse do anything. It is about bringing boundaries into the relationship to provide a context in which both mates can grow.

> *This book is not about changing, fixing, or making your spouse do anything.*

Thus, more often than not, the first boundaries we set in marriage are with ourselves. We deny ourselves certain freedoms to say or do whatever we'd like in order to achieve a higher purpose. Like Lynn, we learn to restrict ourselves from confronting someone when that has proven futile. As the Bible teaches, "Do not rebuke a mocker or he will hate you; rebuke a wise man and he will love you" (Proverbs 9:8).

> *No matter what the issue in your marriage, you need to take the initiative to solve it.*

Many spouses use the concept of boundaries to go on the hunt to "make" their mate change his ways. Instead of a "marriage" problem, they see a "spouse" problem. We aren't denying a spouse's responsibility for problems. However, blaming one's spouse oversimplifies the issue and often doesn't solve the problem.

The reality of boundaries in marriage is that *no matter what the issue in your marriage, you need to take the initiative to solve it.* You may have a spouse who

- Is chronically late like Tom
- Is financially irresponsible
- Withdraws and avoids relationship
- Becomes angry
- Attempts to control you

Though you may share no blame in creating these problems, you probably need to take some initiative in solving them. This often seems unfair to people. They will say, "Why should I have to solve a problem I didn't cause?" This is a legitimate question. However, the question exposes a demand for fairness that will never exist in a fallen world. Such a question keeps people protesting and complaining while still mired in the problem.

God sees it another way. He says that no matter who causes a problem, we are to take steps to solve it. If our brother has something against us, we are to go to him (Matthew 5:23–24). And at the same time, if our brother sins against us, we are to go to him (Matthew 18:15). Fault is irrelevant; we need to work to resolve the problem. God works this way also. He saw our lost state and the problems we had caused ourselves and took the first step of sending his Son to die to reconcile a problem that was never his. As the old song goes, "We owed a debt we could not pay; He paid a debt he did not owe."

Removing the Plank

Another reason we need to look first at our own boundaries on ourselves is that, more often than not, we aren't blameless. Typically, spouses are performing a dance they don't even talk about. But the dance perpetuates the problem and generally involves a payoff for the innocent spouse.

For example, Molly continually overdrew the checking account. She would get in a rush and lose track of checks. The inevitable service charge would show up on the statement, and Scott would hit the roof about her irresponsibility. Molly would be hurt and withdraw. She would try to keep better accounts for a few days, then lose track again.

When I asked Scott why he didn't close the account or make Molly responsible for the service charges, he said, "It wouldn't do any good." However, as we talked, I discovered that Scott was one of those people who always become angry with irresponsible people. Much of his conversation revolved around how unreliable politicians, co-workers, the kids, and Molly were. He prided himself on being dependable.

It finally came out that Scott needed Molly to stay irresponsible so that he could continue his protest against all those irresponsible people in life. Were she to get her financial act together, he couldn't stay as angry about the human race. So he sabotaged any real attempts to help her learn from the consequences. Blowing up at her made him feel less helpless.

Once Scott realized this, he understood that underneath his anger was fear about things beyond his control. He talked about his fears and his sadness that he couldn't change people and about the person he would like to change: Molly. And he and she agreed on a successful plan for her to become responsible for the checking account.

The "innocent" spouse needs to see what part, active or passive, he plays in the problem. Jesus called this the plank in our eyes: "First take the plank out of your own eye, and then you will see clearly to remove the speck from your brother's eye" (Matthew 7:5). This plank may be some attitude or emotion we aren't aware of that encourages the problem to continue. Once Scott dealt with his plank of defensive anger, he could be more mature with Molly.

Taking Ownership of Our Lives

An important aspect of setting boundaries with ourselves is that of taking ownership of our lives. We need to take responsibility for our hearts, our loves, our time, and our talents. We are to own our lives and live in God's light, growing up and maturing our character along the way: "Speaking the truth in love, we will in all things grow up into him who is the Head, that is, Christ" (Ephesians 4:15). This is our job, and no one else's.

However, this is not as easy as it sounds. We are more concerned about the person who is making us crazy or miserable than we are about the state of our own souls. Blaming someone else shifts the light of truth from us to someone else. We come by this trait honestly. Adam and Eve, as we saw earlier, both blamed someone else for their own failings (Genesis 3:11–13).

When we neglect setting boundaries with ourselves and focus instead on setting boundaries with those we think sorely need limits, we have limited our own spiritual growth. As in any growth process, spiritual growth proceeds to the level that we invest in it. When we only invest in changing someone else, they get the benefit of our efforts, but the important work we have to do has been neglected.

For example, you may have the following reactions to your spouse:

- Withdrawal from his anger
- Resentment at his irresponsibility
- Letting go of your responsibilities due to his inattention
- Becoming self-centered out of his self-centeredness

Let's assume your spouse is all of these things—angry, irresponsible, inattentive, and self-centered. You will not grow if you continue to react to his sins. This is not seeking first God's kingdom and righteousness (Matthew 6:33); it is seeking satisfaction from another person.

> *We must become more deeply concerned about our own issues than our spouse's.*

We must become more deeply concerned about our own issues than our spouse's. We cannot overstate the importance of this idea. One of the most frightening facts in existence is that God will someday call us to account for our lives here on earth: "For we must all appear before the judgment seat of Christ, that each one may receive what is due him for the things done while in the body, whether good or bad" (2 Corinthians 5:10). At that meeting, we will not be able to blame, hide behind, or deflect to the sins and problems of our spouse. It will be a one-on-one conversation with God.

Boundaries with yourself are a much bigger issue than boundaries in your marriage. In the end, while we are only partly responsible for growing our marriages, we are completely responsible to God for developing our very souls. You are responsible for half of your marriage and all of your soul. Boundaries on yourself are between you and God.

Being the "Good" Spouse

Another aspect of setting limits with ourselves in marriage is the difficulty that comes in being the "good" spouse. In many marriages, one mate is more obviously selfish, irresponsible, withdrawn, or controlling. The other is perceived as a suffering saint, and people wonder how he tolerates the pain of living with such a problem person. This often makes it hard for the "good" spouse to set appropriate boundaries for himself.

There are a number of reasons for this. First, the suffering spouse may focus more on his spouse's problems than on his own. The more apparent the flaws, the more friends will talk about the flaws of the spouse rather than the problems of the sufferer.

A friend of mine was devastated when his wife left him. But it took him years to finally see how his own people-pleasing behavior led to her leaving. All his friends helped to keep him away from this awareness by constantly criticizing the abandoning spouse. They would tell him, "How selfish she was to leave a loving, nice person like you!" What they would not tell him—and what he needed to hear—was, "She certainly was selfish, but you were indirect, passive, and withheld your feelings from her."

Second, the "good" spouse often feels helpless in the relationship. He has tried to love better and more, yet the problem continues. Because being "good" generally means being caring and compassionate, he doesn't have access to other helpful tools, such as truthfulness, honesty, limits, and consequences.

Third, the "good" spouse can easily take a morally superior position toward his spouse. Since his contributions to the problem may not be as obvious, he may think, *I am not capable of being as destructive as my mate.* This is a dangerous position to take. We are all capable of just about anything, due to our own sinful nature (Romans 3:10–18). We need to be careful about this: "So, if you think you are standing firm, be careful that you don't fall!" (1 Corinthians 10:12). Any time we focus on our goodness, we turn our hearts away from our need for love and forgiveness.

Living by the Same Rules

We need to realize our need for limits because we need to submit ourselves to the same rules we want our partner to submit to. Submitting to the boundary process is the great equalizer in marriage and keeps both spouses in a mutual relationship instead of in a one-up or one-down one. Both need to accept and respect the limits of the other; no one plays God, doing what he wants and expecting the other to comply. When one mate protests her spouse's disorganization yet will not look at her own controlling tendencies, she stands little chance of seeing him change. She is being a hypocrite in that she is demanding of him what she isn't doing herself. Sooner or later, this hypocrisy will break down any good influence on the other spouse.

A couple I know struggled with the husband's tendency to withdraw if he thought his wife was not hearing him. She, in turn, would become angry that he was isolating himself. They argued about this for a long time. Finally, the next time he withdrew, she said to him, "Tell me what I did to hurt you." He broke down crying, thereby moving out of isolation. When he saw her set limits on her own anger and frustration, and instead show concern about his hurt, he moved back into relationship with her.

Freeing Your Spouse by Setting Limits with Yourself

When you set limits on yourself, you create an environment in which your spouse can become free to choose and grow. It is tempting to try to change your spouse. Controlling, nagging, complying to seek approval, and blaming are all futile in helping your spouse to grow. Your spouse will only react to your control. He won't experience his loneliness, need for love, gratitude, healthy guilt, or the consequences of his actions. He will be more concerned with staying free of your attempts to change him, or even with retaliating, to show you how it feels to be him.

For example, Brian suffered from the Peter Pan syndrome: He didn't want to grow up. He was into good times and fun and tried to stay away from boring tasks and responsibilities. As you can imagine, he had many career and financial problems. Andie, his wife, felt saddled with Brian's burdens. So she tried to nag him into growing up and into feeling guilty. She would tell him, "Don't you realize what you're doing to me? After all I've done for you, and this is how you treat me!"

These statements were similar to what Brian's mother would say when he was irresponsible as a child. With Mom, he would feel a momentary guilt, then do whatever he could to escape her. And he did the same with Andie. The more she protested, the further Brian ran, feeling the same smothering guilt that had been so difficult for him as a child.

Finally, Andie set limits on her attempts to control Brian. She became loving and caring toward him, without being critical. And she set firm limits on his job and money problems. She asked a financial counselor at their church for help. Brian lost some rights to his money for a while until he proved himself more mature. He changed because Andie freed him by limiting her nagging. Before that, Brian had

> *You cannot make your spouse grow up.*

only been reacting to Andie/Mother. Now Brian became free to experience her love, which he desperately needed. And he became free to experience the pain of loss of money and being with the financial counselor, who set up an accountability structure from which he couldn't run. And he began growing up.

You cannot make your spouse grow up—that is between him and God. But you can make it easier for him to experience the love and limits he needs. When he faces the consequences of his immaturity, he stands a better chance of changing than if he faces your nagging and hounding. Become truthful, not controlling.

In the rest of this chapter, we will deal with the two major areas in which we need to set boundaries with ourselves in marriage. The first is our own character issues. The second is how we relate to our spouse's.

Setting Boundaries with Our Own Character

Liz and Greg are friends of mine. Liz illustrates the idea of setting boundaries on our own character as well as anyone I know. Her marriage to Greg is less than satisfying. He's a good person, but he's self-absorbed and uninterested in personal growth. He will listen to Liz talk about a seminar she has been to, or page through a book she wants him to read, but that's about it.

Greg's disinterest in personal growth has been a loss for Liz over the years of their marriage. She had wanted to pair with someone who seeks after God and wants to continue to grow as she does. However, she has adapted to the holes in her marriage. While she loves her husband and invests in their life together, she also has deep, regular contact with others who are into growth. She has stayed connected to these people for many years.

What Liz does that has so impressed me is that on a regular basis she will ask Greg, "What do you see me doing that hurts or bothers you?" And whatever Greg says, Liz will take it to heart. If he mentions a truly troublesome part of her character, Liz will work on changing and maturing that part of her. She takes initiative to humble herself to a husband who, as of yet, has never asked her the same question: "What do you see *me* doing that hurts or bothers *you?*"

Liz has no hidden agenda with Greg, such as "I'll change for you if you'll change for me." She simply wants to be what God intended her to be, and she believes Greg is a source of good insight into the weaknesses she needs to address. Whether or not Greg ever gets curious about his own growth is irrelevant to her own journey, though she deeply desires and prays for this to happen.

The highest calling of a spouse is the call to love, just as it is the highest calling of our faith: loving God and each other (Matthew 22:37–40). Love means doing what you can for your spouse. And setting boundaries on your own character weaknesses is one of the most loving things you can do in your marriage. When you grow, you become more tender, more empathic, and yet more honest and firm in your convictions. You become someone who is better to live with. It always saddens me to see a person get into the spiritual growth process and immediately alienate her spouse with her intrusiveness, judgmentalism, and self-centeredness. The spouse of someone who is growing spiritually should be better off, not worse off!

Process, Not Perfection

When we look at our own character issues, we cannot *will* ourselves to maturity. We don't have the power to change our spouse; nor can we change our destructive behaviors and attitudes by "just saying no." As the Bible teaches, we are unable to change ourselves, in and of ourselves: "I do not understand what I do. For what I want to do I do not do, but what I hate I do" (Romans 7:15).

> *We cannot* will *ourselves to maturity.*

However, we do have some power and choices. We can choose to tell the truth about our faults. We can choose to bring those faults into the light of relationship. We can choose to repent of them and to work them out and mature them. Setting limits on ourselves sometimes simply involves taking a troublesome emotion, behavior, or attitude to a supportive relationship, instead of acting on it.

Here are some character issues in our own lives on which we can set limits:

Playing God

By human nature, we try to play God instead of seeking him. We need to continually own this worst and most hurtful aspect of our character. By playing God, we miss the mark in loving, being responsible, and caring about the welfare of our spouse.

Submit this part of yourself to God's authority. Let him know that the desire to play God is larger than your power to stop it, and ask for his help. Stay connected to the life of God and his people. Practice the spiritual disciplines of worship, prayer, fellowship, and Scripture reading: "Do not offer the parts of your body to sin, as instruments of wickedness, but rather offer yourselves to God, as those who have been brought from death to life" (Romans 6:13). As you stay in God's love, his presence in your life limits sin. Because you love him, you want to obey him (John 14:23).

Denial

When we do not admit the truth about who we are, we give our spouse no one with whom to connect. "If we claim to be without sin, we deceive ourselves and the truth is not in us" (1 John 1:8). What we deny about ourselves is absent from love. If, for example, you deny your struggle with insecurity by attempting to be strong, your spouse cannot love and have compassion for your insecure parts. This impoverishes the marriage bond and prevents a deeper connection with your spouse.

Learn to set limits on your bent toward denying who you are. The opposite of denial is confession, or agreeing with the truth. Most likely, your mate knows the truth anyway. Work on your tendency to deny and rationalize your failure, weakness, selfishness, or hurtfulness. When you confess who you are, you are being emotionally present with your spouse. Not only that, but you are also allowing your mate to minister to the vulnerable parts of you.

So many husbands and wives I've talked to over the years have been quite surprised at the warm reception they received from their mates when they came out of denial. Their spouses understood the great risk their partners took to admit their weaknesses, and they were compassionate and supportive. Remember that God has also placed inside your spouse a desire to live and grow in the light of his love: He has set eternity in her heart (Ecclesiastes 3:11). Help stir that part to life with your own openness.

Withdrawal from Relationship

Failing to make and keep emotional connections is a serious character issue. One or both spouses pull away and avoid being open and vulnerable with the other. There are numerous reasons for this. Some people have basic trust injuries. Others fear that the relationship will control or hurt them. Still others can only feel free or set limits by cutting off the relationship itself. Whatever the cause, emotional isolation withdraws the most basic part of ourselves from the source of life: relatedness to God and others.

Sometimes withdrawal manifests itself in the marriage as emotional absence. A wife will report that her husband is "there but not there." In other cases, one spouse will be able to give love and support, but will be unable to receive it. In still other cases, the spouse can stay connected at some level; however, when the connection becomes deeper and more emotional, he disengages.

Though the ideal of marriage is that all parts of one spouse connect to all parts of the other, most couples struggle with their tendency to withdraw their hearts from each other. Withdrawal makes them feel safer and more protected. However, when they allow withdrawal to continue unchecked, they can condemn their union to slow starvation. Marriage requires love to sustain itself.

If you find yourself enticed by withdrawal and avoidance, you can do the following to help you set boundaries on this tendency:

- Enlist the aid of your spouse. Ask her to let you know when she notices you pulling away. Ask her how it affects her. Does it hurt her? Make her lonely? Finding out how your avoidance influences others is a way to limit your disconnection.
- Discover why you withdraw. You could fear rejection, being controlled, or being judged. You could be

punishing your spouse for hurting you. Understanding the reasons can help you set limits on the behavior.
- Say no to your tendency to avoid relationships, and expose yourself to others who can help you connect.

Irresponsibility

Ever since the Fall, we have protested the reality that our lives are our problem and no one else's. All of us desire either to have someone else take responsibility for us or to avoid the consequences of our actions. This is how children and immature adults go through life. They argue that "it's not fair" that they have to shoulder their own burdens. They drive their spouses crazy trying to shirk their jobs in life.

Some of us have more difficulty with taking responsibility than others do. For example, you may leave certain projects, chores, or financial tasks undone at work or in your marriage for someone else to finish up. Or you may argue when others say no to you. The inability to accept another's no indicates a difficulty in taking ownership of your own disappointment and sadness and a struggle in allowing others freedom. If you have problems with responsibility, here's what you can do to help (if you don't think you have a problem here, ask your spouse in the off chance that you may!):

- Submit yourself to safe people who can confront you on your irresponsibility. For example, I have a friend who is "unconventional." She starts things and doesn't finish them; she forgets lunch dates; she keeps people waiting. She regularly asks her friends, "I want you to tell me when I bug you with my flakiness. It really helps me to change." And they do.
- Accept both consequences and feedback for your problem. Tell others to stop enabling you and, for example, to leave for the party without you if you're late. Realize that the consequences will help you structure your life better.

- Tell your spouse that his silence and/or nagging aren't helping you. Ask him to love you, but at the same time to provide limits for you when you don't set them on yourself.

Self-Centeredness

Nothing is more natural than to think more of our own situation than another's. Thinking that the sun rises and sets only on us is one of the most destructive, marriage-busting character issues. Marriage cannot be successfully navigated without our giving more of ourselves than we are comfortable giving. Yet self-absorbed people often attempt to live as a single person within marriage, thinking they can get what is important to them and still pull off the relationship. The result is that the spouse feels like an object, or feels that her own thoughts and feelings aren't valued.

The structure of marriage itself is anti-selfish. Marriage exposes our weaknesses and failings to the other person. It shows us the limits to our goodness. It takes away the sense that everything revolves around us. And not addressing our own egocentrism can hurt.

A couple I know had to work on this issue. When their children were in elementary and junior high school, the husband had tremendous struggles when he would arrive home at the end of his workday. He had always dreamed of coming home, having his wife and kids run to the door to greet him, and sitting in the kitchen talking about his day. In reality, everyone was happy to see him, but no one jumped up to meet him. They sat there and said, "Hi, Dad," and whatever was happening when he walked through the door wasn't automatically put on hold while he reviewed his day. He had to work hard to avoid blaming them and withdrawing from the family as he gave up his unrealistic dreams.

Here are some ideas to help set boundaries on your self-centeredness:

- Ask your spouse to tell you when he doesn't feel that things are mutual between you, or when he thinks he has to constantly see reality your way.

- Learn to let go of the demand to be perfect or special. Accept instead being loved for the real you, warts and all.
- Say no to the urge to be "good," and learn the skills of forgiveness and grief. Forgiveness and grief will help you accept the reality of who you are and who your spouse is.

Judgmentalism

Many spouses struggle with judging, criticizing, and condemning others. They have difficulty accepting differences in others and see the differences as black and white. And they often misread a person's actions out of a need to be loved and accepted: they hate both the sin and the sinner.

Nothing kills love in a marriage more than judgmentalism. When you live with a judge, you are always on trial. This creates an atmosphere of fear as the judged spouse walks on eggshells to avoid the wrath to come. Love cannot grow in a climate of fear: "There is no fear in love.... fear has to do with punishment" (1 John 4:18). A spouse's love can grow if she knows the consequences for her actions. This is the loving discipline of growth. But the fear of punishment is very different. Her very soul and character are tried and condemned, and then cast out of relationship.

If you have the "judge" role in your marriage, these tasks will help you grow out of this position:

- Ask for feedback on how your attitude hurts those you love. Judgmental people are often surprised at how wounding they can be.
- Become aware of your own attacking conscience. Most judging types have a very strict internal judge that punishes them. Learn to receive compassion and forgiveness from God and others for your own failings. This can help soften the conscience.
- Develop compassion for the faults of others. Remember that we all are lost without God's help.

The above character issues can be major sources of distance and disharmony in marriage. Yet, when you own them, set limits on their hurtfulness, and submit them to God's process of growth, love can flourish.

Boundaries on Our Attempts to Control

Of all the aspects of ourselves we need to set limits on, our tendency to control our spouse is probably the most crucial. Ever since the Garden of Eden, we have tried to run each other's lives. The strategies, manipulations, and tactics spouses employ to change their mate are endless. And if there is any sure-fire way to destroy trust and love, control is it. We must give our love freely. We may not say, "I will love you if you do this or that." As the Bible teaches, "It is for freedom that Christ has set us free.

> *If there is any sure-fire way to destroy trust and love, control is it.*

Stand firm, then, and do not let yourselves be burdened again by a yoke of slavery" (Galatians 5:1). When we feel controlled, freedom disappears, and love is threatened.

"Other-control" is the antithesis of having boundaries in marriage. Boundaries relinquish other-control for self-control (Galatians 5:23). Boundaries preserve the freedom of one's spouse without at the same time enabling the irresponsibility of that spouse.

How can you determine if someone is attempting control? Here are several indicators:

- Not respecting the other's no. The husband will make several attempts to change the decision of his spouse and disregard her feelings.
- Punishing a "wrong" choice. When the husband chooses to do something the wife doesn't like, the wife will act put out or like a victim, or she will accuse her husband of not being loving or caring.
- Not valuing freedom. The husband will be more interested in his wife's making the "right" decision, than in her free, heartfelt choice.

- Bad results. The wife who is being controlled will be resentful, act out, or retaliate.

God is the only one who could justifiably control our decisions, and yet he refrains from doing so. He gives us freedom to choose, and he weeps when our choices lead to ruin: "O Jerusalem, Jerusalem, you who kill the prophets and stone those sent to you, how often I have longed to gather your children together, as a hen gathers her chicks under her wings, but you were not willing" (Matthew 23:37). God places such a high premium on our freedom that he shies away from forcing us to do things that would benefit us. He understands that we will never learn to love or respond to him without that costly freedom.

In this section we will shed light on the ways we attempt to control our partners, and we will also provide ways to set boundaries on this unfortunate tendency.

Control Comes in Different Flavors

Connor felt a sense of déjà vu. He had had this argument with Stacy so many times that he could almost predict her lines. As usual, it started with a small thing that mushroomed. Connor had grudgingly agreed to go to the opera with Stacy a few weeks earlier. He didn't enjoy opera, but she had insisted. In the back of his mind, however, Connor kept a little scoreboard. On it, he had logged the opera date as a point for leveraging his way to an event he wanted to go to.

A friend offered Connor tickets to a pro baseball game, and he eagerly anticipated going. However, Stacy reminded him that her mom was coming for a long-planned visit on that day. Connor reminded Stacy about his opera sacrifice. Stacy stood firm. Then he exploded, saying, "This is the payment I get for all I do for you! How could you be so ungrateful!"

At this, Stacy collapsed in tears, even though she had experienced Connor's tantrums many times. She sobbed, "Why did you ever marry me, if you want to hurt me so much?" With that, she ran upstairs.

Immediately feeling guilty over his hurtfulness, Connor followed his wife upstairs. He finally calmed her down and promised he would be at home when her mom came over. Both Connor and Stacy tried to take freedom from each other, which is the essence of control. He still felt resentful inside, but his guilt covered it up for now.

Connor's blowup was an aggressive way to intimidate Stacy into changing her mind and a way to punish her for not keeping the score between them even. Stacy's breakdown was a more indirect way to punish Connor for his anger, and also a means of getting him to change his mind. Neither one valued the free choices of his or her spouse.

Let us look at some of the ways that, like Connor and Stacy, couples attempt to control each other.

Guilt

Guilt messages are intended to make our spouse feel responsible for our welfare. In other words, guilt controls by creating the impression that our spouse's freedom injures us. By choosing differently from us, our spouse has thus been unloving. Statements such as "If you really loved me" or "How could you be so selfish?" and wounded silences convey the message. Stacy's breakdown illustrates the guilt message.

Anger

Often, when one spouse wants something the other doesn't, the disappointed mate will become angry. Anger is our basic protest against the fact that we are not God and that we cannot control reality. Anger can be direct, as in Connor's tantrum. It can be covert, as in passive-aggressive behaviors or sarcastic remarks. It can involve threats of retaliation. It can also, in extreme situations, become dangerous, as in abusive marriages.

Persistent Assaults on the Spouse's Boundary

One person will say no, then the spouse will make attempt after attempt to change the other's mind. Like a strong-willed door-to-door salesperson, the spouse will argue, wheedle, and plead until the other has been worn down. Like a child who has learned to keep asking until he hears the answer he wants, the spouse refuses to live with the boundary of the other.

Withholding Love

Of all the ways we attempt to control, withholding love may be the most powerful. When one spouse disagrees, the other disconnects emotionally until the spouse changes to suit her. This is so powerful because God created us to need love and connection as our source of life. When someone withdraws this from us, we are without the basis of existence. It puts extreme pressure on us to do anything to connect to the one we love.

Submitting to Boundaries on Our Control

The spouse who truly loves his mate and wants her to grow spiritually will, at some point, desire to give up these attempts to control. He will be willing to relinquish these strategies in favor of granting freedom and love. Here are some of the ways you can set limits on your controlling attempts.

Realize the Cost of Other-Control

The cost of other-control is that you might get external compliance, but lose your spouse's heart. Guilt, anger, assaults, and withholding all negate freedom and love. The spouse will go along, but will often be resentful or emotionally absent. Set limits on your desire for other-control as you place a higher value on love.

Ask Your Spouse to Let You Know How Your Control Affects Him

Since marriage is at its core a bond of empathy, your mate's feelings are important to you. Often, when the controlled spouse lets the controlling spouse know how hurtful and distant the attempts make him, the controlling spouse feels compassion for the pain and is able to better set limits on the control.

Experience Your Own Helplessness to Change Your Spouse

No matter how much you would like to believe the opposite, your spouse will not change her decisions, opinions, or feelings until she is ready to. You may need to realize that you live with someone whom you can't "make" do the right thing. This helplessness is often a very painful emotion. Angry control moves may give us the illusion that we have power over our spouse that we don't have. Accepting helplessness hurts, but it's where reality lies.

Learn to Grieve

Grief helps us to accept the truth and to let go of things we can't change or have. When you allow your spouse freedom, you will often feel loss and sadness about losing what you desired from him. Allowing yourself to feel this grief frees you to accept reality and find new ways to adapt to your marriage.

Work Through Dependency Issues

If your spouse is the only person through whom you can get needs met, you will have a bent toward controlling him. Find sources of love, approval, truth, or forgiveness that include your mate, but are not limited to him. For example, you may have a need for recognition of the good things you accomplish. Don't expect your spouse to provide all of the kudos. Use your friends to meet this need as well. When you have other places to get your needs met, you are better able to give your spouse freedom.

Be a Separate Person with Your Spouse

Sometimes one mate will define herself by her mate and not be her own individual soul. Then, when her spouse disagrees or makes a different decision, she personalizes the difference as an attack against her. For example, a husband will become angry with his wife for something. She will feel that he hates her and will lash back to protect herself. Her inability to be separate from her husband's feelings is the problem. As you become more defined by your own boundaries, you will experience your mate's feelings and decisions as having more to do with him than with you. This will free you to allow him to be free.

Value Your Spouse's Freedom As You Want Your Freedom Valued

Jesus' Golden Rule of doing to others as you would have them do to you (Matthew 7:12) is the basis for how spouses are to treat each other. Remember how it felt the last time someone attacked you for your freedom to choose and therefore have compassion on your spouse's choices.

Set Boundaries with Your Spouse Instead of Controlling Him

Often, a wife will resort to control strategies because she feels unable to say no or be free with her husband. She may be afraid of her partner's reactions and may feel she can't protect herself. Control becomes a substitute for establishing boundaries of self-control with her spouse. As you set appropriate limits, you can feel safe and give up controlling your partner.

As you can see, marriage has more to do with bringing yourself under the control of God and his principles than it does with controlling your spouse. However, as you relinquish control of your partner, you are able to better love him, protect your own freedom, and provide a context for both of you to grow.

In the next chapter we will show you how important it is for you to be a separate person from your spouse. Ironically, being an individual is the key to becoming one with your mate.

Part Two

Building Boundaries in Marriage

Chapter 4

It Takes Two to Make One

Oneness. It's the word romance is made of. It's the thing couples dream about when they first meet. Listen to a friend's description when she feels she has finally found "the one." Watch an old movie, and you'll see the leading man and the leading lady gazing into each other's eyes with the fantasy of total oneness.

In reality, this oneness is not a fantasy at all. It's God's very design for marriage. It's the Bible's description of marriage. From the beginning, in the Garden of Eden, God decided that it was "not good for the man to be alone," and he put man and woman together to establish this oneness everyone seeks (Genesis 2:18). And Jesus told us, "'A man will leave his father and mother and be united to his wife, and the two will become one flesh.' So they are no longer two, but one" (Mark 10:7–8). So the movies are right after all: Oneness is real life.

What the movies don't show, however, is what it takes to get there! Most people have felt the initial fantasy of oneness. In the first stage of falling in love, a couple give up all internal boundaries and feel a euphoric sense of merging with each other. You hear them say things like "He's everything I've dreamed of" and "She's a goddess!" and "We are so perfectly matched." This initial stage of a relationship can be wonderful as couples experience the state of "oneness" for which they have longed. But these experiences are not real oneness. They are only a "preview." Oneness is built over time as a relationship grows and as "two become one."

The movies don't show us this part—the part where the initial euphoria goes away, the oneness disappears, and the couple become disillusioned. They wonder, "What went wrong? Did I marry the wrong person?" At this point more than half give up and part ways. They think they can "do better" with someone else, not knowing that the remedy probably lies in their own growth, not in finding a new person. A new relationship will require the same growing pains, both as individuals and as a couple, that they are avoiding now.

In this chapter we will examine how every married couple needs to grow. We will look first at the prerequisite of "two becoming one." This prerequisite is that, for "two to become one," we must have *two* at the outset. *Two complete individuals*. What does this mean? And what does this have to do with boundaries?

"Twoness"

The requirement for oneness is *two complete people*. The Bible defines a complete person as a mature person. A complete person is able to do all the things that adult life and relationship requires: give love and receive love, be independent and self-sufficient, live out values honestly, be responsible, have self-confidence, deal with problems and failures, live out their talents, and have a life. If two people who marry are complete, the oneness they establish will be complete. To the degree that either is less than complete as a person, the oneness will suffer under the strain of that incompleteness. The incomplete partner's longing for completeness will take precedence over what he is able to give to the relationship, and the relationship will suffer.

> *Marriage is not meant to be the place where one gets completed as a person.*

So, if one or both are coming to the marriage asking the marriage to complete them as people, the marriage will break down. Marriage is not meant to be the place where one gets completed as a person. It is meant for complete persons to come together and build a "we" that is bigger and better than either one of the "I's" involved. As Frederick Buechner says in *Whistling in the Dark*, "A marriage made in Heaven is one where a man and a woman become more richly themselves together than the chances are either of them could ever have managed to become alone."

But marriage is an adult contract, and you should not attempt it without two adults present! For a marriage to work, two separate individuals need to have some elements of adulthood. No one has ever made it to adulthood ready for all that it requires. The good news is that you can grow toward this adulthood, or completeness, and as you do, your relationship will attain more and more oneness as well. Before we take a look at the requirements of adulthood, we would like to make one more important point about two becoming one.

Completing Versus Complementing Each Other

As we said above, marriage was not designed to complete a person. It was designed for two complete people to enter into and form something different than either of them is on his or her own. It was designed, not to make you a whole person, but to give your wholeness a new range of experience.

But many people see marriage as a ticket to short-cut completeness, or maturity. Therefore they don't marry out of strength, but out of weakness. They marry someone to make up for what they do not possess on their own. They marry out of their incompleteness, and doing so erodes the possibility for oneness.

You may have heard couples say, "We are such a good balance for each other." This can be good if, for example, he is good at business and she is good at building the nest, or vice versa. But it is not good if it means that she could not survive in the real world of work and commerce on her own without him. If this is true, she has married a "meal ticket," or someone to take care of her in a childlike dependency. And he has married a "mother" to make the home that he could not build for himself while he goes off and plays during the day.

This point is so important that we are going to say it again: The crucial element of "two becoming one" is that the two people must be complete in and of themselves—they must be adults—before they marry. This does not mean that the husband and wife possess all of the same talents and abilities, or even the same style. It does mean, however, that they possess all of adult functioning in key areas of personhood.

> *The crucial element of "two becoming one" is that the two people must be complete in and of themselves—they must be adults—before they marry.*

He might not have her business acumen. She might not have his creativity or his ability to be the extroverted life of the party. This is not what we are talking about. These characteristics *complement* each other, not *complete* each other.

Complementing means bringing different perspectives, talents, abilities, experiences, and other gifts to the relationship and forming a partnership. A couple I know runs a family business. The husband is good at operations while the wife is good at sales. Another couple may complement each other in financial management and ability to create income. One might be good at seeing the problems in a new opportunity while the other is good at finding the opportunities. But all of these facets help the couple work together as a team.

Completing means *making up for one's immaturity as a person.* It is an attempt to use another person to balance an imbalance in one's character, and it never works. Each person is responsible for developing these character imbalances on one's own and then bringing a whole, balanced self into the relationship.

Areas of Completeness That Marriage Cannot Provide

As we said above, many times people will marry to make up for what they do not possess in their own character. This is often what is behind the head-over-heels, "falling in love" experience. Someone who is incomplete in some area will meet someone

who has a strength in that area and feel an intoxicating "wholeness." Let us give you an example.

Amanda was milling around at a gathering at her company.
And then it happened. She saw him across the room: suave,
strong, and assertive. His confidence was apparent as she
watched him talk to others and mingle. She could feel herself
tingle as she saw Eric's command of the situation.

She made her way over to the circle of people around Eric
and was introduced. Eric took control of the conversation and
made her and everyone around him feel at ease. Her initial
attraction multiplied, and by the end of the party she was getting that "swept off her feet" feeling. He seemed very much in
command. What a prince she had found!

They began dating, and her initial impression turned out to
be correct. He was suave, strong, and assertive. Sometimes she
felt that he was too strong, and he didn't listen to what she had
to say. But their "love" was strong, and her need for him was
more powerful than her reason and ability to see the significance
of the problem.

They soon married, and what initially attracted Amanda to
Eric became her worst nightmare. In reality, he was more than
strong and assertive. He was smooth and domineering. As the
relationship progressed, she felt more and more walked over and
less and less able to have a say-so in what went on. A few months
down the road, they came in for counseling.

Her complaint was that he was too domineering. His complaint was that she was always pouting and quietly angry with
him. In reality, what had happened was that each of them had
found their own incompleteness somehow "completed" in the
other, and they soon discovered the problems associated with
that false solution.

Amanda was an attractive, loving, social person, always willing to please others. Everyone loved her. But she had a weakness. She did not have the ability to be as assertive as she needed
to be. She adapted to others rather than confronting them; she
was unable to stand up for herself and what she needed and
wanted. She needed to become more assertive in life. This was

her area of incompleteness. Having grown up under a dominating father, she had not developed her ability to stand up to others. So she desperately needed that function to be whole. And instead of developing it in herself, she found it in Eric. This is why she felt so "completed" when she saw his strength. The problem was that she did not have enough strength to stand up to him in the relationship and was being reduced to a nonperson, an extension of whatever he wanted. She began to resent him.

Eric was the opposite. Compliance to others, vulnerability, and embracing an appropriate sense of powerlessness were the ingredients missing from his personality. He was afraid of those characteristics in himself, and he always took control to avoid feeling them. But, since those are real aspects of a complete person, he also longed to experience them. And he found them in Amanda. Her "sweet spirit" and ability to give in to what others needed and wanted was what he found so attractive—until she stopped being so sweet and resented him for wanting so much. He, just like her, began to hate what he was attracted to initially because he was in conflict with that part of his incompleteness.

Neither Amanda nor Eric was a complete "one," a whole person. They tried to solve their incompleteness by a merger with someone who possessed what they did not. And this always backfires. They battled in the other what they could not come to terms with inside themselves. This is one of the reasons that the Bible so often talks about completeness as a view of maturity (James 1:4).

They had to work to become "two," who could then establish a oneness based on the real intimacy of two people and not on the false sense of security the other provided. Eric had to grow and face his selfishness, his inability to hear and respect no from others, and his fears of adapting and being controlled. Amanda had to learn to be more assertive and speak up for herself and become comfortable with the conflict that came when she did speak up. She had to grow out of the little girl who needed Daddy's approval into a mature adult who could handle her husband's being displeased with her.

Eric and Amanda illustrate that there is no shortcut to growth. You cannot skip out on maturity by "marrying into it." You must become a complete individual on your own in order to have true oneness with your spouse.

Make sure you understand the difference between completing one another versus complementing one another. Eric was still the business whiz that Amanda would never be. She was the organizer and project manager that he would never be. He was creative and entrepreneurial. She was systematic. They had gifts that worked well at creating a team. Those are good complements.

> *You must become a complete individual on your own in order to have true oneness with your spouse.*

But basic human requirements of character are not complements. They are essentials to being a complete person. Below is a partial list of abilities that both partners must possess and that cannot be "borrowed" from each other. The ability to

- Connect emotionally
- Be vulnerable and share feelings
- Have an appropriate sense of power and assertiveness
- Say no
- Have initiative and drive
- Have at least a minimal amount of organization
- Be real, but not perfect
- Accept imperfections and have grace and forgiveness
- Grieve
- Think for oneself and express one's opinions
- Learn and grow
- Take risks
- Grasp and use one's talents
- Be responsible and follow through
- Be free and not controlled by external or internal factors

- Be sexual
- Be spiritual
- Have a moral sense
- Have an intellectual life

These human abilities everyone possesses, although not everyone is able to express them. Make sure that the two of you develop these spiritual and human characteristics on your own. If you do, then you will each become a complete person, and the two of you can "become one."

But how can you go about developing these characteristics? How can you become a complete, mature, and whole person? What exactly are the requirements of adulthood?

Adults Take Responsibility for Their Treasures

In chapter 1 we talked about the importance of your taking responsibility for certain aspects of your soul, the treasures that lie within your boundaries. Remember the list? Here it is again:

- Feelings
- Attitudes
- Behaviors
- Choices
- Limits
- Desires
- Thoughts
- Values
- Talents
- Love

We talked about the importance of people's realizing that they own these treasures and that they need to take responsibility for them. We talked about what happens when they don't. When ownership and responsibility are lacking, blame is shifted and problem solving breaks down.

So the first requirement of adults, or completed persons, is that they take responsibility for all of the treasures of their souls. If they don't, their marriage will stagnate to the degree that they disown aspects of their lives and then either blame the other or require the other to fix it or make up for it.

For example, if a wife does not take responsibility for how she feels, she blames her partner when she feels unhappy. Her kind of irresponsibility translates like this: "If I feel bad, you are doing something wrong. You should be doing something different." How many divorces and how much unhappiness occur because one partner depends on the other for happiness and completeness?

How can this be avoided? First, by each person taking ownership of her own treasures, which we talked about in chapter 1. And second, by each person requiring her spouse to take ownership as well, which we will talk about now.

Requiring Ownership

Remember the term *codependency*, which was a buzzword of the 1980s? Basically, codependency is taking responsibility for another person's problems and not requiring that person to take responsibility for his own. Why do we mention it here in a section on becoming a complete person? Because a mature, complete adult not only takes responsibility for himself, but also requires the same from the people he loves. To be codependent and not require responsibility from others is to not be responsible oneself. Let's look at an example of codependency.

> *A mature, complete adult not only takes responsibility for himself, but also requires the same from the people he loves.*

Scooter had hit a wall in his relationship with Maggie. He came to see me (Dr. Cloud), and his first complaint was about himself. "I just can't seem to be the right kind of husband. I keep letting Maggie down, and I don't know how to do better." He talked for quite a while about how guilty he felt because he was such a failure as a husband.

I empathized with him for what it must feel like to have performed so poorly, and then I asked him to tell me some of the problem areas where he was failing so badly. He gave me such a long list that I could not have kept up if I had not been taking notes. Here are just a few examples:

1. Letting her down by not making enough money to provide for all her needs
2. Working too much and making her unhappy because he was gone so much
3. Forgetting to do things that were important to her
4. Continuing to work with a woman who was a problem

I could see that this was going to take a lot of work if he was so oblivious that he continued to do longstanding hurtful things. Think of it! Financial irresponsibility and non-performance. Abandonment. Treating her as unimportant. Misplaced loyalty. *What an insensitive person*, I thought.

So we went to work, and I asked him about each of these situations. I was amazed at what I found out. Here was reality:

1. Scooter was not making enough money to buy Maggie a new car every two years.
2. Even though he worked at home, Scooter had a handful of meetings during the week for which he had to leave home. He might have to go downtown for three or four hours. Maggie would feel abandoned.
3. Maggie would give Scooter a long list of things to do, and he might not get all of them done in the time period she specified.
4. Maggie did not like a woman with which Scooter had a business deal. The woman was doing a good job on the as-yet-unfinished project, but Maggie did not like her and felt that this was reason enough for him to default on his agreements.

Scooter did have some problems. But the problem he had was not that he was such a bad husband, but that he was so codependent that he did not require Maggie to take responsibility for her own feelings and attitudes. He had to learn that he was not responsible for meeting all of her demands and that it was okay for him to say no to some and not internalize her blame.

Her unrealistic financial wishes were standing in the way of her taking responsibility for her envy and lack of contentment. When he gave in to her, he did not require her to deal with herself and her problems.

One of the greatest gifts we can give to each other is the gift of honesty and confrontation. As Proverbs tells us, "Wounds from a friend can be trusted, but an enemy multiplies kisses" (Proverbs 27:6). We grow when someone who loves us "wounds" us by telling us painful truths we need to hear. Requiring responsibility from each other by telling each other the truth and not giving in to each other's immaturity is indeed a gift.

Adults Value Their Treasures and Those of Their Spouse

In the opening story of this book, Stephanie found herself pulling away from her husband, Steve. She felt that her marriage was more "for Steve" than it was "for them," or even "for her." Stephanie had not valued her own "treasures." She had done what many people do and then find themselves unhappy later. She had ignored her own treasures and had not valued them in the marriage enough to ensure they were getting developed.

Stephanie had ignored her feelings, her attitudes, and her talents while she was "living for Steve." Her treasures were going to waste. But since they were a living part of her, they continued to speak to her in the form of a deep sense of discontentment in her life. Finally, she had to value them because they were getting the best of her.

We can't ignore aspects of our soul God has placed in us. Sooner or later, brushing them aside catches up with us.

In the same way, we must value the treasures of our spouses. Mature people think of nurturing, developing, and taking care of the treasures of the people with whom they are in relationship. They are always thinking of how their loved ones are doing, how they are feeling, and how they could help them grow. Mature husbands and wives place a great value on the feelings, thoughts, and attitudes of their spouse.

During a break at a meeting I attended recently, a couple of men were talking about making some plans for the near future. One man asked the other to meet with him over breakfast to discuss a potential investment. The other said, "Let me see how my wife feels about it, and I will get back to you." The first man, clearly annoyed, asked, "Why do you have to check with her? Can't you make your own decisions?"

> *Mature people think of nurturing, developing, and taking care of the treasures of the people with whom they are in relationship.*

The first man did not realize that it was not a matter of his friend being unable to make his own decisions. It was a matter of seeing how his wife would be affected by his plans. But more than that, he really wanted to know what she thought. He wanted her wisdom and her opinion on his plans. In short, *he valued her treasures.* They were important to him. This didn't mean that he was dependent on his wife and couldn't think for himself. He knew what he thought. But he placed such a high value on what his wife thought that he did not want to miss out on her perspective.

"Not wanting to miss out" is a good way to think of valuing the treasures of your spouse's soul. God has given you each other to know and to share. To value the treasures in the soul of the other is to not miss out on a wonderful gift from God to the both of you. This process of valuing others' treasures is something that mature people do and is part of being a complete person. It also acknowledges the separateness and completeness of the other person. It says, "I know you are a person, too, and I am interested in the person you are."

Adults Understand the Concept of "You Are Not Me"

The concept of "you are not me" is one of the most important aspects of boundaries. We are not extensions of each other. Instead, we are all individuals in our own right. We all need to overcome the basic egocentricity of life, the inborn feeling that "the world revolves around me." There are several components to this issue.

Seeing the Other As a Person, Not My Object

The first component is the ability to see your spouse as a separate person, distinct from you, with her own needs and feelings. In other words, she doesn't exist just to meet your needs. A very young child feels this way toward his mother. He feels that his every wish should be her command. It never occurs to him that she might have a life apart from him, or feelings apart from what he needs at the moment.

We all need to overcome the basic egocentricity of life, the inborn feeling that "the world revolves around me."

This mindset is acceptable in an infant or toddler. But in an adult spouse it can be a relationship wrecker.

Sally and Jim came to see me with "conflicts," as they put it. What was happening was that neither one could see the other as a person in his or her own right. When Sally wanted to talk with Jim, she could not see that he had been working hard, was tired, and wanted to go to bed. She would interpret his need for sleep as not caring about her.

In like fashion, when Jim wanted something done and it was not done the same day, he would become angry. "Where is my blue shirt?" would be more of an accusation than a question. He neglected to understand that Sally was taking care of a thousand other things that day and didn't get around to what he needed.

Whenever we view others only in terms of how they affect us, we are in big trouble.

Whenever we view others only in terms of how they affect us, we are in big trouble. This is self-centeredness. We reduce others to objects of our own needs, and we don't see them as real people. And whenever we don't see people for who they really are, love breaks down.

Allowing the Other's Experience

The second way in which we allow others to exist in their own right is to allow their experience. We need to put our own experience aside and join in the other's experience. We need to understand the other's experience, identify with it, and have compassion for the other in it. The ability to do this is called *empathy*. Empathy is a bedrock of intimacy.

If I can't allow you to be a person in your own right, then I can't empathize with you. I'll always take your experience as meaning something about me. Or I'll react to your feelings by thinking of myself, not you.

Karen and Will had this problem. In one of their sessions, they reported an incident the night before in which Karen had tried to share her feelings on what was going on in their relationship.

"I don't feel close to you lately," Karen said.

"What do you mean?" asked Will.

"I just feel disconnected."

"Great! Just great," Will said. "All I do is bust my butt for you and try to give you all my time and energy apart from work, and you don't even appreciate it. I don't even know why I try."

At this point Karen started to sob. She felt alone and not listened to. This had been a pattern in their relationship. Whenever Karen would try to tell Will how she felt about something, he would take it as an accusation of him; he couldn't listen to her and be with her in the experience. He didn't have the ability to empathize with her because he could not get past himself. Karen felt stuck in her attempts to get him to connect with her at a deep level.

To have good boundaries is to be separate enough from the other person that you can allow her to have her own experience without reacting with your own. Such a clear stance of separateness allows you not to react, but to care and empathize. Not allowing the other's experience can be a major cause of fighting and of feeling misunderstood.

Allowing the Freedom to Be Different

The third way in which we allow others to exist in their own right is allowing them the freedom to be different from us. What do a couple do when they differ? It all depends on how separate they are. Whether or not they can get to oneness will depend on how okay it is to have two opinions, moods, tastes, or needs in the relationship at once.

What if one wants sex and the other doesn't? What if they desire a different frequency? What if one feels like going out and the other doesn't? What if one wants a big house and the other one wants to save the money and avoid the financial pressure of a bigger mortgage? What happens depends on whether the couple can tolerate differences in each other.

In a good marriage, spouses value each other's differences and treat them with respect. They understand each other, listen, reason, compromise, and give up their own wishes sometimes. Because "twoness" exists, oneness can develop.

In a marriage in which the individuals aren't allowed to be different, things don't go as well. Husbands and wives judge each other as "bad" for the preferences each one has. Or they take the difference as a personal affront or a lack of love.

Simon had this problem with Jeri. Simon did not like the church that Jeri attended. He couldn't connect with the services she found so exciting and meaningful. And she could not accept his preference.

"It seems that if he really loved me, he would want to go to church with me," she would say in our sessions. "I don't know why he does this to me. He knows how important it is to me."

Simon would try to explain to her that the amount of overt expressionism in her church was too overwhelming to him and that it made him feel distant from everything. But she could not hear his difference. To her, it just meant that he did not care about what was important to her.

Differences are not bad. They are part of the stuff out of which love grows. The differences are what you like about a person at the beginning of a relationship and then fight about for the rest of your lives! Why is that? Differences are exciting and bring a sense of getting to enjoy something we don't possess. But differences threaten us if we have not matured enough to be truly separate people from each other. To immature people, differences imply distance, a lack of love, abandonment, rejection, or, in some cases, a challenge for *us* to grow. And under this threat, love gets put on the back burner for self-protection.

The ability to tolerate your spouse's differences is an important aspect of boundaries in marriage.

Cherishing the Other's Existence

"I just want to hear her describe it," Robert said about Susan's dance class.

"But you hate dancing," I said to him, wondering why he wanted to hear a play-by-play recap.

"I just want to hear it and see it through her eyes and ears. She gets things out of it that I just can't."

Robert loved Susan. And one of the things he loved about her was her ability to experience things like dancing at a very deep sensual level. He loved the way she processed life. In other words, he *cherished* her experience of life. He loved her essence, who she was apart from him.

What was so neat about what Robert did was that he loved something about Susan *that had nothing to do with him.* She was in no way meeting some need or interest of his. She was just being herself, and he was gaining pleasure from just knowing her and experiencing her. He cherished her just as she was, for just who she was. Even when she was not giving to him, she was important to him and loved by him.

Another part of the "you are not me" concept is the ability to see another person for who she is apart from what we want or need from her and to love and appreciate that person for who she is. To cherish someone's existence apart from you and apart from what you get from that person is a neat aspect of love. It requires very good boundaries, the ability to see the other person as distinct and separate from you—a person in her own right, with value and wonderful things about her that have nothing to do with gratifying you in any way other than pure appreciation. This is the joy of just knowing a person. This neat aspect of love is one of the ones that gives the most pleasure as couples grow together.

Adults Respect Each Other's Freedom

Freedom is a prerequisite of love. If someone controls us, love is not possible. Control results in slavery, not love. The ability for each partner to allow the other to be a free, separate person is one of the hallmarks of a solid relationship.

Free to Have Space

Rich was describing his relationship with Mary in one of our sessions. He had been single for a long time. All of his friends had pretty much decided that he would never marry. A successful attorney, a spiritual guy, and a generally nice man, Rich was a desirable catch. Many single women pursued him to no avail. And then it happened.

He fell head over heels in love with Mary. Everyone was amazed, but also convinced it wouldn't last. But months went by, and then two years, and Rich and Mary were still dating. Still, his friends knew the eventual Rich "bailout" was coming. What came instead was the proposal. And he followed through with marrying Mary.

In his descriptions of Mary that day, I could sense his pure joy in knowing her. And then he said something that should be a message to all married people, male or female. He said, "I am so thankful for the way she does not try to control me. I can feel free to do things at times with my friends and have some time on my own for my own interests. [He was an avid car-racing junkie.] She gives me space. And she was the first one I ever dated who did that."

I knew Mary. What he said was true. She liked the connection with Rich, but she also allowed him to be his own person with his own time and space. And this was not just a sacrifice on her part. It was part of her completeness as a person. She had her own interests as well. She was an avid tennis player and did a lot of volunteer work in her spare time. She was not just "giving Rich his space." She was exhibiting her own freedom and living it out reciprocally with him. He did not feel tied down, and neither did she.

Proverbs 31 gives a great picture of this kind of relationship. It describes a woman who has lots of activities of her own going on apart from her husband, while he has the same. She is out buying and selling, and he is sitting with his colleagues and praising her. They are both exhibiting their own separateness, yet they are deeply connected.

This balance of being deeply connected as well as free to be individuals is one of the most important aspects of completeness. It allows the development and growth of the individual partners as well as the marriage.

But many people struggle with allowing each other to be free. They operate on the philosophy of the old bumper sticker: "If you love someone, set them free. If they love you, they will return. And if they don't, hunt them down and kill them!" Freedom is okay until it displeases us in some way.

A good marriage among two complete people is one in which they keep their individuality and space, and this actually serves to strengthen their relationship. After they have been apart, they come together and share each partner's experience. Relishing these experiences with each other adds to intimacy.

The problem marriage is one in which one partner sees time apart, separateness, and space as a threat. This spouse may feel that separateness means a lack of love, or abandonment. She can only feel loved when with the other person. For example, I counseled a couple in which the wife was very upset and accused her husband of "not caring" because he wanted to go bowling with a group of friends once a week. Another person may fear that if his spouse has some degree of separateness, she will leave him or find someone else. Having separateness and feeling secure in love does not register for him.

Not that there is a certain "amount" of separateness that is good or bad for all couples. The amount has to be negotiated with wisdom so that the "we" does not suffer. There is no absolute. But couples who have a fundamental orientation toward freedom—the ones who do not see separateness as a threat—are able to work out those details

One of the most successful married couples I know sits down at the beginning of a year and decides the structure for that year. As an entertainment lawyer, he travels a lot for business. They decide ahead of time how many nights he will be gone that year. For example, if they decide the limit is one hundred nights, they say no to any engagement that brings the total over this limit. Notice I say, "*They* say no." They decide together. They assume that each partner is free, then they talk about how to spend the freedom, not whether or not it exists.

But freedom is the scariest of all human privileges. Adam and Eve used their freedom destructively to sin against God. In the same way, we can use freedom against each other. As Paul warns, "You, my brothers, were called to be free. But do not use your freedom to indulge the sinful nature; rather, serve one another in love. The entire law is summed up in a single command: 'Love your neighbor as yourself'" (Galatians 5:13–14). The call to relationship with God and each other is a call to freedom. But that freedom is not to be used to gratify self-centeredness.

Some spouses use their freedom to indulge their own desires at the expense of the marriage. Any trip to the grill room at a local golf course can testify to how many golfing widows there are, as their husbands spend most of their waking hours "with the guys." Wives of hunters and fishermen know this scenario as well as do husbands of over-committed wives. This misuse of freedom is selfish and does not serve anyone's growth and development, much less the growth of the marriage. Anyone can get selfish and fall back into the inborn egocentricity we talked about earlier.

So the Bible's warning offers the best solution for that danger: "Love your neighbor as yourself." In other words, in your exercise of separateness, make sure that you are seeing how your freedom and separateness are affecting your spouse. Would you want to be treated with disregard? Certainly not. Practice the Golden Rule.

But remember, it goes both ways. You are free to be separate, but you are also free to be controlling! No one can stop you except yourself. So, if you are trying to control your spouse's separateness and freedom with guilt and prohibition, then ask yourself the same question: Would you like to be imprisoned? Again, the answer is certainly not. The Golden Rule is the best defense against freedom becoming a license to be self-centered.

Good Fear of Reality

And if the Golden Rule doesn't stop you, maybe fear will. I have seen controlling spouses stop being controlling when the fear of reality—the probable consequences—invaded their hearts. The reality is that humans were created and wired by God to do two things. The first is to separate from their parents and be independent from the parental "guardian and manager" role (Galatians 4:1–2). The second is to be free (Galatians 5:1).

If you are controlling your spouse's freedom and separateness, you are no longer an object of love. You have become two things that your spouse will rebel against because it is part of God's plan. You have become the master of a slave, and you have become a parent. A spouse was never intended to be either.

If you are a controller, remember the price you will pay in the end. Your spouse will fight your control to be a free person and an adult. She was made to be an individual, free from control so that she could freely choose to bring that individuality to you to form a "we." If you take away this freedom, there is no longer a "two" to become "one." You have done away with the plan. The "oneness" will only be an extension of yourself.

Also, if you take away this freedom, she will "leave" that parental function you are providing and "cleave" to someone else. Children, not adults, were designed to be under "guardians and managers." Do not become a parent to your spouse by trying to manage her freedom. You will receive an active or a passive rebellion in return.

Rebelling against control is the motivation behind many affairs and other problems. The spouse who feels controlled is not mature enough to stand up to control with responsible boundaries, and he acts out in an affair to "gain a sense of freedom." He finds someone who accepts him, or so it feels in the lie of an affair. The freedom becomes intoxicating, and he falls like a sheep to the slaughter. As Proverbs warns of the adulteress, "With persuasive words she led him astray; she seduced him with her smooth talk. All at once he followed her like an ox going to the slaughter, like a deer stepping into a noose till an arrow pierces his liver, like a bird darting into a snare, little knowing it will cost him his life" (Proverbs 7:21–23).

Persuasive words are often words of flattery and freedom, words that give "relief" to the nagging and guilty feeling of control that a husband or wife is getting at home. Do not become this nagging parent. Give freedom, and require responsible use of that freedom in the service of love.

Longing

What brought you together to begin with? Lots of things, for sure—some of them healthy, some not. But one thing did for certain. God designed relationship to combat the problem he pronounced when Adam was not doing well as a bachelor: "It is not good for the man to be alone" (Genesis 2:18).

God designed human beings with a longing for relationship, with a longing to come together and not go through life alone. We all have this longing. While single people satisfy this longing with friends and relatives, married people go one step further; they meet part of this longing by finding a life partner. God designed marriage particularly to satisfy this longing for relationship, to give companionship on life's journey.

This drive for companionship must be kept at the forefront of our discussion of freedom. If one of you is controlling, if you restrict your partner's freedom, companionship is destroyed. But beyond that, freedom nourishes separateness, which is in and of itself *an undesirable state.* Therefore, freedom from each other ironically creates the very longing that will bring you together over and over again. You must build freedom into your marriage so that you have enough separateness to desire to come together to solve the problem that separateness creates!

This paradox is one of the balancing truths in God's universe. Separateness and togetherness go hand in hand. If you have too much separateness, you have no relationship because you become too disconnected. But if you have no separateness, you also have no relationship because there are no longer two people involved.

Therefore, see the need for freedom as part of God's design, and find the right balance between togetherness and freedom for the two of you. Make sure you have both. If you give freedom, you will have longing. If you have togetherness, you will create more love that gives rise to more freedom to express who you are becoming with the other. Friends, hobbies, work, time apart are all part of the mix. Nurture them, and they will come back to you many times over.

Chapter 5

What You Value Is What You'll Have

_J_ (Dr. Cloud) don't remember where I first heard this saying, but I have come to believe it: "You get what you tolerate." In other words, in an imperfect world, imperfection will always seek you out, and if you tolerate it, you will certainly find all of it that you can handle. Unpleasant things seek the level they are allowed to exist in your life, especially in a marriage.

While you might get all the bad stuff you tolerate, what about the good things in a marriage? Where do they come from? They generally come from the same place from which "tolerance" comes: _your values._ On both the positive and the negative side, ultimately what you value is what you will have. If you value something in a relationship, you will not tolerate anything that destroys this value, and you will also seek to make sure it is present and growing. And because of these values, the relationship takes on an identity and form, a character of its own. Certain things happen in the relationship, and other things don't. What you value happens and what you don't value will be absent. In marriage, for example, it works like this:

1. We will not tolerate anything that violates our value of honesty.
2. We both will actively seek to build and increase the presence of honesty in our marriage.

Your values make sure that certain bad things are not present in the marriage and that certain good things are. The values become the ultimate identity and protective boundaries of the marriage.

In chapter 1 we said that a boundary is a property line that defines where something ends and something else begins. Your values are the ultimate boundaries of your marriage. They form it, protect it, and give it a place to grow. They dictate what the nature of the relationship is going to be, what is not going to be allowed to grow there, as well as what is going to be sought after and maintained. The values of your relationship become like the frame of a house; they give it shape. What you value determines the kind of relationship you most likely will have in the end.

For this reason, we want to introduce in this chapter the values that will give a certain shape and identity to your marriage, some values that will serve to protect it and cause it to grow in the direction God intends.

In 1 Samuel 26:24 the Bible uses a Hebrew word for "value" that means "to make large, to lift up, or to magnify." Our hope is that you will do that with these six values. We want you to make them large items in your relationship. We want you to lift them up and to magnify their importance. For if you will hold these things up high, esteem them, and pursue them as a couple, we believe you will be building your relationship on solid ground. And what Proverbs says of wisdom shall be true for you: "Do not forsake wisdom, and she will protect you; love her, and she will watch over you" (Proverbs 4:6).

But before we look at the six important values we want you to lift up, let's first look at the worst value ever.

The Worst Value Ever

I was talking to a young man one day about his girlfriend. He was thinking about getting married, and he had questions about their relationship. Several times during the conversation, he said that something she did or something about the relationship did not "make him happy." It was clear that this was a theme for him. She was not "making him happy."

When I asked, I found that she wanted him to deal with some things in the relationship. He needed to do some work that took effort. It was not a "happy" time. When he had to work on the relationship, he no longer liked it.

At first, I was trying to understand what the difficulties were, but the more I listened, the more I saw that *he* was the difficulty. His attitude was, "If I'm not happy, something bad must be happening." And his immediate conclusion was always that the "bad" was in someone else, not him. From his perspective, he was not part of any problem, much less part of the solution. Finally I had heard about as much as I could take of his self-centered ramblings.

"I think I know what you should do," I said.

"What?" he asked.

"I think you should get a goldfish."

Looking at me as if I were a little crazy, he asked, "What are you talking about? Why do you say that?"

"It sounds to me like that is about the highest level of relationship you are ready for. Forget the marriage thing."

"What do you mean by 'the highest level of relationship'?"

"Well, even a dog makes demands on you. A dog has to be let out to go to the bathroom. You have to clean up after it. Other times, it requires time from you when you don't want to give it. A dog might interfere with your happiness. Better get a goldfish. A goldfish doesn't ask for much. But a woman is completely out of the question."

Now we had something to talk about.

This person's greatest value was his own happiness and his own immediate comfort. And I can't think of a worse value in life, especially a life that includes marriage. Why? Is this a killjoy attitude? Hardly. I am not advocating misery. I hate pain. But I do know this: *People who always want to be happy and pursue it above all else are some of the most miserable people in the world.*

> *People who always want to be happy and pursue it above all else are some of the most miserable people in the world.*

The reason is that happiness is a *result*. It is sometimes the result of having good things happen. But usually it is the result of our being in a good place inside ourselves and our having done the character work we need to do so that we are content and joyful in whatever circumstance we find ourselves. Happiness is a fruit of a lot of hard work in relationships, career, spiritual growth, or a host of other arenas of life. But nowhere is this as true as in marriage.

Marriage is a lot of work, period. I don't know anyone who has been married very long who does not attest to that. When couples do the right kind of work—character work—they find that they can gain more happiness in their marriage than they thought possible. But it always comes as a result of going through some difficult moments. Conflicts, fears, and old traumas. Big and small rejections, arguments, and hurt feelings. The disillusionment of someone being different than was imagined. The difficult task of accepting imperfections and immaturity that are larger than one thinks they should be.

All of these things are normal, and all of these things are workable. And if people work through them, they reach happiness again, usually a happiness of a deeper and better sort. But if they hit these inevitable walls and have the attitude that this problem is "interfering with my happiness," they are in real trouble. They will be angry with the "inconvenience" of their happiness being interrupted and will refuse to solve the issues or will just leave the relationship. If happiness is our guide and it goes away momentarily, we will assume that something is wrong.

> *The truth is that when we are not happy, something good may be happening.*

The truth is (and this is why happiness is such a horrible value) that when we are not happy, something good may be happening. You may have been brought to that moment of crisis because of a need for growth, and that crisis may be the solution to much of what is wrong with your life. If you could grasp whatever it is that this situation is asking you to learn, it could change your entire life. This is why James tells us to "consider it pure joy, my brothers, whenever you face trials of many kinds, because you know that the testing of your faith develops perseverance. Perseverance must finish its work so that you may be mature and complete, not lacking anything. If any of you lacks wisdom, he should ask God, who gives generously to all without finding fault, and it will be given to him" (James 1:2–5).

When you hit a problem in marriage, your happiness will go away. James's message is that you are probably at an opportunity for great growth, an opportunity to get to "completeness." The two of you can work through whatever it is that was causing you this problem, and then you will be free of it forever. You will have gotten past whatever it was. In that area, you will be "lacking in nothing." You will have grown.

An analogy might be someone who drives a car and runs into trees a few times. Nothing life-threatening happens, but it does cause trouble. He goes out again and hits a few more trees. Finally he says, "Enough of this," and sells the car. "I hate this car! It just keeps running into trees." And he thinks that he will just go get a new one and be happy. He never understands the part he played in the scenario. He thinks that a new car will solve his problem. This one is *not making him happy*.

But if he were to work on his driving, he could graduate from hitting trees and arrive at a place where he no longer has this kind of wreck. And then he would find the "happiness" of tree-free driving. He would finally be a "complete" driver, in James's terms. The happiness would be a result of doing the hard work and getting past the issue causing him pain. But if happiness were his biggest value, then working on driving might interfere.

Many things are better to worry about than happiness. And these are the things that ultimately will produce happiness. Don't get the cart before the horse. Don't think like a little child, who feels that being happy today is all that matters. People like this see marriage existing just to gratify them in the moment, which is a very self-centered and ultimately self-destructive way to live. Be willing to do the hard work of growth now, no matter how it feels, and happiness will likely find you. Don't have the worst value ever: "I must be happy at all times, and I value that more than anything else. Even more than growth." Happiness will certainly elude you.

If not happiness, then what should you value? What should you magnify and lift up to guide you? Certainly we cannot decide all of your values for you. But there are a few values the Bible holds in very high esteem, and these values work to produce great boundaries in marriage. Below is a list of those six values. In the next six brief chapters we will take a closer look at why each can help you build a marriage that lasts.

1. Love of God
2. Love of Your Spouse
3. Honesty
4. Faithfulness
5. Compassion and Forgiveness
6. Holiness

The Big Picture

There are two kinds of people in the world: those who focus on what they want, always desiring it and never attaining it, and those who focus on what it takes to obtain what they want. The latter do the work, delay gratification, make sacrifices, and ultimately get the rewards of their work.

In marriage, if you focus on what you want and desire and just stay angry and disappointed that you are not getting it, you will remain there. But if you focus on cultivating the garden instead of demanding the fruit, then your garden will yield a huge harvest.

So it is with values. Make cultivating the ones we mention here of prime concern. Work on them. *Stand against anything in yourself or your spouse that would destroy them.* This is righteous indignation, and your marriage may depend on it. But also, do everything you can to increase the presence of these things. Give time, money, energy, focus, and other resources to developing the love of God and each other, honesty, faithfulness, compassion, forgiveness, and holiness. Pursue them with everything the two of you can muster. They will not fail you in the end.

Chapter 6

Value One

Love of God

I (Dr. Cloud) was once meeting with a couple who had given up hope in their relationship. I knew that they were at the end of themselves. From their perspective, divorce was the next option. At the same time, I knew that their problems were curable. They were suffering from many of the issues we discussed in chapter 4 on the theme that "it takes two to become one."

I felt that we first needed to put this couple's hopelessness on the table. "Do either of you have any hope for this marriage?" I asked.

"No, we don't," they both finally admitted.

Then I said something that threw them: "Good! Now we can get to work."

"What do you mean?" they asked, surprised.

What they did not know was that I knew they both had a deep love for God and, although they were ready and willing to forsake each other, they were not ready to forsake him. I trusted their faith in God. I knew that if they could stop lying to themselves about wanting to change "for the other," we could get to someone for whom they would change: God. So I told them so.

"I think that both of you are so disappointed in each other and in your relationship that you have very little hope of solving your problems for each other. In reality, there is not enough love between the two of you to hold you together. I'm glad you are facing that reality, because deep down you both know it. But I know something else about you. You both love God enough to make the changes that he wants you to make, and if you do that, I promise you that you will do very well in your relationship. Will you both commit to that kind of love? Can you both commit to doing what God is going to ask of you in this process?"

Both said that they could, but both were downhearted about it. They thought that I meant that just because God says he is against divorce, I was asking them to remain faithful to him and just stick it out in a miserable relationship. In a sense, I was. But I knew better than that. I knew that if they could submit to the changes God would ask them to make, the marriage would get better. But since they could not believe that, they had to take it on faith.

Jesus said that the greatest commandment is to love God with every ounce of yourself: "with all your heart and with all your soul and with all your mind and with all your strength" (Mark 12:30). Why did he place this value above all others?

Although we could point to many reasons, one in particular relates to marriage. When loving God is our orienting principle in life, *we are always adjusting to what he requires from us.* When things get tough in a marriage and when some change is required from us, we might not want to do it. We might feel that it is unfair that we have to change, or it might be too difficult or painful to change. At those moments, it is much easier to just please ourselves. But if we know that it's God with whom we ultimately have to deal, we submit to this reality and his higher calling to us to grow. In the end, the relationship wins.

> *When loving God is our orienting principle in life, we are always adjusting to what he requires from us.*

The "hope-less" couple and I worked hard for a while. And they learned something. She learned that at times she would want to be judgmental of her husband but God said no. She would be very angry toward her husband, but she would submit to God and give up her judgmentalism. At times the husband would get so angry toward his wife that he would want to snap back with sarcasm, something he was very skilled at. But he knew that someone higher was asking him to deny himself that little treat. He would submit to God and bite his tongue.

At other times he wanted to give in to the temptation to avoid listening to her complaints about him. He hated conflict. But he learned that God wanted him to listen and not react defensively. He would submit to God and remain in the conflict long enough to work it out. Before, he would turn to his hobbies and avoid her.

She learned as well that she had a lot of bitterness and fears in her own life for which she was blaming her husband. She found out that God wanted her to take responsibility for feelings with which she had never dealt, so she submitted to God and did the work of change. She got healthier.

Just recently, about a year after the hopeless conversation mentioned above, we had an interesting session. This couple did not have anything to work on. They were doing so well they had nothing to talk about!

She was a little giddy, reminding me of a teenager. "We are just having so much fun together! It is everything that I married him for in the beginning. I never thought we would be here."

"I can't believe what I was missing," he joined in. "I just love being with her. None of that other stuff—mostly work—that I used to spend all of my energy on matters very much any more. I just want to be with her and talk."

Then we reflected on where they had been a year earlier, when it had all seemed so hopeless.

"I did not know what to do," one of them said, "so we just trusted you when you said there was a way out. And it worked."

I clarified something for them. "It may have seemed to you that you were trusting me. But in reality you weren't. I was telling you that I knew that God's ways worked and that, if you could do them, your relationship would work. You made that commitment to God, and both of you followed through with the day-to-day work that he asked you to do. When God asked you to grow and change, you submitted to him. And now you have the fruit that God promises. You might have thought that you were trusting me, but I was just representing him. When you committed to follow him and whatever he showed you, I knew that you would make it."

It was a neat moment. I have no doubt that they will make it now for the rest of their lives. They now have a real love between the two of them that they did not have before. But it came as a result of "loving God." They loved God enough to do what he asked of them, and they grew to love each other as a result. The love that they now have for each other is a fruit of loving God.

This is why loving God must be first. He empowers us to change. He tells us *how* to change. And, most of all, God becomes the one that keeps us from being ultimately in charge. If we try to be in charge, we will do it our way, and then our own limitations become the limitations of the relationship as well. We all need someone bigger to answer to so we will make the changes we need to make.

Love God first, with all of your heart, mind, soul, and strength. Lose your life to him, and you will gain it.

Now let's look at some further values that build sound marriages.

———— *Chapter 7* ————

Value Two

Love of Your Spouse

---

*W*e hear a lot about love, and we all have our own ideas about what love means. To some it is romance, and to others it is security. To still others, it is the feeling of being attracted to some quality that another possesses, such as power and achievement. We all say, "I love that about you." What we mean when we say this is that there is something in the other person that gratifies us in some way, and we like it. These are all wonderful aspects of loving another person. We celebrate who that person is. He or she adds to our existence. Love is a part of the relationship.

But what happens when we don't see "what we love" about our spouse? What happens when our "love" disappears?

The love that builds a marriage is the kind of love God has for us. It is called "agape." Agape is love that seeks the welfare of the other. It is love that has nothing to do with how someone is gratifying us at the moment. It has to do with what is good for *the other*. In short, agape is concerned with the good of the other person.

Jesus said it this way in the second greatest commandment: "Love your neighbor as yourself." When we do that, we are truly loving someone.

> *A*gape is concerned with the good of the other person.

What does it mean to love someone "as yourself" in marriage? It means three things: you so deeply identify with your spouse that you feel the effects of your own behavior on your spouse, you think first of making your spouse's life better, and you want the best for your spouse even when your spouse can't see what that is.

First, you so deeply identify with your spouse that you feel the effects of your own behavior on your spouse. When people do things in marriage that hurt the relationship, selfishness—and a lack of thinking about how that selfishness will affect the other person—is usually at the root.

Scott became angry with Maria in our session. When he was threatened, he would become heated and aggressive in communicating with Maria. And when he became angry with her, she would blame him for something.

But behind her blame I saw something she was not showing.

I stopped him in the middle of his tirade and turned to her. "What are you feeling?" I asked.

"I hate it when he gets like that," she said.

"No, what are you *feeling?*" I pressed.

She broke down and cried. Then she told me how scared of him she becomes when he is angry. She sobbed, shaking with fear.

I looked at him and saw something I had never seen in him before. He was softening toward her. Tears were in his eyes. He was feeling the damage he was doing to her. He was "identifying with her." In Jesus' words, he was seeing her as if she were he.

> To deeply identify with another person is to think about the effects of your behavior on that other person.

"Would you like it if you felt that way?" I asked him.

He looked at her in shame and empathy. "I never knew. I'm sorry."

Perhaps for the first time in their marriage, he looked past his behavior to *the effects of his behavior.* He was seeing what it was like to be on the other end of a relationship with him. He was seeing life through her eyes. He was seeing her "as if she were he." Would he like to be treated that way? Certainly not. And when he began to focus on how he would feel if he were on the receiving end of his actions, he changed his behavior.

To deeply identify with another person is to think about the effects of your behavior on that other person. It is to get out of the self-centeredness of just acting to please oneself. To love someone "as yourself" is to put yourself in the other person's shoes and see what it feels like to be her. This empowers you to seek the best for the other person because it puts you in touch with her life and how it feels to be her, especially on the other end of a relationship with you.

How do you like to be treated? Would you like your spouse to do to you what you are doing to your spouse? This identifying with another's experience is called empathy.

Second, loving your spouse as yourself means you think of making your spouse's life better. You think first about what it would be like to be in the situation or state of life she is in. Then what would you like if you were in this situation? If you have been working hard all day with a bunch of kids, what would you like from your partner? How about some relief? Wouldn't that feel good?

What about other big issues in life? How would you feel if you did not get an opportunity to develop yourself and your talents? You would feel stagnant and stale. You would want an opportunity to grow and develop. You would want someone to give you the freedom and the resources to do that too.

Think of the marital arguments this kind of orientation would instantly stop. When one partner wants to take some money from the budget to invest in personal growth, it becomes a team effort, because both people feel the effect of that person's need. You feel the other person's need as your own (empathy), and you sacrifice to meet it. You also find joy in the happiness and fulfillment that she finds.

Third—and this is the most difficult to grasp—loving your spouse as yourself means you want the best for your spouse even when your spouse can't see what that is. It may be a difficult confrontation, or a healing in your spouse's life. A good example of this is when a person does an intervention on an addicted spouse and puts him into treatment, even if the spouse does not realize that this is good for him. Or, it may mean a need for spiritual growth and a person tries to get her spouse closer to God. Or, it may mean a relief from duties, as when one spouse gets a job to lighten the workload of the other. The key concept is that this is done for the benefit of the other, not for oneself. An intervention is *for the addict,* even if the entire family benefits.

This kind of love may cost you. It may put you out. It may be difficult for you. But if you were the other, it would be good. And to love her as yourself means that you want it for your spouse as desperately as you would want it for yourself.

Commitment

In addition to being based in empathy, this love is based in commitment. Again, this is best seen in the kind of love God has for us. God's word for this kind of commitment is *covenant.* By making a covenant with us, God promised that he is committed to us, and he does not break his promises.

"I will never leave you nor forsake you," he says (Joshua 1:5; see Hebrews 13:5). The Greek word that the Bible uses for "forsake" is a word that means "to desert or to leave." To commit to someone means that you will be there and that you will stay, even when things get difficult. Why is this so important?

If someone is not committed to a marriage, when the marriage gets difficult, he is tempted to leave the marriage instead of working through the difficulty. If leaving is an option, why go through the pain? Why go through the work? A problem in a relationship is usually a sign that both parties need to grow and change, and without commitment, avoidance is often the easier way out. Some do not leave physically, but they leave emotionally. They forsake the relationship by taking their heart out of it.

But as we have seen above, hanging in there and going through the necessary changes often brings great rewards. The problem is that a runner can never see the finish line in the middle of a marathon, and often only the commitment to finish can keep the runner running the race. In life, commitment provides the time, structure, and security needed for the change to take place.

To use another metaphor, a relationship must often go through some deep surgery to get better. Think of surgery without commitment! What if the patient decides in the middle of a heart bypass to get off the table? He would die before the operation that could have saved his life is finished. In marriage, God often wants to do surgery that would save the life of the relationship, but the patient jumps off the table before the surgery is complete. Commitment keeps the patient on the table until the surgery is finished.

Commitment also provides something else necessary for growth: security. Without the security that commitment provides, partners know at some deep level that if they do not perform up to some expectation, they could be "forsaken." This insecurity gives way to a whole host of growth-stopping cancers. Performance anxiety always inhibits real change.

A college friend of mine was a nice guy but suffered from insecurity. He was always trying to impress the people he was around, and he was not someone whom I experienced as "real." About ten years later, I saw him at a friend's wedding, and I was amazed at the change in him. He was so different! He was relaxed and a lot easier to be around. I invited him to dinner, and we talked about the ways each of us had changed over the last decade.

As he talked, my friend attributed his growth to his marriage. The key point in his growth, he said, was commitment. As he put it, "It is a totally different life when you know that the one who loves you is never going to go away. It changes you at a very deep level." What a beautiful testimony to the power of commitment!

Commitment drives the *need* for growth as well as the *security*. If you're going to be with someone for the long term, it's best to work things out; otherwise, you're certain to be miserable! Commitment often drives one toward resolution.

Action

Without action, James says, faith is dead (James 2:17). There is no such thing as a faith that doesn't produce action. The same is true for love. Love is not just a feeling or an attachment to a person. Love is an expression of that attachment. The love that brings good boundaries to a marriage is the love that brings action to the relationship as well.

The more familiar they are with someone, the lazier people get. Usually, in the beginning stages of courtship, the couple are working hard to express and show their love to one another. But as the relationship proceeds, and the knot has been tied, one or both begin to "work less" at showing, expressing, and giving love. They settle into a mutual "taking the other for granted."

True love will not allow itself to go cold. When it does, there is a call to action, a call to rekindling the flame. As Jesus says of our relationship to God, "do the things you did at first" (Revelation 2:5). I know a husband who writes his wife a note every day, communicating something about her that he values and loves. He connects the note to a specific action he has seen her do. He is active in communicating his love in this way. The need for action in a love relationship never goes away.

A Picture

Love is the foundation for marriage: love for God and love for another person. It expresses itself in seeking the best for the other person no matter whether they deserve it or not. It places the other person above one's own selfish needs and desires. It sacrifices, gives, and suffers. It weathers hurts and storms for the long-term preservation of the covenant. It preserves itself as if it is fighting for life. And in the end, that is exactly what is happening, for love and life were meant to be partners from the beginning of creation.

Make love your highest value in your marriage, and it is likely to return the commitment you make to it. It will pay you back multifold, much more than you ever thought possible. For in the end, love is the strongest power at our disposal:

> Love is patient, love is kind. It does not envy, it does not boast, it is not proud. It is not rude, it is not self-seeking, it is not easily angered, it keeps no record of wrongs. Love does not delight in evil but rejoices with the truth. It always protects, always trusts,

always hopes, always perseveres. Love never fails (1 Corinthians 13:4–8a).

None of us is able to live out this description of love completely, but as we try, love will serve as a powerful boundary against all sorts of evil. It will protect your relationship and give you many, many returns for all that you invest in its enduring power.

Chapter 8

Value Three

Honesty

$\mathcal{R}$achel had just received another piece of bad news. Their car was not paid off as her husband, Richard, had led her to believe. She was furious. This was another in a long series of ways he had misled her about their financial state. First it was the late payments on their mortgage. Then it was loans she did not know about from friends. Then it was several unpaid bills she had thought had long ago been paid. Now this, after all of his reassurances that they were back on solid financial ground.

"I just need to know the truth," she explained to me. "I can deal with whatever it is. This is what he does not understand. If he would just tell me the truth, I could handle it. But I can't handle all the surprises. The lies are killing me."

She did not have to tell me. I knew that she was a courageous problem-solver. She would have joined with Richard and been a loyal teammate in trying to defeat their financial difficulties.

But he did not know that. He was afraid to tell her the extent of their financial difficulties because he felt ashamed of how things had been going in his sales job. He was not making it, and he felt too bad to let her know. But he underestimated the power of deception to undermine a relationship. She was getting more and more furious each time she found out he had told her one thing and another was true.

> *The act of lying is much more damaging than the things that are being lied about.*

As she summarized, "I just don't know him. I think I do, and then I find out I don't know him at all."

Deception damages a relationship. The act of lying is much more damaging than the things that are being lied about, because lying undermines the knowing of one another and the connection itself. The point at which deception enters is the point at which relatedness ends. As someone once told me about his fiancée, "I think she has told me everything, and then I find out one more thing that she fudged on." Ultimately, he called off their marriage because his trust had been seriously eroded.

> *Anything, large or small, is forgivable and able to be worked through in a relationship—except deception.*

Couples deceive each other in many ways. Sometimes spouses lie over small things, such as spending too much. At other times, they lie about serious things, such as affairs. In our way of thinking, anything, large or small, is forgivable and able to be worked through in a relationship—except deception. Deception is the one thing that cannot be worked through because it denies the problem. It is the one unforgivable sin of a relationship because it makes forgiveness unattainable.

Some Guidelines

We believe in total honesty. But, honesty must go along with the other values we have discussed. Honesty without love and commitment can wreck a tenuous connection. Honesty without forgiveness can do the same. Honesty without a commitment to holiness does not give the offended spouse a reason for hope that the problem will not reoccur.

Here are some areas that couples find difficult to be honest about:

- Feelings
- Disappointments
- Desires, likes, and dislikes

- Hurts
- Anger and hatred
- Sex
- Sins
- Failure
- Needs and vulnerabilities

Deeper Intimacy

Christy and Dennis had been married for five years. He loved their relationship. To him, everything was fine. But, in reality, things were far from fine. Christy felt alone, unfulfilled, and emotionally cut off. She felt as if she were slowly dying.

Yet she had never told Dennis. Everyone loved Dennis and thought highly of him. He was such a "nice guy" and a good provider that she felt her desire for something deeper was a sign of something wrong with her.

But she still found herself longing for more. Her fantasies about another, more fulfilling relationship were increasing. Not that she would ever act on these desires, but she wished that what she had were different. She wanted more passion and more excitement.

Whenever she would hint to Dennis about how she felt, he would subtly discount her feelings and then try to overcome her discontent with being "nicer" to her. But his "niceness" was driving her crazy. Sometimes she wished that he would be angry with her so that she would feel more alive. Slowly her mood around him was getting flatter.

Then finally, one day, she lost it. "I hate our marriage!" she screamed. "I hate everything about it!"

Dennis was shocked. Stunned! He could not believe what she was saying. He started telling her how great their marriage really was. When he did, she just grew angrier. Finally he realized that they were in trouble and agreed to obtain some help.

In counseling, Christy was totally honest with Dennis. She talked about his lack of passion and how his being "nice" all the time left her feeling as if he had no feelings. She was completely honest for the first time about her resentments and her deeper needs.

In the beginning stages of counseling, Dennis tried his old ways of taking care of her. He tried to placate her by being sweet and nice, but this was not what she wanted. She wanted to know more of him, his feelings, his likes and dislikes, his soul. She was finally complaining out loud.

And then it happened. The scenario had set itself up with Christy being the "complainer" and Dennis being on trial. But something different occurred one day. Dennis exploded. Mr. Nice Guy let her have it. He expressed his anger with her at trying so hard to please her and his never feeling as if it was enough, or done in the right way. He talked about his dying for her to want him in the ways that he wanted her, something of which she was totally unaware. He poured out his secret fantasies about her and how he had never felt that she was really interested in very deep desires.

Now Christy was stunned. Far from being defensive, she fell into his arms. She felt relieved that there was a real person underneath Mr. Nice Guy. The honesty had made the connection real. From this point on, they established the connection they both longed for.

Intimacy comes from "knowing" the other person at a deep level. If there are barriers to honesty, knowing is ruled out and the false takes over. As Paul tells us in the Bible, "Therefore each of you must put off falsehood and speak truthfully to his neighbor, for we are all members of one body" (Ephesians 4:25). Couples often live out years of falsehood trying to protect and save a relationship, all the while destroying any chance of real relationship.

> *Couples often live out years of falsehood trying to protect and save a relationship, all the while destroying any chance of real relationship.*

We can't stress enough the importance of being able to share with each other your deepest feelings, needs, hurts, desires, failures, or whatever else is in your soul. If you and your spouse can feel safe enough in your marriage to be totally vulnerable, if you can remove each other's fig leaves, then once again your marriage can return to a state of paradise. True intimacy is the closest thing to heaven we can know.

For a Reason

Most of the time, in otherwise good marriages, deception takes place for "defensive" reasons. In other words, the dishonest spouse is often lying not for evil reasons, but to protect himself. Fears drive the deception. This does not excuse the lying, but it does complicate matters. For spouses to tell the whole truth, they must deal with their fears first.

Here are some common fears:

- Fear of real closeness and being known
- Fears of abandonment and loss of love if they are known
- Fears of being controlled and possessed if they are known
- Fears of being seen as "bad" or not good enough if some part of them is known
- Fears of their own desires, needs, and feelings

This book will not deal with all of your fears. We have written two other books—*Changes That Heal* and *Hiding from Love*—on that topic. But we will tell you that to live a life of total honesty you will need to work out the deeper issues that get in the way.

What you can do in your marriage is make a total commitment between the two of you to:

1. Have enough grace to tell the truth. Promise that you will never punish your spouse for being honest. This doesn't mean that there will be no consequences, but punishment, shame, and condemnation should not be part of those consequences.
2. Give each other free rein to question and check out things with each other. Don't be offended by the other spouse's

need to understand some facts that do not add up. Don't retort defensively, "What? Don't you trust me?"

3. Police each other when you see your spouse not being totally honest. This can even be harmless and fun, but hold each other to the truth.

4. Become a partner in your spouse's life to heal the underlying fears of being honest. If your spouse's issue is abandonment, for example, show him that you are not going to treat him like whoever abandoned him before.

5. Take responsibility for your own dishonesty and its underlying fears, and make a commitment to resolving them. Become a person of the truth, and find someone else besides your spouse to hold you accountable. Get a friend to help you tell the truth when you are afraid.

6. Use discernment. While total honesty is the ideal, every relationship is not ready for total knowing and being known. Some truths are not ready to be dealt with yet. Some people are too fragile or are in special circumstances, and they need help to deal with some things, or the timing needs to be right. Use wisdom to know what your relationship can handle and what it is not ready for. Check out other resources, such as counseling, healing, time, or other people, that may be needed for honesty to work.

If you are to build a strong relationship, make a commitment to each other of total honesty. But remember, honesty must be accompanied by enough grace to hear and deal with the truth it brings. God always asks us to be honest with him in light of his grace for us, so you have to be able to deal with and accept the truth expressed to you as well.

> *Honesty must be accompanied by enough grace to hear and deal with the truth it brings.*

Talk with each other about how this value can become the bedrock of all that you do together, and then protect against deception and build in honesty. It will pay you back many, many times.

Chapter 9

Value Four

Faithfulness

*T*hink about these words:

- Trust
- Confidence
- Assuredness
- Conviction
- Fidelity
- Truth
- Certainty
- Permanence
- Rest

Now put these words into the context of a marriage:

- Trust each other
- Have confidence in each other
- Be assured of each other's character and dependability
- Be convicted of your ability to trust each other
- Be certain of each other's fidelity
- Be true to one another
- Be certain of one another
- Be permanent to each other
- Rest in each other

All of these words hint at what faithfulness is. *A faithful spouse is one who can be trusted, depended upon, and believed in, and one in whom you can rest.*

Our notion of faithfulness in marriage is too often shallow. We generally think of it only in the physical realm. Yet, in many marriages spouses are physically faithful but not emotionally faithful. They are faithful with their bodies but not with their hearts. The partners can't depend on each other in the ways listed above. There is little trust, little certainty, little safety. Especially in religious circles, people think that if they are not sleeping with someone other than their spouse, they are being faithful.

> *Our notion of faithfulness in marriage is too often shallow.*

But faithfulness means to be trusted in all areas, not just the sexual, trusted in matters of the heart as well as those of the body. Being faithful to your spouse means that you can be depended upon to do what you have promised, to follow through on what your spouse has entrusted to you. It means that your spouse can be certain that you will deliver on what you have promised. It could mean being sexually faithful, but it could also mean doing chores faithfully! It could mean staying within the monthly budget and coming home when you say you will. It could mean sharing without fear of reprisal or condemnation.

One of the words the Bible uses for trust (the Hebrew word *batach*) means to be so confident that you can be "care-less." In other words, you don't have to worry. You are so "taken care of" that you don't have to take care yourself. You can trust that what was promised will be done. The children will be picked up from day care. The milk will be bought at the store. The bill will be paid. The appointment will be made. You can rest in the knowledge that what needs to get done will get done. This is a beautiful picture of faithfulness.

What Drives People Apart

Faithfulness, of course, also means that you will not stray from the one you love. Physical adultery means giving yourself to someone else sexually. But you can commit emotional adultery as well; you can have an "affair of the heart." An affair of the heart means taking aspects of yourself and intentionally keeping them away from the marriage.

This does not mean that you cannot have deep, sustaining, healing, and supportive emotional relationships with other people. We strongly believe in the power of friends to heal, sustain, and support. Sometimes, in fact, you need others to help you become whole enough to be able to get closer to your spouse. A friend, counselor, or support group may help you to feel safer and learn to trust more, and this will carry over into your marriage.

What we are talking about here is when you use other things in life, whether or not they be relationships, to avoid your spouse. The crush at work keeps some part of you split from your spouse. A hobby takes more time and energy than your marriage. Or an addiction becomes more important than the person to whom you are committed.

"Objects" of unfaithfulness are numerous. Some are people, some are not. But the bottom line is that they come between you and your spouse. Some part of you avoids the relationship. We are not referring to the situations in which you are unable to take certain parts into marital intimacy, or in which the relationship is not safe enough for certain aspects of who you are. This dynamic is about deliberately splitting yourself into two people, one of whom is not connected to the marriage.

This commonly occurs in a marriage where there is conflict or a need for growth and one of the partners is not facing the need. To avoid the conflict and the spouse, this partner uses some "outside" relationship.

Leigh and Charlie had been married for ten years. Most outsiders would have thought they had a "good marriage." They got along well with other couples and were everyone's favorite companions. Both were fun, interesting people.

But a dynamic had been driving them apart and keeping them apart for several years. Leigh controlled and criticized Charlie. Charlie avoided Leigh. This combination was leaving them separated at a deep level.

The "driving apart" came from Leigh's anxious control of Charlie. When she felt insecure, she would harp on him about all the things he had not yet done, or about ways she thought he could be a better person.

The "keeping apart" came from Charlie. Because he felt a lot of shame and fear of criticism, he could not go directly to her and talk to her. He would either get defensive or agree with her and then withdraw emotionally. She would think that things were fine when he would agree to "do better." She would feel heard and understood as he agreed with her about how "bad" he was. This would lull her into a false sense of security.

The truth was that Charlie was retreating into an addiction. He would turn to two sources of gratification to obtain what he was not getting from Leigh. He would go to pornography in magazines, on videos, and on the Internet. And he would flirt with a few flattering women at work.

In these escapes, Charlie would find relief. Leigh was displeased with him; his fantasy relationships were not. He would fantasize about the women in the magazines, about how they loved and adored him and were excited by him. He would feel so good about himself when the women at work would stroke his ego and make him think he was wonderful. Then, deep in his heart, he would resent Leigh for failing to see him as these women did. Why didn't she appreciate him the way everyone else did?

In reality, Charlie was unfaithful. He took his heart to an addiction to deal with what he should have been dealing with directly with Leigh. He had a double life. He would try to please her on the outside, but inside take his deepest needs and desires to his fantasy life. He was split, and this was keeping the couple from resolving their problems.

When they finally came in for counseling, both had to face their unfaithfulness. Leigh was not faithful in what had been entrusted to her—Charlie's heart. As we saw above, Charlie was not faithful to Leigh because he took his heart outside of the relationship to his addictions. Leigh had to learn to be safer and not so condemning. Charlie had to learn to work out their problems directly and to cure his unfaithfulness.

No Excuses

Many times one of the partners, like Charlie, will justify unfaithfulness by the other's lack of safety. "Well, if she hadn't been so critical, I wouldn't have had to turn to someone else for love." Or, a wife who has an affair will say, "Well, it wouldn't have happened if he had been meeting my needs."

Nothing is further from the truth. An act of unfaithfulness is something that one person does, not two. As the Bible says of God, "If we are faithless, he will remain faithful, for he cannot disown himself" (2 Timothy 2:13). God does not become unfaithful if we do not love him correctly. He remains faithful no matter what we do. Marriage requires this as well. Do not let your spouse's failures of love be an excuse for your unfaithfulness.

In short, make a commitment to each other that you will not allow anything to come between you. You will be trustworthy. You will be dependable. You will be sexually and emotionally faithful.

> *Do not let your spouse's failures of love be an excuse for your unfaithfulness.*

(Few things are more devastating in life to all parties concerned than marital unfaithfulness. If an affair seems as if it is worth it, run like the wind and find a trusted friend to talk you back into your senses. If you are close to having an affair, you are close to destroying a lot of people, and you need to be rescued. See Proverbs 2:16–19; 5:3–20; 6:23–35.)

If you struggle with wanting to take some part of yourself to someone or something other than your spouse, find out why. Your actions may be okay; your spouse can't identify with all parts of you. Different interests and different aspects of personal identity keep spouses from totally identifying with each other. One person cannot be all that you need in life. Friends can connect with some parts of you better than your spouse. This is okay. For example, you may like skiing, but your spouse hates it. Find some friends to ski with while your spouse pursues the loves that you don't share. A circle of friends can round out your life.

What is not okay is using some lust to keep you split and keep you from integrating your heart to your commitment. Duplicity is taking your heart away from your marriage and bringing it somewhere else. This is unfaithfulness, in love or in deed. As God says, "Remain faithful until the end."

In the next chapter we will look at values that glue all the other values together.

———— *Chapter 10* ————

Value Five

Compassion and Forgiveness

$\mathcal{J}$ (Dr. Cloud) was leading a seminar, and I asked the audience of married couples to stop for a moment and think of their spouse. I told them to think of all of the wonderful things that they love about their spouse and to concentrate on how awesome that person is and how much they love him or her. "Think of the wonderful qualities that you admire and that attracted you to that person. Let those feelings fill you," I told them.

Then, after they were feeling all giddy and in love again, I asked each person to turn to their spouse who was idealizing them at that moment and to repeat after me, "Honey, I am a sinner. I will fail you, and I will hurt you."

You could feel the sense of discombobulation in the room. In one moment, they were shaken from the ideal to the real. Some began to laugh as they got it. Some felt even closer to each other. Some looked up confused as if they did not know what to do with my invitation.

> *We can expect failure from even the best people in our lives.... No failure is larger than grace.*

But that is reality. The person you love the most and have committed your life to is an imperfect being. This person is guaranteed to hurt you and fail you in many ways, some serious and some not. You can expect the failures to come. As the Bible says, "There is not a righteous man on earth who does what is right and never sins" (Ecclesiastes 7:20). And "everyone who sins breaks the law; in fact, sin is lawlessness" (1 John 3:4). We can expect failure from even the best people in our lives.

So the question becomes, "What then?" What do you do when your spouse fails you in some way or is less than you wish for him to be? What happens when she has a weakness or a failure? How about an inability to do something? What about an unresolved childhood hurt that he brings to the relationship?

Other than denial, there are only a couple of options. You can beat him up for his imperfections, or you can love him out of them. The Bible says, "Love covers over a multitude of sins" (1 Peter 4:8). Nothing in a relationship has to permanently destroy that relationship if forgiveness is in the picture. No failure is larger than grace. No hurt exists that love cannot heal. But, for all of these miracles to take place, there must be compassion and tenderheartedness.

What does that mean? I like how the Bible describes God's compassion: "to bend or stoop in kindness to an inferior" (*Strong's Hebrew and Greek Dictionary*). For God to have compassion on our brokenness or sin is certainly to stoop to an inferior. But we need the same attitude toward an equal spouse for two reasons:

First, you forgive what is inferior to the ideal standard. You humble yourself to identify with your loved one, who is experiencing life in a way that is less than you or even he would want. You give up all demands for your spouse to be something he isn't at that moment.

Second, if your spouse is hurting or failing, you are not morally superior, but you are in the stronger position at that moment to be able to help. God never uses the stronger position to hurt, but always to help. As Paul puts it, "Therefore, as God's chosen people, holy and dearly loved, clothe yourselves with compassion, kindness, humility, gentleness and patience. Bear with each other and forgive whatever grievances you may have against one another. Forgive as the Lord forgave you. And over all these virtues put on love, which binds them all together in perfect unity" (Colossians 3:12–14).

What a picture that is! "Clothe yourselves with compassion, kindness, humility, gentleness and patience." What if you "wore" these qualities every time your spouse failed or was hurting? I think we would see a lot more healed marriages.

> *Hardness of heart, much more than failure, is the true relationship killer.*

But that is not the human way. The human way is to harden our hearts when we are hurt or offended.

I was talking to a friend the other day who had offended his wife in a relatively minor way. But to her it was not minor at all. As a result, she did not speak to him for several days. Finally he asked her when she might forgive him. "Will it be before next month? Before Christmas? Just let me know so I can get ready." She finally broke and started laughing, and things were fine again. She saw how unnecessary her "hardness of heart" was to the offense.

Hardness of heart, much more than failure, is the true relationship killer. As Jesus said, failure is not the cause of divorce, but hardness of heart is (see Matthew 19:8). This is why the Bible places such a high value on tenderheartedness.

Tenderheartedness consists of a number of things.

1. An Identification with Sin and Failure

Make sure that you have an attitude of humility toward your spouse's failures. If you think you are above sin, you are in big trouble. If you are very familiar with your own sins, you will have a lot more grace for your spouse's.

2. An Identification with Weakness

Invulnerability is one of the chief causes of hard hearts. If you are staying away from your own hurts and vulnerabilities, you will not be able to identify with the hurts of your spouse either. The Bible tells us that we comfort others out of the empathy we have received for our own struggles (2 Corinthians 1:4). Deal with your own pains and hurts, and you will have more empathy for your spouse.

Don't get angry with your spouse for her weakness! This is the worst thing you can ever do. It is using your strength in that area to destroy. If you have done that, if you have judged your spouse's weakness or inability, put down this book and go apologize, if not for her sake, then for your own (see James 2:13).

Identify with your spouse's weakness or inability as if it were your own. Become a partner in the healing process, not a judge or an impediment. Join with your spouse to heal and strengthen her in whatever area she is injured.

3. A Willingness to Become Vulnerable Again

Sometimes people build up protectiveness from childhood that says, in effect, "I will never let anyone hurt me again." Then they take that strategy into marriage. Whereas it might have been useful earlier in life, this strategy keeps them from having closeness now. When you get hurt, if your spouse is truly repentant and can be trusted, open up again. Be vulnerable again. This is what God does with us.

4. A Willingness to Repent

Forgiveness and tenderheartedness come from the injured party. But, for it to be useful to the future of the relationship, the person who failed must own his failure and show a true change of heart. Without that, opening up oneself to that person makes no sense. We open ourselves up to people when they show that they are trustworthy. This does not mean that they will be perfect, but it does mean that they are truly going to try.

Compassion, tenderheartedness, and forgiveness ensure something very important. These qualities ensure that imperfect people can experience love and relationship for a long time. Clothe yourselves with them.

Chapter 11

Value Six

Holiness

J doubt that Victoria's Secret comes to mind when you think about holiness. Instead, you probably think about something boring and not very romantic. I doubt that holiness sounds like fun. Holiness does sound stiff and boring to most of us, somewhat like some old church experience from childhood.

In reality, holiness is attractive for a marriage. A holy person is someone who is "blameless." The Bible pictures holiness as not just being religious, but also being reality oriented. To be holy means to be pure and blameless. Because God is holy, his reality is ultimate reality; to the extent that we are not holy, we are farther away from the reality of life itself. The equation is that God is life and ultimate reality and, therefore, for us to be unholy is a movement away from the ultimate reality of life.

> *The Bible pictures holiness as not just being religious, but also being reality oriented.*

If every marriage placed value on holiness, the following would be present:

- Confession and ownership of the problems in each individual
- A relentless drive toward growth and development
- A giving up of everything that gets in the way of love
- A surrendering of everything that gets in the way of truth
- A purity of heart where nothing toxic is allowed to grow

This would be a pretty good list of goals for any marriage counselor to have for his clients! If a marriage counselor can get the partners to confess and own their problems and to try to rid themselves of everything that gets in the way of love, he will succeed in healing the marriage. How great it would be if every marriage were doing that on its own!

Kate and David had hit a tough time in their marriage. She had finally decided that she had had enough of his treatment of her. He would vacillate between emotional withdrawal and angry outbursts. Also, he was drinking more and more. Finally, after David had a few too many beers and caused a big blowup, she kicked him out of the house. She told him that he could come back when he faced his problems.

As is the case many times in crisis situations like this, David called a counselor. I (Dr. Cloud) agreed to see them together. It did not take long for me to see that David needed to grow in some significant areas if he were going to maintain a relationship with Kate—or anyone else, for that matter. When threatened, David would get sarcastic, indirect, and angry. He also had a tendency to turn to alcohol or fun when he was close to pain or hurt. I outlined for him the ways I thought he would need to change to make his marriage work.

> *Until "holiness" was important to him apart from what she wanted from him, he was not truly holy.*

David got to work on himself with zeal. But as he was working, I could smell a rat, and so could Kate. Every time David would declare a "victory" of sorts, he would push for Kate to take him back and let him move back in. In short, it became clear that he was cleaning up his act to win her back.

I told David in no uncertain terms that I would not recommend to Kate that she allow him to come back until he convinced me that he was interested in getting better for himself and not for her. Until "holiness" was important to him apart from what she wanted from him, he was not truly holy. I also

told him that he could move back in with her when he was
no longer demanding to move back in.

David got really depressed. This is when his truly hard work
began. I had taken away his goal and motivation for change. He
wanted to change just to get his wife back. In reality, this is not
a bad motivation, but it is never enough, nor should it be primary.
The primary reason for growth must be that one is "hungering
for righteousness"—not for someone else, but for oneself. Ultimately, this is the only way that anyone is going to have life, when
he hungers for it and pursues it with everything he has.

Gradually, I began to see David change. He was no longer driven to change because of Kate's demands. He began to see how
growing into the kind of person God wanted him to be was the
best thing for him. Holiness began to have a different value to
him besides "getting back into the house." David's quest for holiness became larger than the relationship. David was getting free
from Kate's control because he was changing for himself and not
for her. He was getting holy for holiness' sake, not as a result of
being pushed into it from the outside or of trying to get her back.

Then it began to happen, as it usually does. As David became
a person who was being true to life, Kate was attracted to him
again, and she longed for him. She

> *In marriage, holi-
> ness is anything
> but boring.*

saw that he was putting his own
growth first, before even wanting her.
His commitment to getting well, to
getting holy, was getting the time and
energy from him that began to allow
her to trust him to be the kind of person she could give her heart
to again. They got back together and are doing fine.

Don't get holiness confused with some religious picture. Pursuing holiness means that you and your spouse pursue becoming the kind of people who can produce true love and life. You
become whole. You become trustworthy, honest, faithful, and
loving. In marriage, holiness is anything but boring. It is the kind
of purity and trustworthiness from which the deepest kinds of
passion flow.

So, take off your choir robe, and get holy.

Part Three

Resolving Conflict in Marriage

Chapter 12

Three's a Crowd

Protecting Your Marriage from Intruders

*D*enise was in a funk, one that happened this time every year. Her and Roy's twenty-third anniversary approached. Every year, her friends would mention it kindly, ask what their plans were, and congratulate them on their longevity as a couple. And she and Roy would do something special to commemorate their union.

Having a sentimental and reflective nature, Denise would think about the years of marriage to Roy as the day grew near. And she would become sad as she thought about what had happened to their union over the years. It had become less of a union than a warehouse for lots of activities and interests. So many things had come into their lives, many of them good: children, careers, friends, church. But the couple's relationship revolved more around things and people than each other. Within her busy and fulfilling life, Denise often felt lonely and detached.

It hadn't always been that way. During the first few years of their relationship, she and Roy had talked for hours. They had been deeply involved in each other's joys, hurts, and hearts. She thought she had found the soul mate she had prayed for all her life. But, as parenting, work, and life had taken more of their time and energy, interpersonal involvement had waned. It wasn't what many couples report as a normal settling down of intensity as time goes on. It was more that she felt they were not close, except when other people and things were in the room. For Denise, this anniversary was a sad memorial to a seemingly full life that contained a great deal of inexplicable emptiness.

The Outside Affects the Inside

Denise's situation illustrates an important aspect of boundaries in marriage: the marriage union itself needs to be actively protected. God designed both spouses to invest continually in their attachment to each other. Couples need to work to keep their love secure and safe.

Many things compete for your love, as we will see in this section. You cannot assume that the strong connection you had when you first married will always "just be there." Other forces can come between you and your mate and diminish your relationship. As Jesus taught, God himself has forged your marriage: "Therefore what God has joined together, let man not separate" (Mark 10:9). As a bank guards its money, each spouse must guard and protect the core of the marriage: love.

Marriage requires several kinds of boundaries to survive. We need to set limits on our individual needs, desires, and demands. We need to say no to our spouses. And we also need to have boundaries between the marriage and the outside world to preserve what we have. The outside world deeply affects how a marriage operates. The pressures, temptations, and even genuinely good opportunities coming from the outside world are limitless. As stewards of the marriage covenant, you need to know how to structure your relationship so that the outside doesn't control what is inside.

Here are some "intruders" that can weaken the marital bond:

- Work
- Kids
- Outside hobbies and interests
- TV
- In-laws
- Church
- Internet
- Financial involvement
- Friends
- Addictions
- Affairs

Most of these items aren't bad in and of themselves. Yet, when they come in between a couple's love, they can be destructive. You will need to work to protect your marriage. Before we talk in more detail about these "intruders," we need to discuss what drives the problem of intruders in the first place.

A marriage is only as strong as what it costs to protect it. In other words, you value what you invest in. If you have spent time, effort, and sacrifice in preserving your marriage from other influences, your odds of a solid marriage are better. If life has just "happened" to your marriage, you will have a more fragile bond. Like the man who sold all he had for the pearl of great price (Matthew 13:45–46), those who value the preciousness of their marriage will pay a high price to preserve it.

> *A marriage is only as strong as what it costs to protect it.*

Why Two, Not Three

Marriage is an exclusive club. Marriage is a two-person arrangement, leaving out all other parties. This is why wedding vows often include the phrase, "forsaking all others." Marriage is meant to be a safe place for one's soul; third parties can become disruptive to this safety.

Triangulation

Our love often gets segmented into other places. This problem, called triangulation, is one of the great enemies of good marriages. Triangulation occurs when one spouse brings in a third party for an unhealthy reason. A "triangle" is created when, for example, a wife (Person A) goes to a friend (Person C) for something that she should go to her husband (Person B) for. Or in a family setting, a sibling (Person A) calls you (Person C) to talk about "Mom's problem," without first talking to Mom (Person B).

Here are some examples of triangulation that occur in marriage:

- A wife talks to her best friend about her unhappiness with her husband, but doesn't let him know her feelings.
- A husband confides to his secretary that his wife doesn't understand him.
- One spouse makes their child a confidant, becoming closer to the child than to her mate.
- A husband is more invested in his parents than in his wife.

In all these examples, a spouse is taking a part of his heart away from his mate and bringing it to an outside source. This is not only painful, but also unjust. It works against what God intended to develop in marriage—the mysterious unity that brings the couple closer to each other in ever-deepening ways. Triangulation betrays trust and fractures the union.

This is why God is so adamant about honest, direct relationships. He hates the deception and indirectness of triangulation. Gossip, for example, is a form of triangulation. The person who gossips (Person A) relates something about Person B to Person C behind B's back, and "a gossip separates close friends" (Proverbs 16:28). God tells us to speak the truth in love (Ephesians 4:15).

If you happen to be Person C—the one in the middle of two spouses—you may think you are helping the couple. In truth, we all need people to confide in us. But if you are involved in two people moving farther apart, you are being destructive in spite of your good intentions. You may need to tell the person coming to you, "Kathleen, these are hurtful problems between you and Dan. I feel for your struggle and want to support you. But until you are going to him first with these issues, I feel I'm a party to gossip and deception. Will you talk to him about it, and then let me know how I can help?" Remember that "he who conceals his hatred has lying lips, and whoever spreads slander is a fool" (Proverbs 10:18). Don't be either the person in the middle or the one going outside of your marriage in unsafe ways.

Married love requires a great deal of safety for intimacy to grow. Marriage brings out the most vulnerable, fragile parts of us. And these vulnerable parts need a warm, grace-filled, and secure environment in which to grow. If a third party threatens this, those fragile parts cannot be safe enough to emerge, connect, and develop. A wife who has trouble learning to trust others, for example, will have great difficulty investing in her husband if he is kinder to other people than to her or if he discusses with friends what she shares in private with him.

In addition, marriage is designed to mature us. Living in such close proximity for so long with another person helps us come out of our isolation and self-centeredness. But it takes a great deal of work to grow in this context. You can be real with your colleagues and friends, but if you want to get the scoop on what someone is really like, the first person to ask is the spouse. The very exclusivity of marriage is like an oven: there's a lot of heat, and you can't always escape when you'd like to. But this heat can help us grow, also. The heat, or the pressure of living so closely with someone else, can help us face our weaknesses and work on them.

Think about the enormous amount of work it takes to keep a caring connection for a lifetime. This effort would be impossible with the complexities of three involved. The only one who can do it is the Trinity!

Forsaking Is Protecting

Most of us would like to avoid having to say no in life. It's work, it causes anxiety, and it can upset people. Yet reality dictates that in order to say yes to keeping a close marriage, you will have to say no to lots of other things. A life of "yes" to everything else ultimately results in a "no" to your marriage. You simply do not have the time, resources, or energy to do everything you want to do.

Marriage involves much more than two loving people keeping love alive. It means doing some hard work in forsaking, or leaving behind, other things. This is not easy. Many newlyweds are often disheartened to find that they are constantly having to say no to many things to maintain their marriage.

> *Marriage means doing some hard work in forsaking, or leaving behind, other things.*

When she was single, Linda loved being active in lots of things. She had her career, friends, trips, dinners, sports, and classes. She could juggle them all. When she and Tony fell in love and married, she attempted to keep them all going and take Tony along with her. Although he had been less active when single, he gamely went along. Finally he said, "I don't like doing everything you do, but I don't like being home without you all the time, either." Tony's dilemma began the boundary-setting process.

Linda had a hard time putting the brakes on some activities. She felt restricted by the marriage. She even resented Tony for this. But when she noticed that they were really missing each other and their closeness was being affected, she began feeling better about the compromises she was making. Yet, as she put it, "I thought marriage would be like singleness, only you take your husband along." She hadn't factored in the time it takes simply to maintain a connection. She was learning that marriage does involve forsaking some freedom to gain growth. Fortunately, Linda had the character to value Tony and forsake things that weren't as important.

Couples need to normalize the discipline of forsaking and make it a part of everyday life. "I need to check it out with my spouse" and "No, we need to spend some time together" are two of the best things any married person can say to protect his or her union from intruders. All "intruder" problems are ultimately caused by either adding the wrong thing (inappropriate people or bad influences) to the marriage, subtracting the good (closeness and honesty) from the marriage, or both.

When the Outside Isn't an Intruder

Some people feel claustrophobic when they read that they should keep outsiders out of their marriage. They may worry that, although they want their spouse to be their closest relationship, they need more in life than him or her. They may fear a loss of freedom. Or they may be aware that their spouse isn't safe for some part or emotion of their soul, so they wonder whether having boundaries in marriage condemns that part of their soul to be chained exclusively to that unsafe spouse forever.

Sometimes they become concerned that their outside relationships and activities are "bad" and should be avoided. For instance, a dependent and controlling husband may insist that his wife not spend time with her friends. She may think having friends is an act of disloyalty to her marriage, rather than thinking that her husband is dominating her.

When we address the idea of keeping out intruders, we are not saying that marriage is a self-contained unit in which each spouse meets every emotional need of the other. Marriage was not designed to be the source of all life for us. This would be idolatry. God and his resources are our life source: "He is before all things, and in him all things hold together" (Colossians 1:17). The marriage bond is one of God's many avenues of sustenance for us, along with his own love, the Bible, and relationships in the church.

The marriage relationship is a covenant between two adults. They join lives to make a more meaningful and fruitful life together. Marriage is not designed to repair the brokenness of its partners, though it can certainly be a major healing agent. It is not designed to provide everything our families of origin didn't. Nor is it designed to be the only place we go for comfort, help, truth, or growth. To be sole support for another person would put an impossible burden on each spouse.

Marriages that attempt this often end up with a parent-child dynamic. One spouse demands that the other function as the mom or dad he never had. The other gamely attempts to do that, then ends up feeling drained and resentful. Then the "child" spouse feels abandoned and unloved. Or both spouses "parent" each other in different ways. For example, a wife will be the only emotional contact her husband will go to. In turn, he makes all the financial and business decisions. She resents his neediness and resistance to going elsewhere. He wishes she'd help out in decision making and take an accounting course at the local college. Either way, marriage simply does not have all the resources a couple needs.

I read many years ago that Billy Graham's wife, Ruth, was asked, "How is your marriage so successful?" She replied, "Because he plays golf, and I play bridge." Ruth Bell Graham understood the value of outside sources of life for a marriage to flourish.

> *Marriage simply does not have all the resources a couple needs.*

Although these needs are legitimate, God intended them to be met in many other ways than for each spouse to re-parent the other. Jesus referred to these ways when he said, "For whoever does the will of my Father in heaven is my brother and sister and mother" (Matthew 12:50). We can receive the love, structure, or approval we need from those who have God's interests and values in their hearts.

Spouses aren't always the safest places to go for certain aspects of our souls. For example, a husband may be quite nurturing when his wife is feeling weak and lonely. But he may recoil and distance himself from her when she is angry or frustrated. This poses a big problem, as all our parts need to be connected to relationship. Those angry parts, as much as the weak and lonely parts, need relationship to heal and mature them. Because of this reality, we need outside relationships that can handle what the spouse cannot or will not.

A Word of Caution

All good marriages need outside support, so we need to seek out the right and appropriate sources. These should be people who are not only safe, but whose influence on us strengthens the marriage bond. Find people who are "for" your marriage and want to help you grow together. Avoid those who play the game of "poor you, being married to that bad person." This doesn't help a marriage. Even further, avoid those who would like to be destructive to the bond in the guise of being helpful to you.

So many affairs begin with this scenario. A wife finds a co-worker who really understands her in ways her husband can't. She feels better, but her marriage is weaker. Your sources of love should not only be helping you but also be helping you love your mate.

The Intruder as a Symptom of Marriage Struggles

Recently I (Dr. Townsend) was talking to a busy couple, Jerry and Marcia, who felt that their marriage was slipping away from them. They had a full schedule, with lots of involvements, and were seeing more conflict and distance between them. Jerry felt he was being left out more and more by Marcia's schedule. Marcia, however, saw the problem as all those outside things that were besetting them. She felt like their victim. "Where is the time?" she would ask. "With jobs, kids, and everything else, we can't get away from it all."

After some conversations with insightful friends, Marcia realized that she had been busy ever since her mother's death a year before. She had been unable to adequately grieve her major loss and had coped by allowing time intruders to come between her and Jerry.

Often the intruder isn't the issue. The intruder is the result, or symptom, of another issue in marriage. The real issue has more to do with your relationship or your

> *Often the intruder is the result, or symptom, of another issue in marriage.*

character. Sometimes something is broken in the connection. For example, one spouse is unloving or very critical and hurtful to the other. The hurt spouse invests herself outside the marriage. Or the busy spouse needs to deal with some immaturity of her soul.

In Marcia's case, her allowing intruders into the marriage had little to do with her husband and much to do with herself. As we will illustrate, the very nature of marriage lends itself to allowing intruders inside the bond to disrupt it.

Because nature abhors a vacuum, some distance (or vacuum) in the marital bond conveniently becomes filled with busyness.

When a marriage contains conflict or hurt, we tend to busy ourselves in other people and activities. Busyness is less painful than facing some seemingly unsolvable problem in love day after day. So many couples make a few attempts to resolve struggles in closeness or responsibility, then give up and find alternatives to the vacuum they feel in the marriage. Activity anesthetizes the deficits and pain in the connection. The problem doesn't go away, however. It erupts in other ways, such as in covert anger, sarcasm, and emotional unavailability.

Many couples schedule date nights and trips away as the solution for this problem. These are highly important to nourish a marriage. Yet, many couples have been disappointed in date nights and getaways when they misunderstand the underlying problems. Things may keep cropping up so that the dates are constantly rescheduled, or the date night itself is shallow, forced, or distant because of unresolved conflicts in the marriage. Date nights are a necessary but insufficient solution for protecting a marriage.

When you become aware of this situation in your marriage, you need to bring the real issue to light and deal with it.

Intimacy Can Promote Intruders in Marriage

The nature of emotional intimacy itself can make a marriage vulnerable to outside influences. When we are intimate, we experience someone's negative characteristics along with the positive ones. We don't really "know" our spouse until we know his faults, weaknesses, sins, and imperfections. When people spend a great deal of time together, the context of safety causes them to regress. In other words, they relax, feel more dependent, and act weak—like an infant folding into his mother's arms in trust.

Not only do couples regress, but they are also more exposed. It is hard to hide one's flaws in a marriage for very long. By definition, negative traits are hard to live with. The controlling husband, the insecure wife, and the critical spouse all cause conflict and friction in a relationship.

Intimacy, then, causes two threats that leave the marriage open to intruders. The first threat is within ourselves. When we notice our vulnerability and exposure, we become frightened. This fear can have many causes, such as the following:

- Fear of our spouse's rejection of our flaws
- Fear of our own increasing need and dependency
- Fear of our uncomfortable feelings emerging more and more
- Guilt that we are draining our spouse by our problems

Many people distance themselves emotionally when they have these fears. They may shut down and withdraw, for example. Or they may feel blamed and condemned. This distance can cause a breach in the trust relationship. When this breach is allowed to continue, intruders have an opportunity to get in between the love of the couple. For example, a wife may fear that her husband will reject her feelings. She then becomes overinvolved in mothering or with her friends. Yet all the while, at some level, she wants to "come home" to the love she first felt for her husband.

The second threat is not internal, but resides in the marriage relationship itself. When intimacy does its work—and, for example, the wife's frailties are exposed to the husband—the husband can actually distance. What should happen is that increased openness elicits increased grace, compassion, and forgiveness as the husband's love has grown along with the relationship. However, for many reasons, a husband may not be able to handle that part of his wife. Here are some areas that may bring about distance:

- Hurts: your mate wants you to be a stronger person
- Failings: your spouse is disappointed in your imperfections
- Sins: your mate is unable to tolerate living with a sinner
- Negative feelings: your spouse desires only positive emotions
- Aspects of himself: your mate is reminded of his own faults through you

Then, as the husband reacts to his wife's problems, he pulls away emotionally. The vacuum occurs again. And again work, kids, or other people step in.

So, sometimes the vulnerable spouse will distance first, a sort of "I'll leave you before you leave me" approach. And sometimes the other spouse will truly withdraw from the exposed partner. Either way, the result is a threat to the integrity of the connection.

Filling the Vacuum

When couples find themselves with this intimacy problem, it is best for them to take responsibility for the issue and begin to reconnect. For example, the wife who has reacted against her own vulnerability may need to admit her fear that her husband knows awful parts of her and her anxiety that he may disconnect from her. This can warm the husband's heart toward her, or even clarify that it was indeed "all in her head."

I know a couple who had become overinvolved with church and activities. The wife thought that she was no longer an interesting person after all these years and that the busyness would keep her husband from becoming bored with her.

She took a risk and confessed to him, "I've been keeping occupied with other things because I thought I wasn't interesting to you."

He was surprised and saddened. "I just don't feel that way at all, and I've missed our times together."

In situations where the husband has distanced because he can't tolerate some aspect of his mate, he may need to own up to his fears of identifying with his wife's failure, or having a condemning spirit. The wife may need to let her husband know how his withdrawal hurts and ask how they can work it out.

To take another example, a wife may find her husband's anger repulsive because it reminds her of her own underlying rage. She may need to take responsibility for dealing with her own angry feelings safely; her husband may need to let her know how lonely and unloved he feels when she withdraws from him in angry times (unless he is being unsafe or dangerous with her).

Some spouses distance because they have poor boundaries. Withdrawal becomes the only boundary they have. They can't be in relationship with the failings of their mate. When they need to be connected and yet set limits with some problem, they find that they can't stay connected. Or if they connect, they can't address the problem. These spouses need to work on becoming both loving and truthful at the same time.

It is often helpful, for example, for a couple to work on signaling to each other when one feels that love and truth aren't both present. If you can tell you are afraid to say some truth, signal to your spouse that you are scared and want to talk about the fear before you go into the truth. Also, if you notice that your spouse isn't really emotionally present, signal to him that he seems distant to you, and invite him to let you know what is going on.

Not Knowing Your Limits

Dale and Margaret are friends of mine. Dale is the energetic optimist who loves being involved in all sorts of church and civic groups. He coaches all his kids' sports teams and genuinely enjoys his job so much that he works long hours. Margaret, by contrast, is an MBA who feels she is always following Dale around and cleaning up his messes. When he overcommits himself, she helps him decide which meeting to drop and which to attend. When he overspends, she figures out how to get them out of trouble. But even though she sees this as part of their marriage, she is troubled by how little of a priority she feels to her husband. "Dale is a really caring person, and he loves life," she told me. "In fact, he sees life as one great adventure. But he never gets back to us as a couple."

Often couples have problems with intruders because one or both of the mates simply are not aware of their own time, energy, and investment resources. They actually think they'll take care of the fires at home at some point. They sincerely intend to talk, date, and stay involved with their

> *Often couples have problems with intruders because one or both of the mates simply are not aware of their own time, energy, and investment resources.*

spouse, but not at this moment. And, too often, the moments don't come, or at least not often enough. The intruders win, and the couple loses.

This problem usually has to do with the "limitless" spouse's inability to see how his actions have consequences. Someone else is always there picking up the pieces, starting perhaps with a parent, then friends, then co-workers, or a spouse. The lack of anxiety about marriage problems comes from a lack of anxiety about *anything*. This spouse has lived with human safety nets and is secure and confident that either (1) nothing bad will come if he doesn't get to his responsibilities; or (2) if something bad happens, no one will mind; or (3) if anyone is bugged about it, someone else will bail him out, and all will be forgiven. It is a life of happy endings, but not reality-based ones.

When Margaret told Dale her feelings, he was surprised. He thought she felt the same exhilaration he did about being involved in so much stuff. And when she told him, "I love you, but I will no longer support you in things that come between us, like your overinvolvement in committees and work," he was resentful. But as she stopped rescuing Dale, he was finally able to experience the consequences of all his distractions. When he had to face angry people and missed deadlines, he became more realistic. At the same time, he saw how much Margaret had been doing for him. Dale began to appreciate her, and he even felt sad about all the time he'd missed by letting other things get between them. He started responding to the whip of reality and the carrot of love for Margaret.

Taking the Marriage for Granted

A related issue in allowing intruders into a marriage occurs when one or both partners are unaware of the fragility of marriage. They often adopt the mentality that no crises are going on, so everything's okay. And they will tend to the crises or the squeaky wheels of work, parenting, church, and friends. The couple may also feel positive toward each other and so assume they are doing okay.

This is an immature perspective on the institution. It is a little like how a young child feels toward her parents. She is secure and certain in the sense that they will always be there no matter what she does, and they will always be available when she returns to them for help and love. This is right for a young child to feel. But for marriage partners, it can be a problem.

Marriages can go a long time before the influence of intruders is felt. If both spouses are active, structured people, they may shift away without a discernible blip, moving from a deep connection between each other into a comfortably numb one. They may wake up one day feeling that they aren't inside each other's hearts and that other things own their hearts. The saddest cases are those in which the partners become aware of this and think, *It's not that bad as is, let's just keep things this way.*

The reality is that marriage is only as good as the investment people make in it. God has constructed life so that we are always either going forward into the growth process or backing away from it. We can't stay the same. And marriage reflects this reality. The connection either deepens, opening both spouses up to the hearts of each, or it starts to deteriorate, closing them off from each other.

> *Marriage is only as good as the investment people make in it.*

We do not believe in an "out of the blue" marriage problem. So many times a spouse will say, "Everything was fine, and then he started being abusive," or, "I thought we were okay until I found out about the affair." This would not be possible if the marriage was a place for continual emotional investment, risk, vulnerability, and honesty. And in hindsight, many couples will say, "We now see the signs we missed before." These signs generally have to do with things like

- Increasing withdrawal of need
- Unresolved differences the couple simply walks away from in resignation

- Preferences for others for needs that the marriage used to meet
- Interests and relationships that are not talked about with the spouse

Do not mistake a lack of crisis as a sign that the marriage is healthy. Couples need to regularly check in with each other and ask the hard questions, such as "How do you feel about us?" and "What am I doing that hurts or bothers you?" Think about how you would feel if your annual physical with your physician consisted only of a chat about sports over a cup of coffee.

Problems in Setting Boundaries with Others

Cindy and Wade had been married only a few years, but already Cindy was feeling like a third wheel. She knew Wade loved her, but he seemed to be owned by the needs, crises, and whims of others. His boss would ask him for extra work time, or their church would request that he head up the missions committee. Wade would say no to hardly anyone.

> *Do not mistake a lack of crisis as a sign that the marriage is healthy.*

Part of why Cindy had fallen in love with Wade was his sensitivity and willingness to be there for her and others. He had seemed so different from the self-centered men she had dated. Yet, he was now apart from her much more than she was happy with. And Wade didn't seem happy with the situation, either. When someone asked for his time, he would sigh, shake his head, look guiltily at her, and then comply. As she put it, "Wade belonged to everyone. So by default, he didn't belong to me." In not saying no to others, Wade was passively saying no to Cindy.

As they talked about it, it became apparent that Wade had tremendous difficulty in setting limits with other people. Sometimes he felt he was letting people down. At other times he was afraid of their displeasure. And at still other times he was concerned that they would leave him. Yet he was torn over his love and obligations to Cindy. He was a man divided (James 1:8) and never at rest. On the one hand, he felt guilty and fearful about letting others down. On the other, he felt the same about letting his wife down.

Cindy vacillated between resenting Wade, feeling guilty for being angry with such a good person, and feeling detached from him. She would find herself berating him with lines about "the cobblers' children having no shoes." Or she would try to be more supportive and patient. Or she would simply feel as if they were floating apart, with all Wade's duties in between them. She felt he, like the church in Ephesus, had forsaken his first love (Revelation 2:4).

Fortunately, Wade *was* a good-hearted man who wanted, above all, to be a good husband. He worked on his fear of others' responses. He saw that the problem wasn't all those demanding people in his life, but his own need for approval and his great fear of loss of love. He became more honest with people about his real limitations, and he faced up to people who demanded much of him. In short, Wade started to become a truthful man. This was very difficult for him, as some people criticized him and called him selfish. He had to face his fears of abandonment and his anxieties about dealing with the rage of others. But he held onto God, Cindy, and several close friends, who all stood by him as he worked on boundaries. And Wade gradually weeded out the intruders between himself and Cindy.

Wade and Cindy's story is a common one. The problem isn't the same as Dale and Margaret's, related earlier, in which Dale simply loved the exhilaration of being with others, with no concept of the cost or pain to Margaret. Wade didn't enjoy the intruders and gave in to them grudgingly. He felt no freedom to choose.

In these situations, the spouse who is left out has become the lesser of two evils. In other words, the boundary-less mate may be less afraid to let his spouse down than the boss or others. It is often because he feels safer with her and knows she won't leave him. But this is a fatal error in perceiving safety. We should be able to trust a safe spouse and relax in her love. However, safety was never meant as a rationalization for neglecting the love obligation. Living in unconditional grace is never an excuse to be irresponsible or hurtful. As the Bible teaches, "What then? Shall we sin because we are not under law but under grace? By no means!" (Romans 6:15). To take for granted that a spouse will "always be there for us" is, at some level, to place burdens upon that spouse's ability to love and trust us back.

If fear and guilt are the reason your marriage has become infested with intruders, you need to do two things. On the one hand, refrain from nagging and threatening your codependent spouse. If you don't refrain, you risk becoming, in his mind, part of those many people he secretly resents and hates for being so demanding on him.

> *Living in unconditional grace is never an excuse to be irresponsible or hurtful.*

On the other hand, stay away from the tendency to ignore the problem and hope it goes away. The best solution is always to love and yet not rescue a spouse's behavior. You may need to tell your spouse, "I am sorry about how pulled apart you feel by work, the church, and me. I do miss you and feel that these things come between us. I hope you can work out your problem, and I will help you. However, I won't be a party to the problem anymore. If you continue to let yourself be dragged apart, I will find other appropriate sources of support, like friends and groups. But let me know if you want to work on your boundaries, and I will do anything I can."

You need to maintain a position of love without rescue and of truth without nagging. Your own caring boundaries then provide hope for your spouse to develop his own sense of self and boundaries.

Inability to Live with Differences

One thing we often hear from couples over dinner or in reflective times is that they feel distress over the differences between them. They will say, "I don't see how we ended up together; we are so diametrically opposed." These polar extremes can run the gamut, from theology to politics, from career to sex, from family to finances, from intimacy to entertainment.

Some couples will open up about how they have let other things get in between them. "We're so different, so we live in two different worlds," they will say. "I have my friends and activities, and he has his. We don't interact a lot." The existence of separate friends and activities is not a red flag, but the tendency to be more invested in them than in the marriage *is* a red flag. Marriage was intended to be home base for our feelings and souls.

This is not the same situation we discussed earlier in the section entitled "When the Outside Isn't an Intruder." There we dealt with the reality that all loving unions need outside sources to grow. In this section, the issue is not about the need for outside influences, but about going to the outside because two people are different.

Actually, this is a huge misperception. Being different should not be a problem in marriage. In fact, it should be a benefit. When your mate has an alternative viewpoint to yours in parenting or home furnishings, you have been enriched. Your world has been enlarged. You are no longer bound to a world of your own making, which is a prison God never intended for us. You are forced to listen to, interact with, and consider the feelings and opinions of another human being in some matter in which you are dead sure you are right. If this is not a solution for human arrogance, what is!

> *Being different should not be a problem in marriage. In fact, it should be a benefit.*

The Bible teaches that we need these differences. Paul discusses the various spiritual gifts God apportions to people: "If the whole body were an eye, where would the sense of hearing be? If the whole body were an ear, where would the sense of smell be? But in fact God has arranged the parts in the body, every one of them, just as he wanted them to be" (1 Corinthians 12:17–18).

In addition, a couple's ability to deal with differences is a sign of their maturity. Children demand that others agree with them. Immature couples do the same. A husband calls his wife "selfish" and has a tantrum when his wife doesn't see things his way. Or a wife gets discouraged when things aren't perfect and withdraws in resignation that "we'll just never see eye to eye." Such spouses will not be able to live in the tension that the other person won't change his or her mind, and they may become the prey of intruders who agree with them. As we mentioned before, triangulation often occurs at this point: we find people who will agree with our opinion, especially about the bad points of our spouse.

Grownups, however, attempt to understand the other's viewpoint while holding on to their own reality. They empathetically appreciate the sentiments of the other and then come to a negotiated agreement, using love, sacrifice, values, and principles. Differences do not create intruder problems. Immaturity does. As spouses own their own weaknesses and issues, what used to drive them crazy often becomes a source of joy for them.

> *Differences do not create intruder problems. Immaturity does.*

For many years I have known a couple in which the wife is highly emotional and flighty. I have fun watching the show, but I don't expect a serious conversation with her. I don't know if the next thing she says will have anything to do with what is being discussed. This used to drive her husband—a logical, obsessive type—crazy. He would say, "There you go again," in a critical tone of voice. Now, after a lot of growth and humility on his part, he sees her as spontaneous and fascinating. He's not in denial. He's in love.

Conflict Avoidance

Because you are not two clones, your differences guarantee conflict in marriage. Two people who feel strongly about how life should be lived will try to resolve the differences. However, some people fear conflict more than others. They may have grown up in homes in which conflict was never experienced as a good thing. As a friend of mine said, "When we saw my parents argue, they would tell us, 'That wasn't an argument; it was a discussion.' Angriest discussion I ever saw!" These people will often then hate conflict, as it means that the love has gone away. They can't feel connected while disagreement and differences are present. So they avoid conflict at all cost, not wanting to lose love. They are vulnerable to intruders, as other people and activities can help keep distance between themselves and the conflicts underlying their marriage.

We will be discussing conflict in the next two chapters, but we will let you in on the principle here: Make conflict your ally, not your enemy. It is the iron that sharpens your marriage (Proverbs 27:17).

The Intruders Themselves

Having laid down the principles underlying intruder issues, we want to deal with some of the intruders that weaken the marriage bond and want to provide ways to guard against them. Your marriage may be uncontaminated, or it may have all of these. Either way, remember that intruders are a fruit, not a root, of the real problem. Deal with the cause, and the intruder will cease to pull you apart.

This is not a complete list of intruders, as time and space would not permit that. There are others, such as parents, television, the Internet, sports, and shopping. These all need to be evaluated as to how they fit into the marriage, how they affect the less-involved spouse, and how to negotiate and compromise so that both people can love and grow.

Work

Everyone is familiar with the stereotypical problem of the workaholic husband whose wife feels that he loves work more than her. More often than not, problems other than a love affair with career are present. Here are some examples of the issues that may be involved:

- *Attachment problems.* A husband's inability to relate emotionally may cause him to flee to work, where he feels more competent. A wife may need to work on helping her husband own the problem and helping him connect on feeling levels.
- *Demands for praise.* A husband may be self-absorbed and desire the affirmation of work over the confrontations of his spouse. A wife may need to help him experience love over admiration and help him give up the demand to be praised at all times.
- *Lack of safety.* A wife may experience hurt in her marriage and withdraw to work for more positive relationships. This couple may need help in making the marriage safe enough to withstand conflict.
- *Lack of freedom.* A husband may be controlling, and the only way a wife can get some freedom is to go away from him. He may need to work on respecting her boundaries, and she may need to work on being more direct about her needs.

In all of these scenarios, the answer is not to quit work, but to deal with the character and relational problems.

Friends

It is common for couples to feel that friends have come between them, even the "safe" platonic ones. A wife may "come to life" when her friends are around and seem bored when only her husband is present. Or a husband may always be finding ways for them to be with friends and avoid one-on-one times. Or there may be a questionable best friend who seems to get in between the couple. The underlying issues might be the following:

- *Superficiality.* A mate is more "broad" than "deep." That is, he relates well on superficial levels, but fears the closeness that comes with intimacy. He may need help in his fear of being abandoned or hurt.
- *Hurt in the marriage.* A spouse may have experienced rejection from her spouse in her deeper parts. For

example, her husband may criticize her weaknesses, frailties, anger, or needs. So friends become the place for these parts. The husband may need to work on accepting all of her, yet allowing her the freedom of investing in friends also for her own growth.

- *Rejection of the spouse.* A self-centered spouse may discover that her mate is not perfect and so gives up on him, investing in others. Here the couple must deal with grieving perfectionistic demands and work on making her life "good enough," even if not ideal.
- *Sharing secrets with friends.* Sometimes a spouse will be hurt because his mate has secret phone times and conversations. In the ideal, spouses should have no serious secrets in a marriage. The deeper the relationship, the greater its ability to withstand the realities of each spouse. But some more frail marriages may have to use healthy settings such as a pastoral counselor or a therapist until the marriage is strong enough to deal with what exists between them.

Again, friends are a treasure in any marriage. As couples work on their issues, friends are not a boundary problem, but a gift that brings them closer.

Kids

Children are built-in intruders on a marriage. They need so much, so often, from a couple. Yet the couple who puts parenting above their marriage has a problem. Here are some of the underlying issues:

> *As couples work on their issues, friends are not a boundary problem, but a gift that brings them closer.*

- *Hiding intimacy conflicts behind children.* The couple has issues with closeness or control, yet neither partner wants to deal with them. You can never give enough time to kids (just ask them!). So the relationship becomes child-centered rather than

marriage-centered. These couples need to bring out their
conflicts with each other safely and work through them.

- *Overidentifying with children.* Some spouses feel
  inordinate guilt and responsibility for their children's
  lives, and they have a hard time letting go. They feel the
  spouse can handle the neglect, and they overinvolve
  themselves in parenting. They need to allow age-
  appropriate space and time with their kids, an action that
  allows the children to separate and the couple to become
  closer. (For more information on this issue, see
  Boundaries with Kids and *Raising Great Kids.*)

- *Having better boundaries with kids than with the spouse.*
  Often a mate will feel, "If she won't listen to my opinion,
  at least the children will." And he will overinvest in his
  children because they will heed his words. This couple
  needs to work on respecting each other's boundaries and
  helping the other feel both love and freedom.

- *Misperceptions about parenting and marriage.* Some
  people have simply never thought through the fact that
  parenting is temporary and marriage is permanent. A
  friend told me once, "We're in a 'childocentric' culture,
  and I want to become more 'familycentric.'" Couples may
  need to adjust their values appropriately.

Affairs

The most hurtful intruder—an affair—has been the death
knell for many a struggling marriage. Yet we believe that, as in
the other cases, the affair is a tragic symptom of other problems,
such as the following:

- *Emptiness in the marriage.* Some spouses have affairs to
  connect with someone when they can't connect with their
  spouse.

- *Demands to be treated as perfect.* Sometimes a spouse
  with narcissistic tendencies will reject his mate's
  mirroring of his imperfections and find someone who will
  stroke and admire him.

- *Victim-perpetrator-rescuer issues.* One spouse will take on the helpless victim role, and the other will be the predatory perpetrator. Then the victim will seek out a rescuer-type to protect her from the evil one—that is, until the rescuer begins to show signs of being flawed, also.
- *Boundary problems.* One spouse will be unable to set limits in the marriage. The affair becomes the only way he has ever said no to his spouse. In other words, it is the only noncompliant thing he has ever done in the marriage.

These examples indicate severe problems in a marriage. We do not believe in automatically divorcing because of affairs. God simply permits, but does not demand, divorce in cases of adultery (Matthew 5:32).

> *Parenting is temporary and marriage is permanent.*

In cases where the spouse is truly repentant, has given up the affair, and is seriously in the growth process for the long haul, the affair serves as a wake-up call for maturity. We have seen many cases in which affairs have led to greater intimacy and strength in the marriage.

Even while you work on protecting your marriage from intruders, you will still have conflicts. The next chapter will help you deal successfully with the different types of conflicts that marriages face.

Chapter 13

Six Kinds of Conflict

*C*onflict is not all the same. The rules are different for different kinds of conflict. If one of you comes home late without calling, for example, then confession and an apology are in order. But if you are disagreeing about where to go for dinner, no one should have to grovel as if he has committed a grievous sin!

Nevertheless, we run into couples who do exactly that. They feel that every conflict has a right and a wrong, and instead of trying to resolve the problem, they argue over which one of them is right. It is amazing how creative someone can get in defending the "rightness" of her position when she might be talking about how the couple is going to spend a vacation! In most conflict there is not a right or wrong. Yet, some spouses can sound like a couple of attorneys in court.

In this chapter we want to help you distinguish what kind of conflict you are having. Then you may be better equipped to find a solution acceptable to both of you and to the relationship as well. Let's look at the list of common marital conflicts and then examine each kind.

- Sin of One Spouse
- Immaturity or Brokenness of One Person
- Hurt Feelings That Are No One's Fault
- Conflicting Desires
- Desires of One Person Versus the Needs of the Relationship
- Known Versus Unknown Problems

Conflict #1: Sin of One Spouse

In this simple scenario, there is a culprit. Someone has done something wrong. One spouse has sinned against the other. There is a true infraction, not an imagined one. And there is no shortage of areas in which we can sin: sexual sin, angry outbursts, loss of self-control, impatience, critical attitudes, judgmentalism, out-of-control spending of the family money (thievery), lying or deception, critical attitude, substance abuse, controlling behavior, emotionally injurious behavior (name calling or belittling), misuse of power, pride, selfishness, greed, jealousy, envy, and conceit.

The first thing to consider in facing the conflict that comes from an individual's sin is the attitude of the spouse confronting the sin. Even the best of people can do what the Bible calls "falling short of the glory of God." The best thing that anyone can do in the face of the sin of a spouse is to demonstrate the same attitude God has toward someone who sins: "Be kind and compassionate to one another, forgiving each other, just as in Christ God forgave you" (Ephesians 4:32).

Jessica and Reggie came into counseling because she discovered he had been looking at pornography on the Internet. At first she was very hurt. She felt betrayed. Then she felt that there must be something wrong with her or he would not have been looking at pictures of other women. But after the initial chaos of such a discovery, she displayed remarkable grace in one of our sessions.

"How do you feel about this?" I (Dr. Cloud) asked her, knowing about her hurt and feelings of betrayal.

"I guess I am past all the hurt now," she said.

"How did you do that?"

"I just started thinking about him," she answered. "When I saw the kind of bondage he was in and how bad he felt about himself, I thought about what would drive him to such a thing. I felt sorry for him and the shame he felt. I just want you to help him find out the reason he does this and help him with it. I know that I am not perfect, either. I don't want him to do this, but I guess I started to understand his hurt."

Reggie began to cry. The grace his wife showed him was far different from what he had ever received in his life, and much different from how he responded to himself. He turned to her, cried in her arms, and said, "I'm so sorry I've hurt you like this."

From this point on, Reggie was a different guy. He grasped the work of therapy and recovery with a passion, seeing it as a project he must do to not fall short of the grace he had been given. I was reminded of the verse about the grace of God that tells us that it is his kindness that leads us to repentance (Romans 2:4).

Jessica had offered the two most important attitudinal things that the Bible suggests in dealing with someone else's sin: humility and grace. She did not approach the sin of her husband with the idea that she was someone "better than he." As Paul puts it, "Brothers, if someone is caught in a sin, you who are spiritual should restore him gently. But watch yourself, or you also may be tempted. Carry each other's burdens, and in this way you will fulfill the law of Christ" (Galatians 6:1–2).

Jessica did not lord it over Reggie, saying that this was his sin and not hers. She identified with the mutual position they both had before God as sinners. She realized she was not perfect, either, and then gave him the same kind of grace God gives to her. She restored him gently and watched herself and her own attitudes to make sure she remained humble. It proved to be an important aspect of Reggie's own repentance.

At the same time, she did not minimize the sin. This is one of the most difficult things for some people. These people feel that if they are going to be full of grace and humility, they can't be tough on the sin. But a friend of mine once said, "Go soft on the person and hard on the issue." This is what Jessica did. She was honest, called Internet pornography sin, and talked about her hurt and betrayal, but did not let Reggie's sin go unconfronted. She took a stance according to her values, just as we talked about in chapter 5. Couples need to take a hard stand against anything that violates their values. Pornography violates several values: faithfulness, honesty, holiness, loving God, and loving the other.

Do not minimize the sin of your spouse, and ask him or her not to minimize yours. Ultimately this will be best for both of you and for the relationship. Go tough on the issue, but remember, as God is with you, go soft on the person. Like Jesus, face sin with both grace and truth.

> *Couples need to take a hard stand against anything that violates their values.*

The process looks like this:

1. Look at your own attitude. Rid yourself of judgmentalism, condemnation, shame, or pride. Look at the log in your own eye, show mercy, and identify with your spouse as a fellow sinner.
2. Speak to the issue directly. Let your spouse know that you know, and tell him that what he is doing is not right. If the sin is against you, let him know how you feel. Talk about the hurt and how it affects you and whoever else is involved. Don't shame him, but be honest. Use "I" statements.
3. A boundary-loving spouse will acknowledge the wrong and apologize. Accept it; offer forgiveness. Reaffirm your love and acceptance.
4. When emotions are not strong, talk about the problem to see if there is any further help he might need. Even though he might have confessed and repented, underlying issues may need to be addressed, and he might need outside help. Offer your support and help to solve the problem.
5. Agree on a follow-up plan. "If I notice something again, how do you want me to help you? What do you want me to do?" This way you become a team member to deal with the problem and not a police officer. You might want to talk to him about bringing other resources to the problem as well, such as friends to hold him accountable. The important issue is that you are together as a team to fight the reoccurrence.

Conflict #2: Immaturity or Brokenness of One Person

Jerry was frustrated with his wife, Genie. They had decided early on in the marriage that it was important for her to be at home with the children, so they had divided the duties. He worked hard making a living for the family. Running the household was her responsibility.

But Genie was not "pulling her weight." Many things were not getting done. For example, Jerry expected her to clean the house, do the laundry, and have dinner ready when he got home from work. But he would come home to a messy house, undone laundry, and no dinner. In addition, she was tired when he came home, and more and more of the parenting responsibilities fell on his shoulders.

Jerry nagged Genie to do more, and she became angry with him, telling him she was doing all she could. He couldn't understand why she couldn't do more and would tell her, "That's how life is! You just have to buckle down and do it. I am working hard, too." She would not feel very helped by his "advice." She alternated between feeling bad and feeling resentment toward him for pushing her.

Finally they decided to get some counseling.

After I talked with them for a while, it was clear to me that Genie had some significant problems and that Jerry had some significant shortcomings in empathy and understanding. I felt for him in that he was having to carry much more of the load than he had agreed to. But the way he was handling his wife was way out of line. In reality, his behavior was going to make her improvement more difficult.

Genie was depressed. This was the first reality that they both had to deal with. Just trying harder was not going to fix her depression. Until she dealt with her depression, she would lack energy and concentration. In addition, she did not have the structure in her character to manage a house in the way both of them desired.

Growth was needed on both sides. First, Jerry had to "get it." I had to do several things with him. He had to learn how to accept the reality of who Genie was, depression and disorganization included. He had to learn that he was married to all of her, her infirmities included. And he had to learn what unconditional love means. I had to coach him in the realities of depression and also Genie's very real inabilities. She did not have the ability to "just snap out of it," nor did she have the ability to just "get organized." Both were real limitations he was going to have to accept and love her in the midst of.

Second, Jerry had to learn not to be judgmental of her, but be supportive and find ways he could work with her. This included giving up some of the things he wanted that she could not do. Giving up expectations was not easy for him, but he was open and teachable, albeit frustrated! It helped when he looked at some of his own inabilities and could empathize and identify with hers. He had some failures in his own life. I helped him to see that she was no different.

And Genie had to accept herself. She had been fighting the fact that she had a problem. She had not faced the realty of her inability. This realization is an important step in fixing anything. She had been stuck in the "should's." She had been saying, "I *should* be able to do more. I *should* not be so unorganized." She was still protesting the reality of who she was. She had to get to the point of saying, "I would like to be not depressed and to be more organized. But the reality is that this is where I am. Now the question is, this being reality, what am I going to do about it?"

Once Genie owned this, change could begin to take place. Once she faced her inability, she could get to work. We developed the following plan.

1. *Work on the depression.* Genie saw her long-standing depression as a real problem and began treatment for it. She took medication and sought counseling. In a matter of months, she saw real progress. She had much more energy and concentration to face and solve some of her other problems.

2. *Adjust to reality.* Both Jerry and Genie had to reorganize their life. They had to give up some of their ambitious plans for a while until their problems were better. Their original plan had included two fully functioning people, and they did not have

that, at least for a while. So they agreed to cut back on what they wanted until they got to a better place.

3. Work on the disorganization. Genie saw that her lack of structure was a real problem and that one more New Year's Resolution was not going to make her more disciplined. She joined an accountability group with friends who helped her take some steps toward organization. She asked them to check up on her and make sure she had complied with the plans she had agreed to. She asked an older woman in her church to help her acquire some skills she had never learned. Making commitments to certain schedules and jobs was new for her, but very helpful. Soon she was getting her work done and feeling much better about life.

Jerry and Genie did very well. She worked through her depression and began to run the home in an acceptable way for both of them to reach their goals as a family. And Jerry turned into a much more compassionate, helpful person. (Part of me secretly thought that God had put them together to help Jerry become more flexible, though I kept such unprovable theological musings to myself!) I was proud of Jerry and Genie.

> *Most people get married totally unaware of their spouse's shortcomings.*

Their story teaches some valuable lessons for dealing with the conflict that comes from one spouse's inability. All of us will fall short of the demands of life. This is a difficult concept for some people to understand. Most people get married totally unaware of their spouse's shortcomings. In fact, part of "falling in love" is idealizing an imperfect person, not even seeing where he or she falls short of that ideal. But in every relationship, reality eventually surfaces. When it does, it is very important to face it in the following helpful ways.

1. Accept Reality

Accept reality about yourself and your spouse. Both of you will be unprepared for some of the realities life brings. You will not have the emotional ability to weather some stresses in the way you would like. Or you will not have the skill needed to be a mature adult. When this happens, do not be surprised. Below are some common areas where normal people find they have brokenness from the past or some immaturity where they are not equipped to perform as they or their spouse would like:

- Relational abilities to get close, communicate, or sustain intimacy
- Parenting abilities
- Emotional problems from the past or from their family of origin
- Lack of structure, self-discipline, or follow-through
- Financial inabilities to make or manage money
- Sexual difficulties from fear, past trauma, shame, or other emotional factors
- Not having completed the "twoness" and identity formation talked about in chapter 4
- Not having completely left home and become an adult, ready for marriage

None of these are "sins." They are areas in which you are immature and need to grow. If one of you makes them out to be sin, or demands that they not be present because you wanted an "ideal" partner, you are prolonging the problem. Accept reality.

2. Communicate Your Support to Your Spouse

We do not grow when we are judged, nagged, condemned, resented, or subjected to some other lack of grace. We all need to feel that someone is on our side and supporting us. Let your partner know that you are her biggest supporter and reaffirm your absolute unconditional love and acceptance for her just like she is. As 1 Thessalonians 5:14 tells us, "Encourage the timid, help the weak, be patient with everyone." Let your spouse know that her weakness or inability is something with which you will be supportive and patient.

3. Face Issues as Real Problems

Although we don't wish to be nonsupportive or lack grace, we also wish to be honest about problems. It would not have been truly loving for Jerry to ignore Genie's depression or her disorganized life. Part of love, remember, is honesty and requiring holiness and growth from each other. So, where your spouse is not mature, let her know.

Be direct. Tell her what you see as a problem. Let your spouse know how you feel and how it affects you. But be careful to stay away from shame and condemnation: "I understand your difficulty, Genie. I really do. But, at the same time, I would like us to be able to do some things together again. I get lonely. I want you to get your depression treated so we can have fun again." This kind of communication can be motivating, not condemning. But make sure that you are both clear that there is a need for growth.

4. Own Your Problems

If you are the one confronted with your immaturity, own it. Be a "boundary lover." Be the kind of wise man or woman who loves to get feedback and heeds it. Don't be defensive, and try to learn what the person who sees you every day is learning about you. (We will talk more about how to be a boundary lover in the next chapter.) Don't fight the truth as well as the problem itself.

5. Get a Plan

Genie and Jerry designed a plan to deal with their immaturity issues. They received help from others. You will have to do that as well, no matter who you are. We need help, mentoring, support, and teaching. No one ever grew up on his own.

Some need therapy. Others need financial counseling. Still others need support groups or recovery groups. Some need accountability systems. But make sure that your immaturity or brokenness does not rule you. Overcome it by being intentional about dealing with it. Devote resources, time, and energy to the problem.

6. Make It Mutual

Guard against labeling one spouse "the problem person." This is never true. Just because Genie had the more noticeable problems did not mean that she was the only one who had some growing up to do. Neither of you is a complete person yet; you are both still growing up. Guard against the one who is the most functional being seen as "the okay one." God says that you are equal in his eyes, and you should be equal in each other's as well.

> *God says that you are equal in his eyes, and you should be equal in each other's as well.*

Usually one of you has to grow more in the *relational* area, such as expressing feelings and confronting problems, and the other in the *functional* area of life, such as advancing in a career and getting things done. Help each other in your areas of weakness. Remember: you are one now. And if one of you is suffering, so is the other. As Paul tells us, both of you are in this together:

> Husbands ought to love their wives as their own bodies. He who loves his wife loves himself. After all, no one ever hated his own body, but he feeds and cares for it, just as Christ does the church—for we are members of his body. "For this reason a man will leave his father and mother and be united to his wife, and the two will become one flesh." This is a profound mystery— but I am talking about Christ and the church. However, each one of you also must love his wife as he loves himself, and the wife must respect her husband (Ephesians 5:28–33).

There is no "one-upmanship" here. Both of you are loving the other as part of yourself. You are one. You are both in need of growth. Equality and mutuality can solve a lot of problems if you are working as a team. You are no longer individuals in the way singles are. Make the equality mutual, and make the problems mutual so that you help each other.

Conflict #3: Hurt Feelings That Are No One's Fault

George arrived home from work to find the house empty. He had thought Mary would be there, as it was after 6:00 p.m. She usually was home in the late afternoon. He was surprised, but did not think a lot about it. He started reading the paper and watching CNN.

When she did come in, she was excited to see him. She went over to him and gave him a big kiss. He gave her a weak smile. Thinking that he had just had a hard day, she let it pass.

Later, at dinner, George was not very talkative. He took his plate and went to watch TV. She finished her dinner and started doing some chores. George went to bed, and when she went to their room, he was asleep.

By this time, she thought something was wrong, so she woke him up. At first, he was defensive, and then he began to get teary-eyed. Finally he let her know that he was feeling sad and alone.

"Why?" Mary wanted to know, sensing that it had something to do with her.

"Well, I came home to see you, and you were gone. You didn't get here until a long time later. You just ignored me."

"What do you mean? It was not late when I got here. And besides, I was out getting the shirts you wanted exchanged."

"Great! And just forget that I exist while you are out gallivanting on one of your shopping sprees. I am sure that you found some more to do as well."

"Fine! Get your own shirts next time."

Mary went back to the den and watched a late movie. George went to sleep. Neither one felt very good about what had transpired.

What had transpired was a familiar pattern in their relationship:

- One of them feels hurt
- The hurt person communicates as if the other has sinned against him
- The accused party gets defensive
- They "go to court" defending their innocence
- They end up alienated

- The problem never gets resolved, and they go on, "forgetting" about it the next day

Sadly, this pattern happens in many relationships. In reality, neither George nor Mary had committed a transgression. But George was hurt. This hurt was no one's fault. It was not a sin for her to run errands. She had not committed to being home to meet him at a certain time. Neither had George done anything to "get his feelings hurt." It had just happened.

Growing up, George was a latch-key kid, never having anyone home when he came home from school. So he was sensitive to feelings of abandonment and to feeling ignored. Mary had done nothing "wrong," but George was hurt just the same.

This is common. Because we all have hurts and things to which we are sensitive, innocent things will set us off. What is important is that we learn how to deal with this kind of hurt where no one is really "wrong." Here are some hints:

> *What is important is that we learn how to deal with the kind of hurt where no one is really "wrong."*

1. When You Are Hurt, Acknowledge It to Yourself

Know yourself well enough to know when something is bothering you, and own your feelings. George did not really observe what was going on inside himself. Don't ignore how you feel. Figure out what is bothering you. If you don't know what it is, at least acknowledge that it is "something."

2. Communicate

Tell your spouse you are hurt by something she did. Don't blame your spouse as if she has sinned. Unlike George, take ownership for the hurt as coming from inside of you. Communicate that you know it is your problem, that you just want your spouse to understand. This couple's evening would have been different if George had said, "I know you did not do anything wrong. But I felt all alone and sad earlier when I came home and you weren't here. It reminded me of a lot of feelings I used to have."

Again, use "I" statements and talk about your own feelings, making sure that you don't sound as if you are blaming your spouse.

3. Empathize

If you are on the other end of the hurt, show empathy for your spouse's feelings. Know that by caring and offering empathy you are not saying that it is your "fault." If you can identify with your spouse's feelings, offer that as well: "I know what that feels like. I can understand why you felt so sad. I don't like feeling alone either."

Be a healing agent for the hurt of the past. When you offer understanding instead of devaluing your spouse's feelings, you are doing the opposite of the one who caused the original hurt and are becoming part of the healing instead of part of the problem.

4. Identify Patterns and Plan

Learn what hurts you. Then you can anticipate things that might hurt you in the future. And when it happens, you can take precautions to respond helpfully or, better yet, avoid the hurt altogether. If you see situations coming up, you can plan for them so that hurt does not happen.

I talked to a couple the other day who were planning for a few hectic weeks. They knew that the wife was subject to feeling imposed upon and taken for granted when things grew busy. They talked about how she would feel in advance and took some steps to make sure it would not happen. One was for her to give an early warning signal. "If you start to feel imposed upon or taken for granted, let me know immediately," he said.

5. Be in a Healing Mode

We are all responsible for the hurts we carry around inside. If you have become aware of a repetitive theme of hurt, call it a problem and obtain some help. Do something to pursue healing in that area so that it stops interfering in your life. That is part of becoming a complete, healed person.

6. Guard Against "Going to Court"

What George and Mary did is what gets couples stuck. They tried to find out who was "wrong." Of course, they never could, for no one was. Validate each other's feelings because what your spouse is feeling is real and true for him or her. Remember, you don't need to win or to be right. You are not in court, and there is no judge and jury. What is important is that your hearts connect with empathy for whoever is hurting.

Marriage is a place where old hurts get stepped on. This is inevitable. But old hurts can heal as you respond differently to your spouse than he has been responded to in his "past life." Become a healing agent, with empathy, understanding, nondefensiveness, and care.

Conflict #4: Conflicting Desires

Think of the following inevitable conflicts:

- One person likes adventure movies, the other likes romantic comedies
- One wants to spend money on the house, the other wants to save for the future
- One likes the church that focuses on contemporary worship, the other likes traditional liturgy
- One wants to go out, the other wants to stay home
- One wants more children, the other wants no more

Wherever you have two people, you will have conflicting desires. It is one of the things that makes a relationship what it is. Two different people bring differences to the table. In fact, your differences are part of what brought you together. You complement each other, as we mentioned in an earlier chapter.

> *Your differences are part of what brought you together. You complement each other.*

Normally, two giving people develop a pattern of give and take, and differences get negotiated. But sometimes they hit a stalemate. A few principles can help:

1. Avoid Moralizing Your Preference

I was working with a couple who differed in how they liked to spend "free time." Joe liked to spend downtime leisurely hanging around the house. He would play games with the kids or watch sports on TV. On Saturday afternoons he would sometimes take a nap.

Susan was more of a doer. She liked to do projects around the house when she had free time. But after organizing the house and "working on projects" while Joe was napping, she would begin to grow annoyed that he wasn't helping.

Soon an argument would ensue. She would feel that he was being "lazy," and he would feel that she was being "compulsive." They would "go to court." Susan would moralize her position, thinking that work was good and TV was bad. He "should" be helping. He would feel as strongly about his choice, saying that he had worked hard all week and deserved a rest.

Although this was not an issue of right and wrong, each would make a case for being on the moral high ground. And they would not get anywhere.

I was able to show them that these are areas of "preference," not right or wrong. Humans tend to see what they prefer as right, especially if one of the preferences has a moral-sounding quality to it, like working and accomplishing something. For some spouses, relationships could be the moral high ground, while the partner might prefer solitude.

Make sure you realize that your desire is not a higher one than your spouse's. Do not try to win by making yours right and your spouse's wrong. These are preferences, not laws.

2. Empathize with and Understand the Importance of Your Spouse's Desires

Avoid devaluing what your spouse wants. Stay away from statements that make it sound as if what she wants is less important than what you want. Her desires are just as real to her as yours are to you. Validate her desires as real and good.

If she likes movies that have more drama than action, saying that you don't want to go to "some cheesy chick-flick" is not helpful. Say, "Okay, I see why you would want to see that film. It sounds as if it has a lot of meaningful things to you."

3. Move to Meet Your Spouse's Desires Before You Meet Your Own

Paul gives some great advice: "Do nothing out of selfish ambition or vain conceit, but in humility consider others better than yourselves. Each of you should look not only to your own interests, but also to the interests of others" (Philippians 2:3–4). If you are trying to make sure that your mate gets what he or she wants first, your arguments will be over who gets to give that day, not who gets his or her own way!

Seek to make sure that your spouse gets his or her desires met before yours are met, and you will avoid most arguments. In reality, this is not going to happen often, but your attitude is what is important.

Let your spouse pick the car, or the movie, or the vacation this time. There will always be a next one.

4. If Necessary, Keep an Account of Yours, Mine, and Ours

I worked with a couple who always argued about how they spend their time and money. I finally told them that there are two kinds of relationships in the world: those operated by love, and those operated by rules. Loving relationships do not require rules, for these couples live by the Golden Rule of doing unto others as you would have them do unto you. But unloving relationships have to have rules. Since these two people were not loving each other, I was going to make some rules.

I told them to make two columns on a piece of paper and to keep score of how much time and money they had to spend. Figure out whose "turn" it was to get to have their way with that night or that dollar. Then alternate. One could choose the restaurant or the movie one night, and the other the next. One could spend the first one hundred dollars, and then the other. And so on.

At first they were insulted. "We are not children. We don't need stupid rules like that," they protested. But I seriously disagreed.

"Oh, yes, you are!" I said. "You are acting just like children. Each of you wants your own way. So I am going to chaperone and make sure that it is all fair. Bring your report to me next week."

They finally agreed, although they were embarrassed by their level of maturity. But the system worked. They fell into the habit of remembering that two people shared finite resources like time and money. There was just so much to go around, and they had to share.

This system is valuable for couples with differing personalities who drift into unconscious patterns. Remember the opening story of the book? Steve was more assertive than Stephanie and got his way more because she was more adaptive. They had drifted into a pattern of the strong person dominating most of the time. Ultimately it became destructive.

If you keep an account, you will guard against the passive spouse becoming the perpetual loser. The more assertive one will finally get some limits.

5. Don't Define an "I" Choice as a "We" Choice

Some spouses who enjoy "togetherness" define what they want as being for the *relationship,* when it is really for *themselves.* They might choose to spend all of their free time doing things together, thinking that it is a "we" choice when in reality it is an "I" choice. What they should be saying is, "I am choosing to spend my allotted time with you, and that must come out of my account."

Such people feel cheated when the other spouse wants to do something by himself or herself. They feel as if they always give to the relationship and as if the other person is being selfish. This is not true. They are not "giving" to the relationship; they are making personal choices that include the other person because they don't like doing things alone or apart from the relationship.

Make sure that when you want your spouse to do a "we" thing, he or she is really wanting to do that as well. If not, and he or she goes along, remember it is for you and not for the both of you. Count it in your own column.

6. Make Sure "We's" Are Agreed Upon

Make sure you both sign off on activities that are really for the two of you. I talked to a couple recently who had lived for three years in a big house that she finally admitted she resented and hated. He was astonished. He thought they had both wanted and loved the large house, even though it took money away from the family for doing other things.

The wife had gone along and had never spoken up in the beginning. It had really been something for him, but he had thought it was truly a "we" thing. He was appalled that she felt the way she did.

When you both have to sacrifice for something, make sure that you are on the same page in wanting it and agreeing to it. Otherwise, make sure that you are freely giving in to the other person and will not carry a grudge or an emotional debt.

7. Question Your Preferences

Some of the things on which you take strong stances may not be true desires. Susan's preference for working around the house turned out to be a false desire. We examined her desire further and found out that it was really neurotic. In reality, she did not like being busy, but she just *had* to be busy. She became very anxious if she was not doing something.

We worked on Susan's anxiety. She had to learn how to relax and not push everyone around her to the same drivenness she felt. She later changed and did not prefer to be working all the time. We cured her "workaholism."

Others find out the same thing about money. One man I counseled was having marital conflict because of his spending. He bought expensive cars and other pricey items that left his family without the ability to buy other things that would have been better for them. As it turned out, these purchases were not the man's real desires, either. They were driven by his desire to prove to others that he was successful; they were motivated by ego. As he grew, his desires changed, and he spent more money on the things his family wanted.

As James tells us, we sometimes want things for wrong motives (James 4:3). God wants to grant to us our real desires, but sometimes what we want are not true desires. They come from motives other than those from our heart. These false desires try to fill empty places and cover feelings of insecurity.

Desires to spend time in certain ways can be similar. Some men are driven to compete in sports, for example, to cover feelings of insecurity. They have to improve their golf game or their time in the next marathon. Or they have to work longer and harder to make more money. Still others do the same thing with church. They try to work out their guilt or some other unresolved feeling by doing service projects. These things, done out of impure motives, often take time away from the family.

The point is that some time spent at church can be for an impure motive and not out of a true desire. It may be that someone compulsively spends time at church to cover up for feelings of guilt, and it may not be real service at all. When we evaluate our motives and get to true desires, sometimes we find time we did not know we had.

Check the motives for your desires. You might find more lasting fulfillment giving to the relationship instead of your "pleasures."

8. Expand and Grow

You might find out that you actually like romantic comedies or Chinese food or a vacation in the mountains, if you try. Instead of fighting for your own way, give in to the preference of your spouse as a learning and stretching experience. You don't like it now because you might never have let yourself try. Your spouse might know something that you don't!

Relationships can grow you and expand you if you let them. Try to see the activity through your spouse's eyes, and you might learn to enjoy something that you never would have thought possible. People like opera for a reason; try to find out what it is. The old adage "don't knock it until you've tried it" might apply to you. And make sure you try it more than once.

Conflict #5: Desires of One Person Versus the Needs of the Relationship

Sometimes the desire of one spouse conflicts with the needs of the relationship. Mom wants to go back to school, but the couple needs the time or the money. Dad wants to relocate for a promotion, but it would disrupt the family. One partner has been working hard for a season and wants to spend some time or money for himself or herself. On the surface, this desire of one member of the family can be seen as selfish because it will cost the relationship or the family something.

The rule here is that there is no rule. If there were a rule, it would be to find balance over the long term. No relationship is going to survive if all the members are not

> *The rule here is that there is no rule.*

getting some desires met; vice versa, no relationship is going to thrive if the members get their individual needs met and the relationship always suffers. It is good for a relationship at times to "serve" its members.

I talked to a family the other day whose mother has found out in middle age that she has a particular talent. Pursuing this talent into a career costs the rest of the family. They all have to pitch in and take up the slack while she invests time and money into pursuing her dream. But it is a team effort. They are all in it together. The husband is more excited about what she is doing than he is about his own work. It is a beautiful thing to watch.

It works because this woman has given much to her family over the years. She has proved that she can sacrifice for the marriage and for the family. Now the family is sacrificing for her growth. It is a good balance for all concerned.

The problem comes when the marriage always serves one member and never the others. Make sure that over the long haul

> *In the end, the marriage benefits as each member grows. But keep it in balance, making sure that the marriage gets served first.*

the marriage goes on the back burner at times for each member and that each member has learned that the marriage is more important than his or her individual wants.

Marriage means giving up some individual "rights" for the sake of the marriage. But sometimes the marriage returns the favor and sacrifices for the individual. In the end, the marriage benefits as each member grows. But keep it in balance, making sure that the marriage gets served first.

Here are some hints:

- Remember that the marriage comes first. Give the best to the relationship before your individual desires. Earn the equity to spend later.
- Be clear about what you want. Don't passively wish. Tell your spouse clearly.
- Be excited about what your spouse wants for himself or herself individually. You are "one," and it is for you as well, even if seems that it is just "for him or her" right now.
- Make sure that your individual desires that take away from the relationship over the long haul are not unbalanced in terms of what your spouse gets.
- As much as possible, make long-term plans for individual things that take away from the marriage. This way you can plan together to sacrifice, and it is not spur of the moment. Immediate requests feel more like demands.

Conflict #6: Known Versus Unknown Problems

Denial has received a bad rap. To be sure, it can be dangerous. When we are in denial about some problem, it can destroy us. And some denial systems are very strategic and intentional. People with substance problems, for example, maneuver a lot to remain unaware of their problem. This kind of denial needs to be assaulted.

But another kind of denial is not intentional. It is the human trait of being "unaware." Some people are not "in denial," but they have a "blind spot." We all have aspects to our personalities and character that we do not know about. As King David said, "Who can discern his errors? *Forgive my hidden faults.* Keep your servant also from willful sins; may they not rule over me. Then will I be blameless, innocent of great transgression" (Psalm 19:12–13, italics added). David knew that there were things about him that he did not know.

> *In marriage, your spouse may know more about you than you do. The trick to growth is becoming partner to this secret knowledge.*

In marriage, your spouse may know more about you than you do. The trick to growth is becoming partner to this secret knowledge. There is a difference between known and unknown problems, however, and they should be handled differently.

Conflict in Known Problems

- If you have talked about a certain pattern before, agree about what you will do if the pattern returns. Agree that the person with the problem is responsible for it once he knows about it, and each party knows what to expect if it happens again. For some, this may mean, "I am not going to tell you again. I am just going to enforce the consequence we agreed upon." In principle, the person knows that he has the problem and should be working on it. If you have talked about one partner's tardiness, for example, then you might agree ahead of time that if the partner is tardy again, he will get left behind. Or if one spends too much again, she will have to work it off.
- If you have talked before and want each other's help, then confronting will be used not for policing, but for

making someone aware. "I cannot see when I am doing that. Please let me know." Then confrontation is an attempt to heal, not to control the problem.

- If you know about the problem, the plan to fix it is your responsibility. You are in charge of your own character issues. Don't blame your spouse in any way for something that you already know about yourself.
- If it is your partner's problem and she knows about it, don't enable her. If you do, you are part of the problem. Follow through with the consequences you have agreed upon.

Conflict in Unknown Problems

- Agree with each other that you have permission to tell each other about what you notice. If you are partners in discovery, then you will experience it as teamwork and not control.
- When you are confronted, be open. Don't be defensive. Accept the feedback, at least agreeing to look at yourself and see if it is true.
- Seek feedback from others also. If your friends tell you the same thing as your spouse, you might believe it more.
- Ask your spouse to show you each time it happens so that you can see the pattern. We tend to think a mistake or problem is a "one-time occurrence" if we don't know that it is true about us. Catching yourself over and over will slowly convince you.
- Give grace to each other. In areas that are new discoveries for your spouse, change is not going to be immediate. Give him time.

In the next chapter we will deal with the process of how to solve conflicts with a spouse who supports the idea of boundaries.

Chapter 14 ────

Resolving Conflict with a Boundary-Loving Spouse

Shellie and I (Dr. Cloud) had had a difficult session. It was her first appointment, and I had not known what to expect.

She had said in the initial phone conversation that she wanted to come to "talk about some things." I didn't want to get into all the details over the phone, so we just set up an appointment. When she did come in, she was in a lot of pain.

"He just doesn't understand how much I'm hurting," she said, referring to her husband, Robbie. "I've talked to him before about both things, but it just doesn't do any good. I'm thinking that there needs to be a serious intervention."

The "intervention" Shellie talked about had to do with Robbie's drinking, but she was also upset about his workaholism. A few years earlier, he had started a chain of retail stores that had become very successful. But the success brought much more work than he had promised. She was very upset with how much time he was spending away from the family.

As I listened to Shellie, I wondered what I would be able to do for the relationship, for she sounded so hopeless. It sounded as if Robbie was unwilling to change anything for her. But, since it was a relationship problem, I told her that I wanted to talk to him as well.

At first she seemed reluctant to agree to my seeing Robbie. When I questioned her, she said that she knew that we were eventually going to have to meet together, but she had hoped I could just help her to feel better "before we got into all of that."

When I asked her what "all of that" was, she explained that she didn't think Robbie would be very open to her complaints. She feared that he might not even participate in the counseling at all. That is why she thought an intervention might be the only way.

I told her that I understood her fears, but that I really did not want to work on the relationship without him unless we knew in fact that he was unwilling. So she agreed to talk to him and invite him to our next session.

A few days later, when I went into the waiting room, she was sitting there with Robbie. I invited them into my office.

Bracing myself for his strong reactions to anyone bringing up problems, I ventured into that unpleasant but very familiar territory of confronting someone with something he does not want to hear.

I began with a question: "Robbie, did Shellie tell you why I asked you to come?"

What came next was a surprise. "Yes, she did. And I'm so grateful that we are doing this. I've been concerned for quite some time. I think I'm way too caught up in work, and I need some help to get more balanced. Shellie also thinks that I'm drinking too much, but I don't know if that's true or not. But I'll do whatever you tell me to do. I really want us to get out of this mess."

I could feel myself letting go inside. I had braced myself for Robbie's denial. It was so refreshing to hear him say, "I have a problem. Please help me." I knew that things were going to go a lot more smoothly than Shellie had imagined.

In fact, we initially had to work on Shellie's fear of confrontation and her expectation that if she got into problems with Robbie, something bad would happen. What occurred was the opposite. He was a true joy to work with and took everything I said to heart. He was open to feedback and really worked on changing. And as he showed that to be true, Shellie followed suit. Many times I left our sessions wishing that all the couples I worked with were like the two of them.

Boundary Lovers

What did I like about Shellie and Robbie? Did they have easy problems? Not at all. In fact, Robbie had a pretty significant depression that drove much of his behavior. He was running from a lot of pain and also a lot of changes that he had to make in how he handled stress, fear of failure, trying to please his father, and other issues. I did not like Shellie and Robbie because their counseling issues were easy. I liked them because the *process* was easy. What's the difference? The answer gets at the heart of all human growth.

> *I liked them because the* process *was easy.*

In any situation requiring change, two major issues appear right off the bat.

1. The issue to be dealt with
2. The ability of the person to deal with the issue

If number two is good, then in most cases, number one will not be a problem. This is what I mean when I say that the issues were tough, but the process was easy. Robbie and Shellie had to do some tough changing, but the process of getting them to see the problems and to face them was easy. Both were open to feedback, willing to look at themselves, and able to see when they were wrong. So I did not have a war to fight when there was an issue to face. They were open to feedback and to the truth about themselves. The biggest problems they had to face were always in category number one: "the issue to be dealt with."

With some couples, category number two is a bigger problem than category number one. They are not open to feedback, cannot see when they are wrong, do not like limits of any kind, and blame everyone else for their problems. These people we call "boundary resisters," and we will cover them in the next chapter. But people who have the ability to hear feedback and listen we call "boundary lovers." That's what Shellie and Robbie were. They welcomed feedback.

> *In the history of people helping from biblical times until now, there are two kinds of people in the world: those who listen to feedback and those who don't.*

In the history of people helping from biblical times until now, there are two kinds of people in the world: those who listen to feedback and those who don't. Modern psychiatry calls the ones who don't listen to feedback and cannot observe their problems "character disorders." Many times professionals do not expect a lot of change from such people. (We disagree. We have seen lots of change in initially resistant people.) The ones who listen to feedback—the "boundary lovers"—are characterized by several traits:

- They are open to feedback and correction from others and gain understanding as a result of confrontation or feedback (Proverbs 15:32).
- They don't become defensive when their spouse shares feedback.
- They take ownership of their own problems, choices, feelings, attitudes, and behaviors.
- They have the ability to see themselves and observe their behavior.
- They value the treasures of their spouse.
- They see their spouse as an individual, separate from themselves, with separate experiences.
- They allow their spouse the freedom to be different from them.
- They respect the freedom and space of their spouse.
- They see their own need for growth and change.

All of these traits show that someone is open to the truth, to the freedom of the other, to responsibility, and to love. Before you read on, it might be good to take a look at these traits with each other and see where you are. Everyone needs improvement, and you are probably not perfect in all of them. But if you do have an attitude of openness, a desire for your spouse and you to experience freedom and love, then you will be able to talk through problems and help each other. If you are both boundary lovers, you have only one problem when you have a conflict, not two! This is very good news indeed.

> *Wherever two are gathered, there will be conflict.*

The other piece of good news is that having the first problem is not bad, either. Conflict is normal. If you didn't have conflict, one of you would be unnecessary in the relationship! Wherever two are gathered, there will be conflict. But this is not bad. Conflict just means that two things come together that are opposed to each other and do not immediately agree. The fun part is working it through.

An Overall Strategy

In the previous chapter we discussed the six different kinds of conflicts, giving numerous examples. There is a pattern to what we have suggested, a process for dealing with conflicts of all kinds. It involves the character traits and the interventions we have discussed throughout the book. For all kinds of conflicts, the Bible suggests the following predictable path over and over again:

1. Observation

You can't fix a problem you do not see. One of you has to notice the problem first and see it as a problem or a conflict.

2. Confrontation

You cannot fix a problem that you don't talk about. Speak honestly with each other. As Paul says, "Therefore each of you must put off falsehood and speak truthfully to his neighbor, for we are all members of one body" (Ephesians 4:25). But speak the truth in love as you let your spouse know what is wrong.

3. Ownership, Grief, and Apology

If you are the problem—or at least part of it—own it. If you have been hurt, own your hurt and communicate it. If you are the one who is doing the hurting, then confess and apologize. If you are the wounded party, forgive as well as express your hurt.

4. Repentance

Once you see your part in something, repent. Change your mind about the problem and change direction. In short, stop it. Commit to change.

5. Involvement in the Process

Problems do not go away immediately. Become involved in whatever process will be necessary for change. It may be counseling or some other form of structured help, but commit to it and stay involved.

6. Reexamination

Have some system of reexamination. Just because you have faced something does not mean it is gone forever. Get a checkup from those to whom you have made yourself accountable. And then continue to get reexamined for other things as well.

If you have a boundary-loving spouse and are one yourself, you are fortunate indeed. It means that you are open to the truth, responsibility, freedom, and love. And if both of you are open to such things, God will help you find them. Keep it up!

Remember, however, that conflict can still be painful even if everyone is open to feedback. Negative things hurt, and losing things hurts as well. So remember the basic rules of all communication:

1. Listen and seek to understand the other before you seek to be understood. Make it your mission to really understand what your spouse is feeling, wanting, or desiring.
2. Actively empathize and use reflective listening to let the other person know you understand. "So it really hurts you when I do that. I get it." Or use statements to let them

know that you know. Active listening really confirms to someone that you are hearing and taking seriously how he or she feels.

3. Do not devalue or explain away what the other person is feeling or saying. Don't defend. Just listen.
4. Clarify to make sure you understand. Ask questions.
5. Use "I" statements that show you are taking responsibility for what you are feeling or wanting. "When you are late, I begin to feel not cared for." This is much better than saying, "You make me feel so unloved." The latter is blaming, and the former is communicating feelings.

Above all, don't be afraid of conflict. There is always a death before a resurrection and conflict before deeper intimacy. Go through it lovingly, and chances are you will find more intimacy with your mate on the other side.

Now let's see what conflict looks like with someone who is not so open.

Chapter 15

Resolving Conflict with a Boundary-Resistant Spouse

*F*or many years I (Dr. Townsend) had been friends with Michael and Sharon. The advantage of longevity in a relationship is that you can observe the husband's and wife's character through many different circumstances. Over time, I learned a great deal about both Michael and Sharon and about boundaries in marriage.

The two were caring, goodhearted people who loved each other deeply. Michael was a successful business owner, and Sharon worked part-time and spent the rest of her time being a mom. The picture seemed almost perfect, except for a chronic problem I saw play out between them over the years. The problem was money: there was never enough.

Michael made a good income, which was subsidized by Sharon's job. But every time we got together, he was always overworked, and they were always behind on bills and credit-card payments.

"It's my fault," he would explain to me guiltily. "I like to see Sharon happy, and it's hard for me to let her down when she has her heart set on something." These "somethings" included expensive furniture, jewelry, clothing, and vacations. Nice things made Sharon happy, and that made Michael happy.

When she overcharged, he would ask her about it. Sharon would say, "But we really need this." And Michael would go along, figuring she was right.

Finally, they got into real financial trouble and almost lost their home. They went through the struggles that go with near bankruptcy, such as conflicts with each other. As they were working through this difficult phase, Michael and I had lunch, and I asked him how things were going.

"Well, the lights are starting to go on for me," he replied.

"What about?"

Michael paused a moment. "Our money crisis unearthed a lot of stuff for me, and one of the most startling things has been how I see myself and Sharon. I've always felt that my husbandly duty was to make enough money to keep up with her spending. That was my way of loving her. I never seemed to make quite enough, and it never went far enough, but I figured that was my problem.

"But one day a friend told me, 'You're working on the wrong problem, Michael. It's not that you don't make enough money. Your problem is that you don't understand that Sharon doesn't like to hear the word no.' And that has changed everything. I've stopped trying to make more. Now we're working on how she hates limits and how afraid I am of setting them with her. And it's slowly starting to help."

Happily, Michael and Sharon have kept working, and they have progressed far beyond this point. He is less guilt-ridden about saying no, and she is more able to accept financial boundaries. But they would have gotten nowhere if his friend had not diagnosed the problem for him. Michael and Sharon had been not allies, but adversaries in their finances. She was resistant to hearing that she couldn't spend when it struck her fancy. And no matter how much more income he produced, Michael would probably never have been able to keep up with Sharon's character issue: a resistance to accepting limits.

Boundaries Aren't Always Welcome in Marriage

Michael and Sharon illustrate a difficult reality: boundaries aren't always welcome in a marriage. But that is not how God intended it. God designed boundaries for some very good reasons, all of which benefit a couple. Boundaries protect love. They enhance freedom. They allow people to be separate and stay connected. They define responsibility so that people know what their

> *Boundaries operate best when both spouses restrict their freedoms so as to better love each other.*

tasks are. It is a wonderful thing when a couple enters the process of boundary building as a team.

This is the ideal. Boundaries operate best when both spouses restrict their freedoms so as to better love each other. Because you love your spouse and want to enhance his life and growth, you restrain your tendencies to be selfish, and you even curb your right to exercise legitimate freedoms. You don't want to use your freedom to hurt the one you love. This is the essence of responding to your mate's boundaries.

Love can only flourish and deepen when two people embrace the pain of receiving and respecting their mate's boundaries. So many good things result when both mates preserve the boundaries of the other:

- You increase your ability to feel compassion for your spouse's needs, desires, and hurts.
- You develop self-control and patience.
- You become humble and self-correcting.
- You appreciate your mate for who he is, not for his usefulness to you.
- You depend less on your spouse's reactions and more on your own values to make you happy.
- You learn about how God respects our boundaries with him.

Yet, sometimes a spouse does not see the benefits of this gift from God. I remember that after our original book, *Boundaries,* came out, Phil, a friend of mine on the East Coast, called me.

"I read your new book," he said.

"What did you think?"

"I don't like it."

"Why not?"

"Because I'm the one in the marriage who busts all the boundaries, and it makes me the bad guy."

We joked about his response to my book, but Phil was making a good point. For people who control others or who don't take ownership of their own lives, the boundary message doesn't come as good news or something that brings freedom. In fact, controlling spouses hear that they are hurting someone they love. They hear that things need to change, and change is difficult and often painful. These changes may involve several things:

- Allowing your spouse to say no to you
- Humbly admitting you have been trying to control your spouse
- Submitting to God's process of learning boundaries and self-control
- Respecting the freedom of your spouse
- Restraining the tendency to withdraw from your spouse, attack her, or make her feel guilty
- Becoming aware of your helplessness to truly control anyone
- Asking for your spouse's feedback when you cross her boundaries

These tasks are not pleasant, and they are a lot of work. So it is understandable that any spouse would experience receiving boundaries as unpleasant. Phil was just stating a fact: accepting boundaries hurts sometimes. It is realistic to identify pain as pain, even if it is growth-producing pain.

> *The painful discipline of boundaries will eventually bear good results in our lives.*

The painful discipline of boundaries will eventually bear good results in our lives. As God says, "No discipline seems pleasant at the time, but painful. Later on, however, it produces a harvest of righteousness and peace for those who have been trained by it" (Hebrews 12:11). And we believe that boundaries are the only way to keep love alive.

Character Is What You Do with the Pain of Boundaries

The issue is different, however, when a mate goes beyond saying, "Ouch, I don't like this," to "I won't accept this," in response to an appropriate limit. This is not a reaction to pain, but a value statement. It says much about the character of the spouse.

Good character welcomes the pain of boundaries, as a person of character wants to love God and others and grow spiritually and emotionally. A person of problem character, however, refuses to accept his status as someone who sometimes needs correction and limits from others. This scary position is the position of a mocker, who hates those who rebuke him (Proverbs 9:8). Even more frightening, it is the position of one who is attempting to take on the role of God, who alone in the universe does not need to be corrected.

Yet there are many "mixed marriages," mixed in terms of the spouses' views of boundaries. It is sad when one spouse finds the other is not willing to carry his load. During all the times I have spoken on boundaries over the years, the scenario that fills my heart with joy is the one in which a couple comes up to say hello and says, "We're here today because we both want better boundaries." They are united in love, truth, and the pursuit of God's growth. The opposite scenario that wrings my heart is the one in which a married person attends alone, saying, "He isn't interested in boundaries," or, "She won't respect my boundaries."

Some common examples of the "mixed marriage" are the following:

- A husband asks his wife to spend less, and she blames him for not making enough money.
- A wife wants her husband to share the housekeeping duties, and he refuses.
- A husband doesn't want to go to a party, and his wife withdraws emotionally from him to punish him.
- A wife says no to sex, and her husband acts like a martyr.

- A husband disagrees with his wife's plans for the weekend, and she blows up at him.
- A wife wants help with the kids, and her husband refuses to help.

In these and many more settings, two factors are prominent. First, one spouse has too much responsibility, and the other has too little. Second, the boundary-busting spouse is refusing to make the right changes.

How the Boundary Buster Sees the Issue

Often one of the greatest problems between couples is that the boundary-loving spouse doesn't understand the perspective of the boundary-resistant one. The boundary lover doesn't grasp that the boundary resister really doesn't see things the same way she does. She is often surprised or shocked to learn how different her spouse thinks and feels about this matter. Understanding his viewpoint will help you do the right things and avoid making mistakes in the process.

People who don't respect others' boundaries have a basic attitude toward life: I should be able to do what I want. Just as Adam and Eve did, they protest the restrictions of being a creature and not the Creator. They demand ultimate freedom as their right. You see this same attitude in small children, one that we hope will mature as they grow up.

> *People who don't respect others' boundaries have a basic attitude toward life: I should be able to do what I want.*

The boundary-resistant spouse may be a wonderful, loving person in normal circumstances. The couple may be genuinely drawn to each other and care deeply for each other—until a boundary issue arises. Then the good feelings go away, and anger, guilt messages, or acting out take their place.

The boundary-resistant spouse reacts this way because he really does feel that the limit—any limit—is unreasonable, unfair, and hurtful. So he is enraged that his mate would be so mean as to say no to him in some area of life. Her request for him to respect her no feels like hate, not righteousness. It is nor-

> *Boundaries say that you cannot do what you want all the time.*

mal to be angry when someone treats us unfairly, but it is immature to be angry when our spouse sets a limit with us for a legitimate reason.

Remember that the boundary-resistant spouse feels that he should be able to do what he wants whenever he wants. With that as his operative

principle in life, he will challenge and protest any boundary until he begins to grow up. Boundaries say that you cannot do what you want all the time.

Ignorance Is Not a Character Problem

We are not saying that all boundary-busting spouses have a character problem. Many times what appears to be selfishness is actually ignorance. The spouse may simply not know that her behavior is hurtful or irritating to the other. And in those "ignorance defense" cases, the spouse will often respond positively when she hears the truth. In fact, she will sometimes feel deep remorse for causing her spouse's pain and will change her behavior or attitude quickly out of love for the other.

Rick and Kim, a couple who are friends of mine, exemplified this recently. When Rick would bring a problem with Kim to her, she would negate his feeling. She would say, "No, your feelings make no sense. I didn't do that," and he would shut down.

Finally he told her, "I'm not looking for you to agree with me. I just want you to understand what I'm saying. And when you tell me I'm wrong without listening, I feel cut off from you."

Kim reacted awesomely. She listened carefully and said, "Tell me what I do. I see that what I'm doing hurts you, and I don't want that." When he told her, she understood and said, "I'm really sorry, Rick. I had no idea. Will you tell me when I do this again?"

Rick broke down crying. He felt as if a heavy weight had been lifted as he regained his connection with Kim. She had crossed emotional boundaries out of ignorance, not out of a character problem. And all it took for her to change was to learn of his hurt.

> *Your spouse may be crossing boundaries with you out of a lack of awareness.*

Your spouse may be crossing boundaries with you out of a lack of awareness. You may not know if this is the reason for the problem. If so, remember that love is hopeful (1 Corinthians 13:7). Approach the problem first as if it is an ignorance issue. You will find out quickly enough whether or not you are right. If you are correct, and he has truly crossed boundaries, either your spouse will love you for telling him (Proverbs 9:8) and will make the changes, or he will resist it. And this resistance is the bigger problem.

The Spouse of the Boundary Buster Needs Scrutiny

Be aware that discovering that your spouse is a boundary buster doesn't mean he is any worse a person than you are. The acting-out, childish, immature, or controlling spouse does have a more obvious problem. Because his issues are more exposed, he can look very bad to others while you look very innocent. This reality has its dangers. Beware of judging and condemning as you figure all this out, as " judgment without mercy will be shown to anyone who has not been merciful" (James 2:13).

> *Discovering that your spouse is a boundary buster doesn't mean he is any worse a person than you are.*

Be merciful in how you think about your spouse. Most of the time, the mate of a boundary-resistant spouse has much to repent of also, such as the following:

- Pretending that everything is all right
- Not speaking the truth

- Being emotionally absent and withdrawing instead of bringing up problems
- Not following up on consequences
- Nagging and not acting responsibly
- Being passively revengeful
- Being self-righteous and condemning
- Gossiping about your spouse but not telling him your feelings

You can see why you may have to carve out time to work on setting boundaries, as it takes so much time to deal first with ourselves.

Causes of Boundary Resistance

Before you address the problem of the boundary-resistant spouse, you need to understand the reasons for boundary resisting to help you know better how to approach the issues.

Empathic Failure

To accept boundaries, a person must be able to see the effects of his lack of boundaries on others. When the husband who is tardy to dinner notices that his behavior disrupts his family, he should feel godly remorse (2 Corinthians 7:10) and compassion for the hurt he has caused them. Love based on empathy is one of the highest and purest motives to change. It is truly treating others as you would like to be treated (Matthew 7:12).

> *To accept boundaries, a person must be able to see the effects of his lack of boundaries on others.*

However, some people have difficulty becoming aware of their effect on people. They have trouble sensing emotionally that they hurt others. This is a problem in compassion. They may do all the right things, but they can't sense the feelings of others. A wife may tell her husband how tough it is when he is late for dinner, and he may not understand why she is bothered. Like Mr. Spock of the old *Star Trek* television show, he may be mystified by her upset feelings and wish she were more "rational" and "logical." Often, people who struggle with understanding feelings tend to be detached and self-absorbed.

Opening up the world of emotions and relationships to this spouse may be very helpful. He may need to have emotions explained to him so that he sees the feelings under people's skin. For example, saying, "I feel lonely when you go straight to the computer after coming home," can be a revelation to a spouse with this issue. He may also need to learn to open his own feelings up and connect in vulnerable ways to the outside world, which will help him to receive comfort that he can then give to others (2 Corinthians 1:4). For instance, inviting him to confess his pain in the following way can help: "When you didn't get the raise, you seemed to shut down. I would have felt hurt and angry. I'd like to know how you felt about it."

Irresponsibility

Some spouses have a low sense of ownership of their actions. They feel that they should be able to do whatever they want and suffer no consequences for it. Like a small child, they aren't anxious about crossing others' boundaries, because they don't see their life as their own problem. It is someone else's.

This character issue is the one the human race has struggled with since Adam and Eve: "Someone else did it!" None of us take responsibility for our own lives gracefully; it has to be built into us by many painful experiences. And some people have escaped this lesson because parents and friends have enabled their behavior and rescued them. Behind an irresponsible spouse is always a safety-net person, either in the past or the present.

For example, a husband may be a nice person, but a poor provider because of his lack of boundaries. He may go from job to job, unable to discipline himself to complete tasks, perform adequately, produce results, and grow in competency. This behavior can severely jeopardize his family's quality of life. However, this individual will often blame the boss, job, or others for his failure, and he will be unable to learn from it.

This person needs to see that he is the major cause of his problems. He will probably need supportive but firm people surrounding him to teach him ownership and self-control. These people can be a neighborhood group, a Bible study, or a support group.

Inability to Receive Limits and Stay Free

At other times, a spouse may resist boundaries because of a split within his own soul. He may be unable to receive confrontation or consequences due to a lack of integration of love and freedom. When his wife asks him to limit himself for their marriage, he may feel that this request makes him too helpless and vulnerable. Therefore, feeling that his own freedom is at risk, he refuses the boundary.

> *A spouse may resist boundaries because of a split within his own soul.*

An example of this is the husband who has come from an enmeshing family. He may have had to struggle greatly to be able to make his own decisions and choices. He may sometimes get too angry or harsh with his wife. When she asks him to be more considerate of her feelings, he may feel that she is trying to control and enmesh him, and he may react against her. In this case, the spouse needs help in preserving his freedom and choices while freely choosing to respond to limits without jeopardizing that freedom. His wife may want to tell him, "It is okay for you to say no to me or to be angry with me. I want you to have that freedom. But I won't tolerate disrespect or harshness."

Control of Others

Some spouses resist boundaries due to their attempts to control, manipulate, or dominate their mates. They are unable to see their spouse as having separate and equal feelings and ideas. Rather, they believe that their way is the only way. Instead of mutually solving problems, they negate and minimize the freedom of their spouse.

An example of this would be the wife who subtly controls her husband's attempts to have wholesome outside friends and interests. Because the wife feels abandoned or unloved by her husband's separateness, she passively withdraws or pouts when he goes out with his buddies. When he tells her this behavior bothers him, instead of owning the problem and taking responsibility for her sad feelings and difficulties with separateness, she blames him for being distant and unloving.

> *Controlling people are dependent on the compliance of others. People who are free do not need to control others.*

An example of more aggressive control would be the husband who raises his voice, threatens, or otherwise intimidates his wife when she disagrees. He directly assaults her separateness and freedom, hoping to make her comply and submit to his opinion or desires. What God intended to be a loving connection is reduced to a fear-based dominance.

When a spouse is either passively or aggressively controlling, he needs to learn that his denial of ownership not only hurts others, but also hurts him and keeps him from being free. Controlling people are dependent on the compliance of others. People who are free do not need to control others. A person with the problem of control sometimes needs love, confrontation, and consequences to help him own the issue. For example, an aggressively controlling husband might need warnings, then consequences such as emotional distance, physical distance, and even the intervention of others (like church leaders and friends) to help him see that the situation is destructive and must change.

Denial of Imperfection

Spouses who refuse to admit weaknesses and faults can be major boundary busters. They stay highly invested in not being "wrong" or "bad." Then, when their mate points out that they didn't take out the trash, for example, they have to resort to several options to protect their "good self." For example, these spouses might

- Deny they have crossed a boundary: "I didn't yell at you. I never yell."
- Rationalize or minimize the offense: "I didn't yell at you, I just raised my voice. You're overreacting."
- Blame the spouse: "You frustrate me so much that I have to yell."
- Reverse the issue: "But what about how much you yell?"

In all of these situations, the mate tries to avoid owning her fault or sin. She may be trying to escape from a harsh and condemning conscience. Or she may lack understanding of her badness. Or she may have a deep sense of entitlement. Whatever the cause, the spouse is unaware of how hurtful her boundary-crossing can be, and she avoids taking responsibility for her badness.

Think about it: children learn about boundaries from the pain they experience when they cross the boundaries. They think, "When I didn't clean up my room, I lost my free time for a week. I need to start cleaning my room." But people who can't admit faults don't start this learning curve. Instead, they think, "Everyone's so unfair. I just didn't have time to clean my room (or, 'It's not that messy, anyway'), and I got a consequence. I have been wronged." This attitude slows down the learning and training process of boundaries immensely. Often spouses with this problem need both consequences when they hurt others and a safe way to explore their bad parts.

Retaliation

Sometimes a marriage can be troubled by a spouse who takes revenge on perceived or real transgressions by his mate. When he feels wronged, he feels justified in more wrongdoing: an eye for an eye. This issue can cause tremendous boundary problems.

For example, a husband I know was quite upset by his wife's lavish spending. So he bought a boat he didn't really want and they certainly couldn't afford. His justification was, "Well, maybe now she'll see how it feels to be broke." She didn't. In fact, she escalated the spending war, and they got into deep financial trouble. The fight didn't end until he stopped trying to punish her and started dealing with the problem itself.

One of the hardest things about marriage, or any relationship, is that revenge isn't an option. Love, vulnerability, and intimacy always cause some hurt. Your mate will not always handle your tender feelings in the most careful way. You may feel justifiably hurt and angry about his treatment of you. Yet, revenge belongs to God, not us (Romans 12:19). Take your hurt feelings to people and places where you can heal, and then learn to solve the problem, not take revenge on the one who hurt you.

Transference

The intimacy generated by marriage can revive old feelings toward other significant relationships. Intimacy begets emotions, and emotions that have not been worked through can come out in confusing ways in marriage, causing boundary problems. The confusing state of having feelings toward a spouse that are about someone else is called *transference*.

For example, Bob and Christie "had problems solving problems." When things were okay with them, they had a great time and were very much in love. However, every time Bob would bring up an issue between them—be it finances, intimacy, or parenting—she would react negatively to him. "You're accusing me and trying to control me!" she would say. Bob wasn't perfect, so he checked out with Christie, his friends, and God to see if that was true. He tended to be too structured, so he worked on that tendency. Yet Christie kept reacting negatively to Bob's bringing up problems.

After much soul-searching, Christie realized that her negative feelings about Bob had a lot to do with her relationship with her critical father. He had used blame and control to keep her in line, and this had hurt Christie deeply. Since she had never worked through these feelings toward her father, they were still inside her heart in a damaged state. When Bob would say, "Christie, it really bothers me that you're not getting the kids to bed on time," she would feel like a little girl being harshly scolded. It took some work, but as Christie dealt with her feelings about her dad, she could see Bob in a more realistic light and receive his confrontations in the loving way he was giving them.

Specific Context of Resistance

Some spouses are empathic, humble, correctable, and respectful to boundaries in all areas but one. This "pocket area" becomes a no man's land for the marriage. Both spouses learn to skirt around it, as it tends to bring out fights, eruptions, and unresolved conflict. For example, a husband may resist boundaries in the sexual arena. He may be insensitive sexually and not hear his wife's needs and desires. Or a wife may be great in all areas except that she is critical and disrespectful of her husband in public, such as at parties and social gatherings. When he shares his hurt, she may dismiss his feelings. These context-specific situations can cause a great deal of distance in an otherwise loving marriage.

Generally speaking, there can be more than one cause for these situations:

- Lack of information and experience. A spouse may simply have no clue as to how this area affects the other person.
- Past hurts in that area. The critical wife may have been shamed by her parents in public and may be reacting in that specific arena.
- Character issues. This one visible problem may be the sign of a deeper, hidden character problem. The deeper you investigate, the more a consistent pattern emerges. The sexually insensitive husband may be self-centered sexually because he can hide his needs in the other arenas of life. However, a discerning eye can see that his lovingness in other areas may be shallow.

Whatever the cause, the specific context—time, money, sex, in-laws, communication, or parenting—may signal a need to look more deeply into the marriage and the hearts of both spouses.

The presenting problem is rarely the real problem, but more likely it is the fruit of a problem root (Matthew 7:17). For example, the husband may have difficulty in receiving love and comfort in his

> *The presenting problem is rarely the real problem.*

marriage and relationships. Sex might be the only place he can feel connected to life. He may need to verbalize his needs for relationship and letting people into his heart in nonsexual ways.

If It Is Character, You Have a Job to Do

Let's suppose your spouse is aware of your feelings and concerns, but ignores, minimizes, or otherwise resists your boundaries. If this is your situation, you have some work ahead of you. It is hard work, but it can also be the most productive thing you will ever do for your marriage. In this section we want to give you a structure to follow to help deal with your resistant-spouse problem in a caring, yet truthful manner.

You must not approach this problem as if you are a team. At this point, you have an adversary. Like a child having a tantrum, your spouse may hate you for entering the world of boundaries. So understand that you are on your own, within the marriage, in approaching the issue. Actually, you are not alone; you have God and your boundary-loving friends. But you don't expect much cooperation from your spouse.

A few things you may be tempted to do will not help the situation at all. Remember these, tape them in your wallet, and DON'T DO THEM!

- Don't deny or minimize the situation if it is a significant boundary problem. Hiding from reality doesn't change reality.
- Don't ignore the situation, hoping it will get better. Time alone does not heal character immaturity.
- Don't become more compliant and pleasing, hoping love will fix everything. Again, character issues demand more than love in order to mature.

- Don't nag. Repeating the same protest over and over never changed anyone (Proverbs 21:9).
- Don't be constantly surprised at your spouse's behavior. This is a sign of a defensive hoping against hope. When out-of-control people have no external forces causing them pain, they generally stay out-of-control. Expect things to stay the same until you initiate changes within the marriage.
- Don't blame. Very few marriage-boundary conflicts involve an all-innocent and an all-guilty party. Take ownership of your part of the issue, taking the log out of your own eye (Matthew 7:5).
- Don't take total ownership of the problem. If you rescue your partner from his part, you will only make the issue worse (Proverbs 19:19).

Your To-Do List

We also want you to have several specific principles of operation in mind. These will give you a way to approach your spouse with grace and truth.

Make Soul Connections

If you deal with a boundary-resistant spouse, you will encounter conflict. Your spouse may become angry with you, withdraw from you, or try to make you feel guilty. This struggle will threaten the closeness you have with him. Your hopes to fulfill your God-given need for love may be jeopardized when you set boundaries with your spouse.

> *Don't nag. Repeating the same protest over and over never changed anyone.*

For many, their spouses are the only deep connection residing within their souls. Some people invest their hearts only within marriage. Then, when their spouses withdraw love, they feel loveless inside. This is why, before you enter the conflict arena, you need to establish healthy, safe, and honest soul connections with God and others. Enlarge your heart to include more than your spouse, and bring your needy, dependent parts to these other people. They will serve as a resource for comfort, encouragement, and strength during the stress of boundary negotiation in your marriage.

We have seen so many cases in which a spouse who had no deep attachments tried to set boundaries with her mate. When her spouse refused to accept a limit, she would give up and sometimes even apologize to her mate to reestablish the relationship she feared losing. What a sad situation when the injured party apologizes to the hurtful party simply to stay connected!

This doesn't have to happen if you will do the time-consuming but rewarding work of opening up to good folks who will support your boundaries. A good resource for picking the right individuals to whom to connect is our book *Safe People*. It describes what people of character are like and how to connect with them.

Grow and Own

God doesn't want you to come into relationship simply to set limits in your marriage. He wants *you*. So, what often happens is what needs to happen. As you open up, confessing your needs and faults to loving people, you grow spiritually and emotionally. Good things happen inside. You deal with old hurts. You become more honest. You "find your heart." You forgive and let go of things. You center your life around God and his life for you. In short, you grow up in him (Ephesians 4:15–16).

> *It makes sense that if you try to help a difficult spouse learn about love and responsibility, you will grow in these capacities as well.*

God does not pull a bait-and-switch scam on you. He simply uses your need within your marriage to reorient you to a growing love relationship with him as the source of your life. It makes sense that if you try to help a difficult spouse learn about love and responsibility, you will grow in these capacities as well.

Many things can happen during this process that can help you prepare for dealing with your boundary problem with your spouse:

- You may discover why your spouse has this particular issue.
- You may find out why you have had trouble setting limits.
- You may learn how to be more honest and confronting in safe relationships to prepare you for confrontation in the marriage.
- You may learn how to receive love and support when you fail in your limits and need grace, encouragement, and feedback.

It is easy for the spouse of a controlling or irresponsible mate to think, *My biggest problem is this spouse of mine.* As long as you believe this, you will guarantee more misery. But you become free the moment you realize that to some extent you have contributed to the problem. Then you have unearthed something you can control, instead of someone else and his problem.

This unearthing will require honest, open exploration between you, God, and your safe people. You may find that you are guilty of one or more of the "don't do" items above. If so, deal with these and correct them in the process of growth.

Identify the Specific Issue

Once you are connected and in the boundary-setting process, you will need to find out what the specific boundary issue is. This important part of the process cannot be completed instantly. You will need to know the following aspects:

- What boundary of yours is being violated: "My husband is chronically late. My boundary of being on time is violated."
- How it affects you and your love for your spouse: "I feel devalued and less important than his other commitments. It distances me from him."

- Whether or not the problem is a pattern or an occasional event: "It happens several times a week, and has for years."
- Why it is important enough to risk conflict over it: "I don't want to resent him. I want to feel close to him. And I want him to be on time for meals and family meetings."

You may find it harder than you think to identify a specific boundary issue. This requires a cool head and the ability to sort through many aspects. Many spouses make the mistake of creating a huge list of requests for change in their mate. It would be discouraging for anyone to learn everything that is wrong with him or her at one time.

> *Many spouses make the mistake of creating a huge list of requests for change in their mate.*

No wonder that after reviewing how bad his condition was, Paul asked to be rescued (Romans 7:24). It is much better to pick and resolve issues one at a time, unless there is a severe situation, such as drugs, abuse, or alcohol, which may require drastic action all at once.

When you deal with a specific issue, the question of character change may arise. Ask yourself, "Am I requesting my spouse to change her heart or simply her behavior? Am I asking for a character change or a boundary change?" For example, suppose your wife is a loving-but-disorganized person. Your house is always a mess, even though you do your part to help. Do you ask her to value your feelings and the concept of organization more, or do you ask her to clean up the house better?

> *When two are one in the growth process, many boundary conflicts are much more easily resolved.*

Any mate's deepest desire is for his spouse to enter into the growth process with him, deepening their love and knowledge of each other and God. Most of us dreamed of and prayed for this kind of marriage all of our single lives. It is the highest state of existence on this earth. In addition, when two are one in the growth process, many boundary conflicts are much more easily resolved. A mate who believes in love, respect, and freedom will desire to work out issues because she loves her spouse and because she believes in God's values.

It is generally best to request the deeper attitude change first for several reasons:

- Solving the internal issue helps solve the outward symptom. A wife who is concerned about your feelings of wanting a pleasant home and who sees that she has a problem with structure will take steps to solve the disorganization problem.
- Asking for internal change often helps you learn about your spouse's attitude toward boundaries. If she is boundary-friendly, she will want to change. If she is boundary-resistant, she will deny, rationalize, and blame.
- Everyone, even a boundary-resistant spouse, needs to be invited to change internally before dealing with consequences. By inviting her to change internally, you put grace before truth and treat her as you would like to be treated.

Sadly, a boundary-resistant spouse will most likely negate your request for internal change. This is the nature of resistance: an opposition to seeing or owning an issue. When you have humbly asked for the internal change, and she resists, move on to the specific behavioral level:

"Honey, I know you think I'm overreacting about the house. I've tried to see it your way and deal with my part. I've talked to objective friends about it. And I guess I must disagree with your opinion. So, even if you think I'm wrong, I really need some changes in the way our home is kept up. So until we can agree on our perspective on the house, I am going to do the following: I'll do my part in housekeeping, but I will not be funding the home improvement projects you want. I hope we can come to better terms, however, as we discuss this."

Validate Your Spouse

Resistant spouses still need to know that you understand their perspective. People have a difficult time changing when their feelings are negated and dismissed. They dig in their heels more, because more is at stake. When they feel misunderstood, they cannot trust that the other person has their best interests in mind. Think how you felt the last time someone wanted you to change and yet was unwilling to see your point of view. This is much like the child who feels he is being criticized yet not being heard.

> *People have a difficult time changing when their feelings are negated and dismissed.*

When you take the initiative to show your spouse that you understand, you are validating his experience. Validation involves several dimensions:

- His feelings are important to you: "Tell me what the problem is from your perspective and how you feel about our conflict."
- You want to understand and articulate his point of view: "Do you think it's not that bad, or that I'm overreacting? I don't want to hurt or distance you."
- You want to appreciate and respond to what is actually true about his viewpoint: "I agree with you that I don't say anything about the problem for weeks and then blow up. That is true, and I'm sorry. I will work on that."

This is how God works with us to change us. He lets us know that our experience is valuable. Yet he also requires change. Jesus' words to the church in Ephesus are a wonderful example of these two aspects. First, he validates all their hard work. Then he corrects their mistakes (Revelation 2:2–5). Remember that change for anyone is difficult. Validation and grace soften the burden of change.

Love Your Spouse

In boundary conflict resolution you need to communicate that your goal is to be close to your spouse, not to hurt her. Boundaries are about protecting love. They are not about changing people, beating them up, punishing them, or showing them their evil ways. Setting boundaries will enhance or repair the loving feelings you have for each other, and you need to convey this to your spouse.

> *Boundaries are about protecting love, not about changing people, beating them up, punishing them, or showing them their evil ways.*

A boundary-resistant spouse can be a defensive spouse. She may feel that you are attacking her person, condemning her, or making her the bad guy. Take some responsibility for helping her see that you need and love her, and that the boundary conflict is an obstacle to the love you want to give. Repairing the boundary problem can reestablish the love you both desire.

Here are some examples of making love the goal:

- "The overspending distances me; I want to solve it so that we can be close again."
- "When you dismiss my feelings, I can't feel the love. I want to fix it so that I can feel it again."
- "Your flirtatiousness hurts me and makes it hard to trust you. I don't want to control you; I want to believe you so that I can feel safe with you again."

If you don't establish that you are trying to solve a problem so that love can reign, you risk being seen as a controlling or critical parent by your spouse. Show her that you value the connection above all. The goal of instruction is love (1 Timothy 1:5).

Create a Level Playing Field

Here is some hard news: you have to earn the right to require your spouse to change. Look actively at how you may be contributing to the problem, and make any necessary changes. This is what we mean by creating a level playing field: don't set yourself up either as a perfect person or as a judge of your spouse. It destroys his motivation to change, and it is not true. None of us is perfect, and we don't have the right to judge each other.

What is even harder is that you need to make your changes, even if your spouse does not. This may sound unfair, but it is one of the more important realities of life. God wants to work in you to grow you up and mature you. He wants to make you more like him. Do not depend on your spouse to grow up before you do. Pray for her, love her, set appropriate boundaries with her. But your growth is between you and God.

> *You need to make your changes, even if your spouse does not.*

Pam and Al illustrate this point. Al, on the one hand, bossed Pam around and disregarded her point of view in decision making. She, on the other hand, would become quiet and withdraw love from him. For example, Al didn't like a dress Pam was going to wear to a party. He said abruptly, "I don't like that on you. Put another one on." Pam complied. However, she didn't say more than ten words to Al at the party or for the rest of the night.

At first blush, we could analyze Pam and Al's problem as simply a couple's issue. That is, if Al would be kinder, Pam would not withdraw. Or conversely, if Pam would be more up front, Al would be less bossy. There is some truth to this, but it hides the fact that there are two issues here: Al is bossy, and Pam withdraws. Al could become the most mutual and fair person in the world, but this would be no guarantee that Pam will not withdraw. Pam could learn to be assertive, but this does not ensure that Al will give up bossiness. The point here is that both spouses are responsible first to God to change.

Look at your own contribution to the boundary conflict. Ask your spouse. Ask honest and safe friends. And ask God to search your heart (Psalm 139:23–24). Make the necessary changes. They do help you earn the right to ask for change. Yet, on a deeper level, they are what molds you into God's likeness.

Request Change

Remember all the above elements as you approach your spouse with a request for him to respect a boundary of yours. Let him know about your love and your own faults. But be clear and specific about your request. Try not to leave room for misinterpretation:

- "I would like for you to stop belittling me when we are with friends."
- "I want you to take more initiative in our parenting, especially in helping the children with their homework."
- "I need for you to settle into a steady job within ninety days."
- "I want you to cook half the meals, since we're both working now."

> *You are responsible to state the boundary problem and your request for change.*

Remember, "where there is no law there is no transgression" (Romans 4:15). You are responsible to state the boundary problem and your request for change. In so doing, you have transferred some responsibility to your spouse.

Give Your Spouse Time and Patience

This may be the first time you have addressed the boundary problem with your spouse. Or it may be the first time you have brought it up appropriately. If so, simply make the request and allow some time to observe her response. Before you set up consequences, see what happens when you ask correctly, appealing to love and empathy. Remember that you are always evaluating yourself, her, and the process during this time. By giving her time to respond, you are learning whether or not consequences are necessary.

Some boundary-resistant spouses need time to adjust to the new reality of a mate with boundaries. She may not be used to your being direct, immediate, and honest about what you don't like in the marriage. This stands to reason, as to some extent you have trained her to bust your boundaries. Now you are changing the rules, and it takes time to adapt.

Your clarity and the time to adapt may be all your spouse needs. If so, you have won her, as the Bible says (Matthew 18:15). Have the grace to see what time can do, once you have brought the issue into the light between you.

Establish Appropriate Consequences

Stating your boundary, however, may not be enough. Ever since Adam and Eve, humanity has known the rules and still crosses the line (Genesis 3:6). Whatever your spouse is doing that is hurting you, the benefits he receives may far outweigh your appeals and requests. At this point, you need to set consequences.

A consequence is an effect, or result, of another act. You need to establish some consequence for your spouse's transgression so that he will experience some discomfort for his irresponsibility. A consequence has to have several very important characteristics:

- *Designed to help with reality and protect you, not designed to control or change your spouse.* Boundaries and consequences are not about fixing someone or making them choose better. They are about allowing appropriate cause and effect so that your spouse will experience the pain of irresponsibility and then change.
- *Deliberate, and not impulsive or set in anger.* Think through, prayerfully and with friends, what an appropriate consequence might be. It is not about getting even. It is about getting out of enabling your spouse and about protecting yourself from evil.
- *As reality-based as possible.* You want reality to be your spouse's instructor. For example, a husband who

becomes enraged should have people leave his presence for a while. No one wants to be around people having tantrums. This is preferable to an unrelated consequence such as having him watch the kids an extra evening.

- *Appropriately severe.* Evaluate how chronic, destructive, and severe the boundary violation is. For example, a spouse who won't clean up the dishes might need to cook some meals for himself to get the idea. But a spouse who is having an affair may need to leave the home. Either way, the consequence needs to be serious enough to matter, but not so severe that *it*, rather than the behavior, becomes the issue.
- *Enforceable.* Make sure this is something you can and will do. You need to make sure you have the power and resources to set the limit. If you can't tell the pastor you are having trouble in your marriage, don't threaten to do that.
- *Preservative of your spouse's freedom.* Don't set a consequence by saying, "You have to," "You must," or, "I will make you. . . ." Consequences are not something you do to control your spouse. They are reactions to his choices. Let him make his choices, but prepare your reactions.
- *As immediate as possible.* Just as kids need quick consequences, so do spouses. Your spouse can make the association between his action and the results if they are close together in time.
- *Respectful of his role as spouse.* Stay away from humiliating or punitive consequences such as making fun of him or making sarcastic remarks.
- *Designed to be modified as your spouse changes.* Consequences don't have to be forever. As your spouse owns and repents, you can change the consequences. However, be sure that change has truly occurred over some period of time. "I'm sorry" is not enough to let go of the consequence. The other side of this, however, is that you may have to escalate the severity of the consequence if

your spouse behaves worse. A spendaholic wife may need to work extra hours to earn the money she spent. But if she gets worse, she may need to lose her credit cards.

Boundary: I want you to	Consequence: I will
Be less messy at home	• Confiscate/give away what I pick up that is yours • Stop doing your laundry
End your chronic lateness	• Leave for the meeting without you
Stop demeaning me in public	• Be emotionally distant • Leave the event
Give up your deception and lying	• Emotionally pull away to protect myself or ask you to leave (depending on severity) until you agree to counseling
Cease your temper tantrums	• Leave the room/home for a period of time • Join a support group for raging spouses • Ask our friends for help
Quit overspending	• Remove your credit cards • Open separate accounts • Stop paying for certain expenses and have you take responsibility for them
End your drinking/substance problems	• Set up an intervention • Have you leave home until treated
Deal with your sexual problems: pornography, prostitution, etc.	• End sexual intimacy • Require that you work on issue in outside relationships to stay in home
End the affair	• Require that you leave home, not returning at the soonest until the affair is over and counseling entered
Stop your abuse	• Leave home and go to safety • Contact authorities: police/church/counselors

Examples of Consequences

Use the above criteria along with the prayerful creativity of yourself and your friends. To help you, here are a few examples of consequences, along with the related problems. Of course, these are general in nature and should be adapted to your own situation.

Warn Your Spouse

Appropriately warn your spouse. If you have requested change and have given time with no result, she needs to be aware that you will now begin setting limits. This accomplishes two purposes. First, your spouse has a chance to repent before suffering (Ezekiel 3:18–19). Second, you are not reacting impulsively or secretly, but in grace and longsuffering. You are demonstrating to your mate that you don't want to trap or punish him. You don't want him to suffer; you just want the problem solved so that you may re-enter love.

Follow Through

A boundary without a consequence is nagging. Be sure to follow through with the limit you have set. Otherwise, you train your spouse that he can do whatever he wants and that nothing worse than words will befall him. As the saying goes, "Don't write a check with your mouth that your actions can't cash."

> *A boundary without a consequence is nagging.*

You may encounter problems following through. Guilt, fear of loss of love, and fear of your spouse's escalating behavior may cause you to hesitate. If this happens, make sure that you surround yourself with loving, honest people who will support you in this process. They can encourage you, protect you, assure you of the rightness of your stance, and be with you in the process (Hebrews 12:12–13).

Observe and Evaluate Over Time

Again, let time pass after you follow through with consequences. Through this experience you will learn to understand your spouse better. Some mates will require only a few examples to see that irresponsibility or selfishness is painful. Others may need more time, and you may even have to change the consequences to fit the situation better. Still others, sadly, will have no interest in changing.

God grieves with you when a spouse continually resists the boundaries of love: "O Jerusalem, Jerusalem, you who kill the prophets and stone those sent to you, how often I have longed to gather your children together, as a hen gathers her chicks under her wings, but you were not willing" (Matthew 23:37). When someone wants to live a life unaffected by the feelings and hurts of others, that behavior goes against everything that is true about God. Yet God gives people great freedom to be selfish and hurtful, because this freedom may one day be the freedom through which they choose his ways. As C. S. Lewis says in *Mere Christianity*, "If a thing is free to be good it is also free to be bad.... Why, then, did God give [humans] free will? Because free will, though it makes evil possible, is also the only thing that makes possible any love or goodness or joy worth having."*

> *God gives people great freedom to be selfish and hurtful, as this freedom may one day be the freedom through which they choose his ways.*

If this is your situation, understand that your boundaries are more for you than for your spouse. They are to protect and structure you, and only secondarily to change and motivate him. Enforce the consequences for your own spiritual and emotional well-being.

Deal with Escalation and Anger

Don't be surprised or shocked if your spouse escalates the behavior that troubles you. Kids do it all the time to test limits and see if parents are serious. Your spouse may get messier, more

---

*C. S. Lewis, *Mere Christianity* (New York: Macmillan, 1952), p. 52.

controlling, or more of a spendthrift. Be prepared for this. Warn again, make the consequences stricter, or simply make sure you are sticking to them consistently. Some spouses wake up and smell the coffee after a few escalations, and some test you longer.

Handle his anger and hatred with firmness. Many spouses back off an appropriate boundary they have set because they can't tolerate being hated. The experience makes them feel unloved and bad. This is very normal, as everyone wants his spouse to love him. Be prepared to be resented. Make sure you have others filling you up with love and support to replace the love you are losing (only temporarily, we hope). Don't take abuse or think it's your job to fix temper tantrums. But allow the hatred to exist. Your spouse is angry with you for saying no to him. He has the right to hate your no. Just understand where it comes from, don't react to it, and stay connected to God and others. Remember how much flak God gets for doing the right thing. It hurts him, but he loves us and keeps the boundary (2 Corinthians 12:7–10).

I know a man whose wife hated him for months because he set a financial boundary. He cut off her credit cards because she was wildly overspending. Her anger hurt him, but he knew he had to do the right thing for both them and their kids. Yet he was afraid that his need for her and his fear of her anger would make him compromise the boundary. To guard against this, he met regularly with trusted friends to keep him loved and sane. He was in

- A healthy church
- A couple's growth group that met twice monthly
- Weekly couple's counseling

And he arranged

- One or two breakfasts or lunches a week with healthy friends
- Regular time with his best friend

It was a large investment of time, but it worked. He could keep loving his wife and keeping the boundary while she worked through her anger at him.

Normalize Doubt

Don't be surprised if you begin questioning yourself. You may do this especially if your mate protests, blames you, becomes angry with you, or intensifies her resistance. You may doubt whether your boundary setting is the right thing to do. After all, it's a new way of looking at things for you, and you may not be doing it correctly. Also, it is your very love for her that will sometimes have you wondering things such as

> *Don't be surprised if you begin questioning yourself.*

- Am I being unfair?
- Does she need another chance before I enforce a consequence?
- Did I explain the situation clearly enough?
- Am I overreacting?
- Is there a better way than boundaries and consequences?
- Am I secretly trying to punish her instead of doing the right thing?

These are all legitimate questions that you'll need to answer for yourself. Think through them. Setting limits with your soul mate is a serious endeavor. At the same time, realize that any new way of operating in life is accompanied by doubt. Expect it. Settle the questions, and continue the process.

Leave Permanently

It is sad but necessary to bring up the ultimate consequence in marriage: divorce. Divorce does not fix a marriage. It ends it. It is much less than God's ideal, but he does allow it in certain circumstances, such as adultery or desertion by an unbelieving spouse (Matthew 5:31–32; 1 Corinthians 7:15). Even then, God does not mandate it.

> *Any new way of operating in life is accompanied by doubt.*

There are many steps to take before you consider divorce, as you can see from this chapter. Divorce can only be the last step in a long process that includes prayer, invitation, change, patience, consequences, and love.

It is best to see boundaries in marriage as just that: they are *in* marriage. Boundaries are meant to be carried out within the framework of the marital structure.

> *It is best to see boundaries in marriage as just that: they are in marriage.*

(In the next chapter we will talk more about how people have misused boundaries to leave their marriages.) Divorce takes the problem outside of the marital framework. Develop your boundaries and consequences so that, ultimately, you aren't the one leaving. Rather, construct them so that your righteousness and God's painful realities will force your spouse over time either to relent and change, or to decide against you and God. In that way, your spouse must be responsible for the consequences of leaving you, not you for leaving him.

This chapter has dealt with some difficult realities about setting boundaries with a spouse who does not support boundaries. Yet, remember that God supports you as you follow his ways. He will not leave you during the conflicts and dark times. Cling to him and your friends as you establish good limits for you and your marriage: "By day the LORD directs his love, at night his song is with me" (Psalm 42:8). Remember his love as you begin the boundary-setting process in your marriage.

But before you begin that process, read the next chapter to avoid the mistakes some have made in setting boundaries.

Part Four

Misunderstanding Boundaries in Marriage

Chapter 16

Avoiding the Misuse of Boundaries in Marriage

J (Dr. Townsend) had a curious experience while speaking on boundaries at a seminar. During a question-and-answer segment, a woman stood up and said, "I'm so glad I learned about boundaries. I was able to break free from an abusive relationship." You could see the approving nods of others in the audience as they affirmed the prisoner who was now out of jail.

Later that day, a man came up to me and said, "I know that I have been a controlling husband. But for a long time I've been working hard on my issues, going to counseling, joining an accountability group, and meeting with my pastor. That woman who mentioned breaking free from an abusive relationship is my wife. Because of these boundary ideas, she has left our home and our kids, and she refuses to meet with our pastor to deal with these problems." I wondered about how easily the audience would have bestowed their approval on this woman had they seen the distress on her husband's face.

> *Misuse of boundaries often results in increased alienation instead of increased love.*

Over the years, we have become concerned about similar misunderstandings about boundaries within the marriage relationship. Our concerns generally stem from one spouse's misusing the role of boundaries in the marriage. Misuse of boundaries often results in increased alienation instead of increased love. Here are some examples:

- A wife whose first and only boundary is to divorce her husband
- A husband who controls his wife but calls his actions "setting boundaries"
- A wife who uses consequences and withdrawal to get revenge on her husband
- A husband who excuses his rage attacks by saying he is simply being truthful

These are all grievous misunderstandings of what the Bible teaches about becoming a righteous, responsible, free person, a person with good boundaries. Boundaries were not designed to end relationships, but to preserve and deepen them. With couples, boundaries are ultimately for working within the marriage, not outside of it.

> *Boundaries were not designed to end relationships, but to preserve and deepen them.*

The purpose of this chapter is to clarify some of these misconceptions about boundaries in marriage. We will look at the purpose of suffering, how boundaries fit into problem solving in marriage, the issue of submission, and the divorce question.

The Purpose of Suffering

Riley and Emily were in their mid-forties. Riley had been your typical compliant, passive "nice guy." He forever gave in to his more dominant wife's inclinations in many areas of life, from how they spent their money to how he spent his spare time.

But by their middle years, Riley had become more and more opposed to Emily's desires and opinions. He demanded changes in the marriage, saying, "You've had things your way all these years. Now it's my turn. We'll do things my way."

Emily wasn't sure what Riley meant by all this. She wondered if it was a midlife crisis. But she told him, "Well, I'm open to your ideas, Riley. I suppose I've been too much in charge sometimes."

But Riley wanted more than openness. He wanted license. He spent money without checking with Emily. He took long trips by himself and didn't tell her where he was going. When she asked him about his behavior, Riley would say, "I'm setting a boundary with you. I don't have to answer to you."

The couple had a long, painful season until a pastor sat down with Riley and told him, "Riley, you're confusing freedom with selfishness." Riley took the pastor's words to heart, and he began to consult Emily more before he acted.

Riley's struggle is an example of the problem of thinking that setting boundaries means we don't have to suffer. It's like thinking that when we say no, we can now do whatever we want. Actually, nothing could be further from the truth. Boundaries are not about an escape from suffering, nor an escape from responsibility. In fact, when we set limits in marriage, sometimes we suffer more, not less. When a wife takes a stand to disagree with her opinionated husband's desire to plan their weekend his way, she will suffer for her stand. Yet it may be the right thing for both of them.

> *Boundaries are not about an escape from suffering, nor an escape from responsibility.*

Suffering is a necessary part of life, growth, and any meaningful relationship. No truly mature person or marriage has ever escaped suffering. In fact, the Bible teaches that suffering produces perseverance, which then produces character (Romans 5:3–4). Suffering, at least the kind that God calls us to experience, is designed to help us adapt to reality the way it really is. Through suffering we learn to get our needs met, give to others, and yet relinquish demands that all creatures in the universe bow down to us. Suffering helps us survive, even thrive, while giving up the wish to be God.

Here are some of the benefits that suffering can bring to marriage:

- Growing in faith that our unseen God is helping and supporting

- Learning to hold onto one's values in tough times
- Becoming a truthful person when it is not popular
- Delaying gratification for a future and better goal
- Staying connected to others instead of withdrawing in self-absorption
- Learning to live in forgiveness with an imperfect spouse
- Learning to accept forgiveness for being an imperfect spouse

In fact, almost all of the processes that strengthen and deepen a marriage involve some pain and discomfort. Suffering pushes us into the learning curve of adulthood.

Suffering for the Wrong Reasons

The confusion about suffering, boundaries, and marriage often comes, not because spouses try to avoid growing up, but because they have been suffering for some time for the wrong reasons.

> *The confusion about suffering, boundaries, and marriage often comes because spouses have been suffering for some time for the wrong reasons.*

Godly suffering, described above, is good for us, but ungodly suffering is not.

Many times a longsuffering wife will become aware that what she has been putting up with is not doing any good. Then she will think, "I have had it. Any type of discomfort is harmful," and she will opt for "It's my turn" thinking, similar to Riley's above. Let's look closely at ungodly suffering to understand it.

Ungodly suffering comes from either doing the wrong thing or not doing the right thing. This type of pain is a signal to us that something bad is happening. It is a warning to change a behavior, an attitude, or a feeling. For example, the Bible teaches that if a spouse rescues a raging mate from his anger, she will experience discomfort: "A hot-tempered man must pay the penalty; if you rescue him, you will have to do it again" (Proverbs 19:19). If she facilitates her husband's immaturity instead of confronting it, the next day she will find herself having to do it again. She will be enabling him. This is painful for her.

Do not misunderstand what is going on here. The rescuing spouse of the rageaholic is not experiencing godly suffering, the kind that comes from doing the right thing; instead, she is experiencing ungodly suffering, the kind that comes from doing the wrong thing. She is reaping what she is sowing. It is to be hoped that she will heed the warning of this pain and change her ways. Ungodly suffering should resolve itself when we stop doing whatever caused it.

> *Ungodly suffering comes from either doing the wrong thing or not doing the right thing.*

Godly suffering changes, also, but in a different way. We keep suffering as we mature in different tasks. For example, the compliant spouse speaks up and tells the truth. This is difficult for her; it is godly suffering. As she matures in truthfulness, it becomes less difficult to be honest. But then she realizes she has a judgmental, condemning spirit. She now begins to work on forgiveness and grief to resolve that problem. That, too, is godly suffering. The process continues as growth continues.

God does not want you to set boundaries in your marriage to end suffering and pain. He wants you to end the ungodly suffering, which produces no growth, and enter his suffering, which always brings good results. The Bible teaches that "he who has suffered in his body is done with sin" (1 Peter 4:1). When we start suffering in our body in righteous, honest, loving ways, this often cures the problem of suffering in sinful, rescuing, fearful, or guilty ways.

> *Ungodly suffering should resolve itself when we stop doing whatever caused it.*

The following table contains examples of how boundaries in marriage can help you stop suffering the wrong way and instead suffer the right way:

Situation	Ungodly Suffering	Godly Suffering
An overspending wife	Nagging or silence	Taking the credit cards and enduring her wrath
A critical husband	Complying to win his approval	Leaving the room when he criticizes and letting him be angry about it
A wife who controls by guilt messages	Resentfully doing what she wants	Confronting her covert control and letting her call him an unloving person
A husband who doesn't help with housework	Pretending he's a cute little boy and overlooking it	Letting him cook his own meals until he helps out, and allowing him to pout

None of these scenarios has a painless response. So if you're going to endure discomfort, you may as well have it do some good. Remember that Jesus endured the pain of the cross for the joy that was set before him (Hebrews 12:2). Don't set limits to live an anesthetized life. Set them to build love, honesty, and freedom in your marriage.

Setting Boundaries to Avoid Growth

Vicki loved Colton, but he had a bad temper. When things were okay, he was warm and loving with her and the kids. But when he had a bad day at work, or things were out of sorts between them, Colton would lash out at his family. He would end up hurting feelings and disrupting the home's peacefulness.

> *If you're going to endure discomfort, you may as well have it do some good.*

Vicki had a hard time confronting Colton on his short fuse, and rarely did so. There were many good things about him, and she hated injecting conflict into the good times. She didn't want to start a fight when it wasn't necessary; yet she knew he wasn't getting better over time.

Finally, a friend told her, "Vicki, set some boundaries before it gets worse." Vicki wasn't really sure what that meant, but she decided to set limits.

The result was like the old saying, "A little knowledge is a dangerous thing." When Colton came home after work, Vicki met him at the door with an ultimatum. Before he had a chance to say hello, she said, "I've had enough of your temper. It hurts me and the kids. If you ever direct your anger at us, we're moving to my mom's. You decide."

Colton was devastated. Of course, he had an immediate temper tantrum, upon which Vicki and the kids spent some nights at her mother's. The next few weeks were not smooth ones. Colton was upset by Vicki's abrupt and reactive boundary. He felt blindsided and attacked out of the blue. The kids were disoriented and divided in their loyalties to their parents. It took a long time—longer than it had to—before Vicki and Colton worked out their affairs and repaired things between them.

Vicki had the right intent, but she did not understand the place of boundaries in her marriage. With no warning, she arbitrarily laid down the rule with Colton. Colton had no chance to feel her love or concern, only her wrath. And he did what most of us do when we feel anger but no love from someone: he became angry back. That is when everything fell apart.

More importantly, Vicki didn't understand that boundaries are not a simple ultimatum in marriage. They are a part of a long and often trying process, which involves more than just limit-setting. Spiritual and emotional growth requires a complex set of situations. It takes a lot for us to mature. God himself does many things over time with us to help us grow up. He knows our frailties and how much time, patience, and effort it takes for us to change. How easy it would be for him to simply set the rules and say to us, "Get your act together or else!" In reality, he goes a much longer, much more difficult route with us: "'Come now, let us reason together,' says the LORD" (Isaiah 1:18), as he works through our sinfulness and childishness with us.

It is the same in marriage. Understand how hard growth and change are for your spouse, especially when she is in denial or out of control. Give her the same grace that you also need to mature. Below are some of the elements you will need to apply in your marriage along with boundaries. As you bring these into your relationship, they will enfold you in the process of growth rather than catch you up in the demand that someone change immediately. Boundaries serve the growth process. They are not a way to change or fix someone.

> *Boundaries are not a simple ultimatum in marriage. They are a part of a long and often trying process, which involves more than just limit-setting.*

Love

Love is the most important element of any relationship. It is the essential framework for how to treat your mate. When you love someone, you are "for" him, and whatever you do or say must be from a loving perspective, not a vengeful or punishing one. When problems arise in marriage, the first thing to do is to establish that you desire the best for your mate, even if he has not been a loving person himself. Some spouses will respond to the love itself as it reaches the soul. Others may not respond. In these cases, the love helps you to balance the pain of boundaries with care for your spouse.

> *When problems arise in marriage, the first thing to do is to establish that you desire the best for your mate, even if he has not been a loving person himself.*

Others

Not only do you need to speak from love, but also you need to be receiving care, support, and encouragement from God and others outside of your marriage. We need relationship with people to fill us up inside, especially when we have marriage struggles. Being connected helps us to bear and tolerate the problem, the distance from our spouse, and what it takes out of us to deal with the problem. Many times, a spouse who is detached from supportive relationships either will set no boundaries or will set extremely reactive boundaries as a response to his own internal emptiness and deprivation.

For example, a husband I know had a hard time forming relationships outside of his marriage. He operated in life as a loner. When he finally confronted his spendthrift wife on her problem, he found himself yelling and being harsh in ways he hadn't wanted to be. His own lack of being loved caused him to set an unnecessarily harsh boundary. And a harsh, angry boundary is almost always received in anger. You rarely get what you want when you set these sorts of boundaries.

> *There are almost no marriage problems in which one spouse contributes one hundred percent and the other, zero percent.*

Ownership

There are almost no marriage problems in which one spouse contributes one hundred percent and the other, zero percent. Humbly take responsibility for what you have done, apologize, ask forgiveness, and change. Perhaps you have not spoken up when you should have. Perhaps you have told others about your problems with your husband, but have not gone directly to him. Your ownership of your part of the problem helps your spouse not to feel judged or put down.

Invitation

Whatever the problem between you and your spouse, invite him to change before you set limits. With empathy and love, request that he make a change. For example, you might say, "Your critical tones hurt my feelings and distance me from you. I want to be closer. Will you work on changing your tone?" Often a husband will feel sad and empathic for the pain he has caused his wife. Invitation can preclude having to set some consequence.

Warning

Giving a warning is one element Vicki had neglected. She went straight to boundary setting with Colton. He felt ambushed and hurt. A warning might have helped both of them obtain what they wanted. When we warn, we tell our spouse two things: first, we tell him that something painful might happen in the future; second, we tell him that his behavior will help determine what happens. Vicki might have said, "If you continue to rage, I will have to put distance between us to protect myself." Give your spouse the benefit of a warning. Often, knowing that a consequence is in our future helps us take ownership of ourselves.

Patience

Many times, a spouse will appear impatient and intolerant of his mate's irresponsibility or control. Once the issue is exposed, he will demand instant change and will be quite critical when she fails, regresses, or resists the process of growth. This often happens because he has been silently suffering for so long that he feels he has indeed been patient.

However, silent suffering is not patience. Such suffering is often driven by fear or avoidance of conflict. Patience is different. Patience allows the process to happen while you are also providing the ingredients of growth. Make sure you are loving and truthful while you allow your spouse time to grow. Remember how long it has taken for you to change, and remember God's patience with us: "He is patient with you, not wanting anyone to perish" (2 Peter 3:9).

> *Silent suffering is not patience.*

Consequence

When love, support, invitation, warning, and patience are in play, you may have to follow through on your consequence. Consequences protect you and also help your spouse deal with the reality of his actions. Be consistent but loving. Don't set your consequence out of anger, revenge, or punishment.

Renegotiation

Many boundaries can be changed over time as a spouse matures and changes. You may not have to keep a limit forever, as what you make external becomes internalized in your marriage, as it becomes a part of who you two are. This is a mark of growing up: what was outside becomes a part of us inside.

> *In marriage, try to operate with as few rules as possible.*

Renegotiation may mean that when your spouse changes, you will again be close to her. Or that you will have less of a need to protect yourself. Or that you will not be so controlling with the finances. In marriage, try to operate with as few rules as possible. The more people grow, the fewer rules they need.

Forgiveness

Finally, be actively and constantly in the process of forgiveness. To forgive is to cancel a debt. You need to both forgive your spouse and request forgiveness from your spouse. What you try to accomplish in boundary setting can be severely hampered if you don't live in forgiveness. You will run many risks that will disrupt the process of marriage growth, such as

- Blaming
- Judging
- Laying guilt trips on your spouse
- Being unable to let go of past problems
- Taking too much responsibility for your spouse's issues

When God wants to help us grow, he does more than simply set a limit. He uses his boundaries as one of several elements to encourage us to change, mature, and become what he intended us to be. The process of growth is difficult, but the alternative—divorce—is worse.

But before we talk about divorce, let's take a brief look at how the idea of submission in marriage has been misused.

Submission

Few passages in the Bible have been subject to more misunderstanding and misuse than this teaching on submission: "Wives, submit to your husbands as to the Lord. For the husband is the head of the wife as Christ is the head of the church, his body, of which he is the Savior.... Husbands, love your wives, just as Christ loved the church and gave himself up for her to make her holy" (Ephesians 5:22–23, 25). Husbands have used the apostle Paul's teaching to justify control and abuse of their wives. In fact, we have rarely seen a client in marriage therapy bring up submission unless a big part of the problem is a controlling husband. Usually a husband wants to control and not serve his wife, and he is in denial of his own controlling behavior. When his wife has finally had enough and stands up to him, he plays the submission card as a way of getting back in control and avoiding whatever problem she is confronting. This is not what this passage has in mind.

Basically this passage establishes a sense of order in a marriage. It places final responsibility for the family on the shoulders of the husband. He is the "head," or the leader of the family, as Christ is the leader of the church. The passage asks the wife to submit to her husband's leadership, as we all submit to Christ's leadership.

What does this leadership look like? It is basically the leadership Christ provides the church: He died for her and makes her whole. He looks out for her growth and best interest, cleanses her from guilt, provides resources for her growth, and protects her from the world, the flesh, and the devil. He helps her to invest her talents, heals her hurts, takes her suffering on himself, supports her in trials, and comes alongside of her when she falls.

The apostle Paul describes this leadership role in Philippians 2 as one of a giving servant: "Your attitude should be the same as that of Christ Jesus: Who, being in very nature God, did not consider equality with God something to be grasped, but made himself nothing, taking the very nature of a servant, being made in human likeness. And being found in appearance as a man, he humbled himself and became obedient to death—even death on a cross!" (vv. 5–8). A leader is a giving servant who is committed to the best for the one(s) he or she is leading. If a wife is resisting a husband who is loving, truthful, protective, and providing for her well-being, then something is wrong. The commandment for her to submit, to respond to her husband assumes he is loving her in this way. So, whether we are speaking of the church or of marriage, the commandment provides a beautiful picture of a sacrificial love and the response to such a love.

What submission does not mean is that a husband just tells a wife what to do. Leadership does not mean domination. Marriages that work best have equal partners with differing roles. Decisions are best made mutually, as both parties with their different strengths bring in different perspectives. A loving man would never make some decision that would hurt his wife. He needs her input, and she needs his. They are interdependent, and they are partners in the marriage. In fact, in the verse before the submission verse, Paul says, "Submit to one another out of reverence for Christ" (Ephesians 5:21). The husband should always submit to his wife's needs as Christ did for ours, even to death on a cross.

Another problem may occur when a wife stands up for the right thing, and her husband tells her she is not being submissive. She may confront her husband's attitudes or addiction or lying or some other ungodly behavior, and then she is called "unsubmissive." Wives are always to submit to God and his laws above those of their husbands. If their husbands are doing something evil, the wives are to stand up to that evil.

There is also the problem of a controlling woman who wants to be in charge of everything. Selfishness knows no gender lines. If a man is so passive and wimpy that a controlling wife is able to take charge of him for fifty years, something is wrong. And likewise, if he finally stands up and becomes a person and she will not submit to him as he takes his responsibilities, she has some problems. The clear teaching of the Scripture passage is that a wife is to submit to her husband's leadership in some big picture way that each couple has to flesh out in a way that works for them.

The idea of submission is never meant to allow someone to overstep another's boundaries. Submission only has meaning in the context of boundaries, for boundaries promote self-control and freedom. If a wife is not free and in control of herself, she is not submitting anyway. She is a slave subject to a slave driver, and *she is out of the will of God.* As Galatians 5:1 says, "It is for freedom that Christ has set us free. Stand firm, then, and do not let yourselves be burdened again by a yoke of slavery." If a wife is being put under some law that says she is "bad" if she does not submit to her husband's cruelty and problems, then she is not free at all. Likewise, if she is not free to say no without being deemed "bad," then she is not free at all. So the concept of boundaries as the "freedom to do good" in no way contrasts with the idea of submission. A free person is the only one who can submit.

The idea of submission aside, selfishness is never good for any relationship. If both of you are not using your freedom and boundaries to give to and to serve each other, then you do not understand love. As Paul tells us in 1 Corinthians 13:5, love "is not self-seeking." Use your freedom to give, sacrifice, and love your spouse, whether you are husband or wife. If you do that, with the result that most of your arguments are over who gets the chance to do the sacrificing, submission will never be an issue. You will be submitting to each other in Christian love. And if it breaks down, you both are responsible for your own behavior to submit back unto love and the other. If one of you discovers that you are being selfish and not serving the other, you can take ownership of that behavior and make a change. Seek each other's best out of freedom, and submission issues will disappear.

Boundaries and Divorce

At nearly every *Boundaries* seminar that we do, we hear a version of the following story.

Kelly married with great expectations. Scott was everything she wanted: outgoing, attractive, successful, and spiritual. Every time she was with him, she felt life was wonderful. Their dating time was heaven on earth. He pursued her, romanced her, and did special things for her. He would send her flowers, plan special outings for her, and pay attention to her almost obsessively. She felt so special.

So, it was easy for her to say yes to Scott's proposal of marriage. She did worry about his desire to get married right away. She felt that they really needed more time than the six months they had been dating, but she knew that she loved him and decided to go ahead.

They married a few months later. Kelly now felt complete. Life was going to be everything she always wanted. But this feeling only lasted for about six months. Scott began to change.

At first he did not seem as warm to her. Then he began to pick at little things she did. Nothing she did pleased him any more. Little things that he used to rave about could not even get his attention now, and if they did, he criticized her. She began to get discouraged.

As time went on, Scott spent more time out with his friends, playing golf. He came home later and later. Or when he was at home, he would watch sports on television, saying little to her. When she asked him questions or tried to talk, he would give one-word answers or just brush her off. This was a long way from the passion and pursuit that had characterized their relationship in the beginning.

First, Kelly tried nagging Scott, but he would get angry and call her a complainer. She wanted him to go to counseling, but he did not believe in telling other people your problems.

So, she tried the "nice wife" approach. She read somewhere that problems like this were because the wife was not building up her husband's self-esteem and meeting his needs. She blamed herself for Scott's unresponsiveness. She went on a full-fledged program to do nice things for him, improve her looks, dress in sexy ways, and meet his needs like a king would expect.

He disdained her every effort. She felt as if she were becoming a groveling person. Scott had very little respect for her, and his anger grew. She was so lonely and needed his love so badly that she grew more and more depressed. Finally, she confided in a friend.

Her friend told her that God never intended for her to live like this and that she deserved a lot better. She needed to have some boundaries, draw some lines in the sand, and not put up with it any more. If he would not change, then end the marriage, her friend said. This advice conflicted with her pastor's. He had said that she should be submitting to Scott, and everything would be OK. But, she had tried that and it had not worked. Her friend's advice sounded better to her at this point. She was miserable, and there were too many nice guys in the world for her to have to live like this. So, she took her friend's advice. She told Scott that he had to change or else.

He just looked at her like she was nuts and went on in his detached ways. She took that as her signal and went to see an attorney. She, in her mind, was "getting some boundaries." She had always been the kind of person whom people walked over and who tried to please everyone. It was now time to please herself.

Eventually, she got the divorce and was now on her own. She explained it in terms of "getting some boundaries."

In a sense, Kelly was right: she certainly needed some boundaries. Her friend was right also: God never intended her to live that way. But, they were both desperately wrong in the way that they solved the problem.

As we said earlier, divorce is not a boundary in a relationship. Divorce is an end to a relationship.

Often people will get to a point in a boundary-less marriage when they just cannot take it anymore. And they are right. God never meant any relationship to be lived without boundaries, for boundaries enforce his righteous principles. But God never meant for divorce to be the boundary either, and he certainly did not mean for it to be the first real stand that someone takes. That move is basically a defense against growth and change.

God's solution for "I can't live that way anymore" is basically, "Good! Don't live that way anymore. Set firm limits against evil behavior that are designed to promote change and redemption. Get the love and support you need from other places to take the kind of stance that I do to help redeem relationship. Suffer long, but suffer in the right way." And when done God's way, chances are much better for redemption.

We wrote this book to help you avoid ungodly suffering. Even if your spouse is not growing and maturing, if you take the stances we suggest here, you can be healthy. We have seen many situations turn around when people stop ineffective behaviors, such as nagging, people pleasing, and angry leaving, and take a firm stance over a process.

> *God never meant for divorce to be the boundary, and certainly not the first real stand that someone takes.*

There are many, many unnecessary divorces. God has always intended that we do everything we can to redeem relationships, and not to leave them.

Jesus does not judge anyone. He brings light to him or her (John 3:19–21). He acts in righteous ways. He will not participate in lies, cruelty, meanness, betrayal, addictions, or irresponsibility. He will bring the boundaries of light to every situation and will live them out. Then, if people respond, they have been won over. If they do not, they go away.

In one sense, people with real boundaries could avoid many divorces. But they might have to take a strong stance; separate, not participate in the behavioral patterns against which they are setting boundaries; and demand righteousness before participating in the relationship again. If they become the light, then the other person either changes or goes away. This is why, in most cases, we say you really should not have to be the one who divorces. If you are doing the right things, and the other person is truly evil, he most likely will leave you. But you can rest in the assurance that you have done everything possible to redeem the relationship.

The problem is that sometimes a person thinks that he is setting boundaries, but in reality all he is doing is continuing to blame his spouse and demand change in her without changing himself first. Make sure that you have "gotten the log out" of your own eye before you demand that someone else take the speck out of his.

Here is a reiteration of the path we suggested in our book *Safe People* on how to repair a relationship. It is a different way of saying the same thing we said in the chapter on boundary-resistant spouses:

1. Start from a supported position so that you have the strength to deal with your spouse.
2. Solve your own problems and act righteously toward your spouse. Don't contribute to the problem with your own issues.
3. Use others to intervene (counselors, pastors, friends, family, other people with leverage).
4. Accept reality and grieve expectations. Forgive what has already happened.
5. Give change a chance. After you have stopped enabling your spouse and have set good boundaries in the relationship, give it time. Your spouse may not believe you at first.
6. Long suffering begins at this point, not earlier when you were contributing to the problem.
7. After doing the right things for a long time, separation is sometimes the only helpful option until someone in denial decides to change. In the separation, do not give your spouse the benefits of marriage if he is not pursuing change. If someone is abusive, addicted, dangerous, or has other significant problems, a separation can change his life.

Boundaries in a marriage seek to change and redeem the relationship. Divorce should *never* be the first boundary. You need to set boundaries in the context of relationship, not for the purpose of ending relationship. Take a stance that you will not participate in the relationship until the destruction ends. This is a boundary that helps. But, if you take that stance, make sure that the problem is truly the other person's and that you have followed all of God's steps above.

Obviously, by writing this book we want ungodly suffering in a relationship to end. But we also want redemption to happen. End your suffering and see if the boundaries you set to end your suffering can be used to bring about redemption and reconciliation as well.

We have seen it happen many times in many "hopeless" situations. When one spouse finally gets true boundaries, the other one turns around. Give it a chance.

Conclusion

*S*ince publishing *Boundaries: When to Say Yes, When to Say No to Take Control of Your Life* in 1992, we've seen many people embrace the struggle of finding real love in a fallen world. And, along the way, we've caught wind of many boundary heroes. To them, our hats go off.

There are the people in regular situations who, married and wanting to grow, find themselves, like Adam and Eve, pointing the finger at their spouse and getting stuck. But, by removing the "log" from their own eyes, they take responsibility for their own actions, and their self-control leads to deeper love. They discover that growth is an ongoing journey, and they travel the road willingly.

There are the people in difficult situations who, because of some odd teaching or their own weaknesses, have not taken the stand they need to take against hurt or evil in their marriage. They have been too afraid or too guilty to stand up to abuse, irresponsibility, control, or other behavior that destroys love. As a result, the behavior and their hurt have continued. Then they read *Boundaries* and discover that God takes a stand for what is good. God stands up for love and against evil. God stands up for responsibility and freedom and against domination and control. And they join God in the fight for what is good. They set boundaries against evil and protect good things, like love and respect. And, as a result of taking a courageous stance, their marriage is turned around and saved.

One of our favorite stories of this kind of person is told when, for example, a husband comes up to us at a seminar to thank us for writing *Boundaries*. When we ask if he has read the book, he replies, "No, my wife did. And when she stopped taking my immature behavior, I had to turn around and grow. I had to learn to stop being so mean [or controlling, or drunk, or whatever evil was destroying the relationship]." In these instances, the brave spouses who take that stance to protect what they value save both a marriage and a person. This is the peaceful fruit of discipline

(Hebrews 12:11). Boundaries have done their work, and a person has repented and grown.

And, finally, there are the people who have done the right thing, who have taken a stand for good, and who have been rejected. They have suffered for their stand. To an abusive or addicted spouse, they may have stood up and said, "This is not right." And the outcome was partially good: the abuse or the infliction of pain stopped. But the abusive spouse did not heed the discipline and turned against them. These people gained freedom from evil, but love eluded them. They had to find love and support from their friends and their communities. To these people, our hearts go out. You have done well, and you have suffered as Jesus did and as we are commanded to (1 Peter 3:13,14). May God bless you for your courage and perseverance.

But we could not end this book without warning you about the opposite of these fine people. There are self-serving people who use boundaries to continue in denial and blame. They don't remove the log from their own eye and seek to control themselves; instead, they blame others and try to judge and control them. Look to yourself first, before blaming others, and make sure that you do not fall into this group. Then, take a stand for what is right and good, all the while guarding against using your freedom as an opportunity for selfishness (Galatians 5:13).

Our prayer is that, in whichever one of these situations you find yourself, embrace boundaries the way God does. He takes control of himself, takes a stand for the good things of life, like love, forgiveness, freedom, and responsibility. Full of mercy, God desires for others to move out of darkness and join him in the light, having firmly entrenched himself there. And God always fights for love, never at the expense of another person, but often at his own expense.

With God as your model, full of grace and truth, we are confident that having good boundaries in marriage is truly attainable. God bless you.

HENRY CLOUD, PH.D.
JOHN TOWNSEND, PH.D.
NEWPORT BEACH, CALIFORNIA

Embark on a Life-Changing Journey of Personal and Spiritual Growth

DR. HENRY CLOUD

DR. JOHN TOWNSEND

Dr. Henry Cloud and Dr. John Townsend have been bringing hope and healing to millions for over two decades. They have helped people everywhere discover solutions to life's most difficult personal and relational challenges. Their material provides solid, practical answers and offers guidance in the areas of *parenting, singles issues, personal growth,* and *leadership.*

Bring either Dr. Cloud or Dr. Townsend to your church or organization. They are available for:

- Seminars on a wide variety of topics
- Training for small group leaders
- Conferences
- Educational events
- Consulting with your organization

Other opportunities to experience Dr. Cloud and Dr. Townsend:

- Ultimate Leadership workshops—held in Southern California throughout the year
- Small group curriculum
- Seminars via Satellite
- Solutions Audio Club—Solutions is a weekly recorded presentation

For other resources, and for dates of seminars and workshops by Dr. Cloud and Dr. Townsend, visit:

www.cloudtownsend.com

For other information **Call (800) 676-HOPE (4673)**

Or write to:
Cloud-Townsend Resources
18092 Sky Park South, Suite A
Irvine, CA 92614

Milton Keynes UK
Ingram Content Group UK Ltd.
UKHW041316080124
435672UK00009B/125

PARIS

A Literary Anthology

Edited and introduced by
Zachary Seager

MACMILLAN COLLECTOR'S LIBRARY

This collection first published 2024 by Macmillan Collector's Library
an imprint of Pan Macmillan
The Smithson, 6 Briset Street, London EC1M 5NR
EU representative: Macmillan Publishers Ireland Ltd,
1st Floor, The Liffey Trust Centre, 117–126 Sheriff Street Upper,
Dublin 1, D01 YC43
Associated companies throughout the world
www.panmacmillan.com

ISBN 978-1-0350-2361-5

Typeset in Plantin by Jouve (UK), Milton Keynes
Printed and bound by TJ Books Ltd, Padstow, Cornwall PL28 8RW

Visit **www.panmacmillan.com** to read more
about all our books and to buy them.

Contents

Introduction

ZACHARY SEAGER

There is a real place called Paris. You can go there, if you like. Perhaps you've already been. In any case, the city is so well known that it hardly needs to be described. The Eiffel Tower, the Seine, Notre-Dame and Montmartre: that ought to be enough to form in many minds a mental image of wide Parisian streets stretching symmetrically out to the horizon, studded here and there by quaint boulangeries and elegant boutiques, filled with dashing locals and romantic possibility.

Unless of course Paris, for you, means cigarettes and unpleasant smells, grey skies and traffic jams. Because however real the city might be – however concrete the facts of its storied history and cultural landmarks may prove – there is no single Paris. Paris is multiple. Paris is endless. Paris is a dream, dreamed by many dreamers. Paris is a network of tales, legends, clichés and stereotypes, shot through with lyrics from half-remembered songs and scenes from half-forgotten films, all overlaid one upon the other into a mesh of many myths.

This anthology gathers some of those mythic threads and weaves them together into a guidebook of Parisian dreams.

There is the myth of an older, grander Paris, the labyrinthine medieval city destroyed by Baron Haussmann. Lost to industry and modernity, this dead city is by turns achingly lamented by poets like Charles Baudelaire and Guillaume Apollinaire, and creatively reconstructed by novelists like Gustave Flaubert and Victor Hugo.

Then there is the myth of that modernity itself, destroyer of the old world and forger of the new. It was meticulously reproduced and ruthlessly critiqued by writers like Honoré de Balzac, who witnessed in nineteenth-century Paris the birth pangs of our modernity.

Later, there grew a myth of a beautiful, wondrous capital, sanctuary to artists and expatriates from Edith Wharton to Ernest Hemingway, a place of endless indulgence and joyful creative communion where even the simplest pleasures are embraced for their own sakes, and where art and thought can thrive unimpeded.

And yet, at the same time, there was Paris the savage city, the modern Babylon ravaged by greed and lust and the cruellest indifference to human life, a paradise of crime and a breeding ground for misery, populated by heartsick criminals and jaded policemen as well as down-and-out émigrés like the young George Orwell.

Or an amorous Paris, perhaps? A city of tender lovers strolling quietly by the Seine, a romantic ideal embraced by countless authors and mocked by countless others. A darker erotic dream stalks the streets of Paris, too. As does the myth of a regal city, a Paris of royal courts and refined salons, aristocratic luxury and staggering sophistication, along with its equally powerful pendant, the Paris of bloody revolutions and popular uprisings, where a righteously angry populace stands forever ready to haul down a new Bastille.

The myths go on. Because Paris is multiple. Paris is endless. This anthology leads you to it. The rest is up to you.

PARIS

A Literary Anthology

LONGING FOR A
LOST PARIS

GUSTAVE EIFFEL
(1832–1923)

An icon of industrial design and one of the engineering marvels of its day, the Eiffel Tower has become indissociably linked to the city of Paris. Used in countless films and photographs as a visual byword for the French capital, it is also among the most visited tourist attractions in the world, to say nothing of the countless key chains, t-shirts and scale models it has provoked. But this much-loved monument wasn't always so admired. Originally conceived for the 1889 Exposition Universelle, it was designed by a brilliant engineer named Gustave Eiffel who, though already well respected, had yet to summit the peak of his career. The tower was only intended to remain in place for a short period, after which point it would have been dismantled and left to an uncertain fate. Even that was too much for some, though. In fact, many of Eiffel's most illustrious contemporaries were furious with the project. The proof: this bombastic protest letter, which appeared at the beginning of the construction process – two full years before the tower was completed. In bemused fury and with searing rhetoric, a host of famous writers, musicians and artists argued that Eiffel's tower would permanently disfigure Paris, putting an end to the unbroken centuries of tasteful artistic development in France. Signatories included writers like Guy de Maupassant and Alexandre Dumas *fils*, along with countless

3

other luminaries of the Parisian art world. The tower so outraged Maupassant that, upon its completion, he is said to have regularly dined in its restaurant. Why? Because it was the only place in Paris from which he couldn't see the tower itself. Vexed by the protest, Gustave Eiffel responded personally and promptly, offering a vigorous and compelling defence of his audacious project.

Artists' Protest against the Eiffel Tower

LE TEMPS (14 FEBRUARY, 1887)

We – writers, painters, sculptors, and architects, passionate devotees of Paris' beauty which, for the moment at least, remains intact – protest with all our force, with all our indignation, in the name of that belittled French taste, of that French art and history which is currently under threat, against the construction, in the very heart of our capital, of this useless, monstrous Eiffel Tower, which public hostility – so often stamped with common sense and the spirit of justice – has already christened the "Tower of Babel".

Without descending into jingoistic enthusiasm, we have the right to loudly proclaim Paris a city without rival in the world. Over its streets and widened boulevards, along its superb river banks, amidst its magnificent walkways rise the noblest monuments yet conceived by human genius. Author of so many masterpieces, the soul of France gleams through this august efflorescence of stone. Italy, Germany, Flanders – so justly proud of their artistic heritage – possess nothing comparable to our own, and from every corner of the universe Paris draws curiosity and admiration. Should we let all this be profaned? Should the city of Paris continue to associate itself with the outlandish and mercenary fancies of some machine-builder, and thereby ruin and dishonour itself irreparably? For the

Eiffel Tower – which even business-minded America itself would not want – will, without doubt, be the dishonour of Paris. All can feel it, all say it, all are profoundly distressed by it; indeed, we are only a feeble echo of this legitimately alarmed universal opinion. When foreigners arrive to visit our Exposition, they shall cry out in astonishment: "What! This is the horror that the French have dredged up to give us an idea of their famous good taste?" And they will be right to laugh at us, because the Paris of sublime gothic, of Jean Goujon, Germain Pilon, Puget, Rudge, Barye, will have become the Paris of monsieur Eiffel.

To better grasp our argument, one must only imagine, for an instant, a giddily ridiculous tower dominating Paris like a colossal black smokestack, crushing with its barbarous mass Notre Dame, the Sainte-Chapelle, the Saint-Jacques Tower, the Louvre, the Invalides' dome, the Arc de Triomphe – all our monuments humiliated, all our architecture shrunken down and dissolved by this mind-boggling fantasy. And for twenty years we shall see – yawning across a city that still quivers with the genius of so many centuries – spreading like an ink stain the odious shadow of an odious column of bolted sheet metal.

It is up to you, then, dear compatriot – you who so love Paris, you who have so richly embellished it, you who have protected it so often from governmental devastation and the vandalism of industry – it is your great privilege to defend Paris once more. We trust you to plead the cause of Paris, because we know that you, sir, will expend every effort and every eloquence that can be inspired in an artist such as yourself by the love of all that is beautiful, great, and right. And if our cry of alarm is not heard, if our arguments are not heeded – if Paris obstinately persists in dishonouring itself – we, at the very least, will have offered a protest that brings honour to us all.

Have already signed:

E. Meissonier, Ch. Gounod, Charles Garnier, Robert Fleury, Victorien Sardou, Édouard Pailleron, H. Gérôme, L. Bonnat, W. Bouguereau, Jean Gigoux, G. Boulanger, J.-E. Lenepveu, Eug. Guillaume, A. Wolff, Ch. Questel, A. Dumas, François Coppée, Leconte de Lisle, Daumet, Français, Sully-Prudhomme, Élie Delaunay, E. Vaudremer, E. Bertrand, G.-J. Thomas, François, Henriquel, A. Lenoir, G. Jacquet, Goubie, E. Duez, de Saint-Marceaux, G. Courtois, P.-A.-J. Dagnan-Bouveret, J. Wencker, L. Doucet, Guy de Maupassant, Henri Amic, Ch. Grandmougin, François Bournaud, Ch. Baude, Jules Lefebvre, A. Mercié, Cheviron, Albert Jullien, André Legrand, Limbo, etc., etc.

Response to the Artist's Protest

LE TEMPS (14 FEBRUARY, 1887)

On what grounds do these artists protest the tower's continued presence in Paris after the Exposition? That it is useless, monstrous! That it is an eyesore! We shall speak of its utility in a moment. Let us focus, for now, on its aesthetic merit, about which the artists are especially competent. I would very much like to know on what they base their arguments. For, note well, monsieur, no one has yet seen my tower, and no one, before its completion, can pronounce on what it shall be. It is for the moment only known through one architect's drawing which has been printed hundreds of thousands of times. Since when does one judge the artistic value of such a monument on the basis of an architectural sketch?

And what if my tower, once erected, instead of being an eyesore, proved to be something beautiful? Would these artists not regret having so quickly and so rashly rushed to campaign against the conservation of a monument that has yet to be constructed? Let them wait and see it first.

I shall tell you all my thoughts on the subject, and all my hopes. I believe, for my part, that my tower will be beautiful. Do people truly believe that, because we are engineers, we are not preoccupied with the beauty of our constructions, and that while we pursue solidity and durability we do not also seek elegance? Are not the true conditions of strength always in accordance with the hidden rules of harmony? The first principle of architectural aesthetics is that the essential forms of a structure should be perfectly in accordance with and appropriate to its purpose. Now, which condition, above all, did I have to account for with my tower? Its wind resistance. Well, I contend that the curves of the monument's four iron piers, such as my calculations rendered them, will give a great impression of beauty, for they shall translate for the eye the boldness of my conception.

There is, moreover, an appeal in the colossal, a particular charm to which standard artistic theories hardly apply. Who should claim that it is by their artistic value that the pyramids have so strongly marked mankind's imagination? After all, are they anything other than artificial mounds? And yet, who remains unmoved in their presence? Who, before them, is not filled with an irresistible admiration? And what is the source of that admiration if not the immensity of the effort and the grandeur of the result? My tower shall be the tallest structure ever built by human hands. Shall it not therefore be grandiose, too, in its way? And why should that which is admirable in Egypt prove unsightly and ridiculous in Paris? I search for a good answer to these questions and, I confess, I do not find one.

The protest letter declares that my tower shall, with its huge barbarous mass, crush Notre Dame, the Sainte-Chappelle, the Saint-Jacques tower, the Louvre, the Invalides' dome, the Arc de Triomphe, all our monuments in short. How much at once – and by a single tower! Truly, it makes one smile. When one wishes to admire Notre Dame, one goes to see it from the cathedral square. How, then, from the Champ de Mars, shall my construction bother such a visitor who, in front of Notre Dame, will not even see it? This is, in passing, one of the falsest ideas around – that the construction of one edifice overwhelms the buildings around it. See for yourself whether, set among the surrounding houses, the Opera does not appear more overpowered than overpowering. Go to the roundabout at l'Étoile: because the Arc de Triomphe is large, do the nearby houses seem smaller for it? On the contrary, the houses appear as tall as they truly are, that is, around 15 metres high, and it takes a real effort of thought to persuade oneself that the Arc de Triomphe is, in fact, 45 metres tall.

Thus, as to the artistic effect of the tower, no one can judge it in advance, not even I, for the dimensions of the foundations astonish even myself, now that they are beginning to rise out of the ground. As to the damage the tower will supposedly do to the other monuments of Paris: mere words.

There remains the question of its utility. Here, seeing as we must leave behind the world of art, permit me to oppose the artists' opinion with that of the public. I do not believe it vain to declare that a project has never been more popular; every day brings me new proof that there isn't a single Parisian, however humble their origin, that does not know the tower and who is not interested by it. Even abroad, when I happen to travel, I'm astonished by the sensation it has caused.

As for the learned among us, the only true judges of the utility question, I can affirm that they are unanimous. Not only does the tower promise fascinating observations for astronomy, chemistry, meteorology, and physics; not only will it allow us, in wartime, to keep Paris constantly linked to the rest of France; it shall also be a dazzling proof of the progress made this century in the art of engineering. It is only in our age, in these last few years, that we have been able to calculate with enough certainty and work iron with enough precision to dream of such a colossal undertaking. Is it then nothing for the glory of Paris that this condensation of contemporary science should be erected within its walls?

Victor Hugo
(1802–1885)

Poet of genius and revolutionary playwright; bestselling novelist and penetrating social critic; gifted artist who produced more than 4,000 drawings; political exile and, later, senator with staunch republican ideals, a deep disgust for capital punishment and an impassioned belief in the future of a united Europe: Victor Hugo was all this and more. Honoured in his native France as something more than a literary legend, almost a national hero, his work is read and admired by millions around the world. He had many detractors during his long career, both from political and literary foes who attacked his penchant for sentimental pieties and his unshakeable belief in the fundamental goodness of humanity. But even his fiercest critics were sometimes dumbfounded by Hugo's undeniable literary powers and his extraordinary cultural influence. His passionate defence of Gothic art and architecture in *The Hunchback of Notre Dame* (1831), for instance, ignited a feverish taste in his contemporaries for all things medieval, and kick-started a successful campaign to restore and maintain the cathedral. Hugo himself knew that this project was the work of many centuries and the responsibility of each passing generation. In this extract, drawn from that beloved novel, he offers a comprehensive description of Paris's great cathedral as it would have appeared in the distant past.

from The Hunchback of Notre Dame

NOTRE-DAME.

The church of Notre-Dame at Paris is no doubt still a sublime and majestic edifice. But, notwithstanding the beauty which it has retained even in its old age, one cannot help feeling grief and indignation at the numberless injuries and mutilations which time and man have inflicted on the venerable structure, regardless of Charlemagne who laid the first stone of it and of Philip Augustus who laid the last.

On the face of this aged queen of our cathedrals we always find a scar beside a wrinkle. *Tempus edax, homo edacior*—which I should translate thus:—Time is blind, man stupid.

If we had leisure to examine with the reader, one by one, the different traces of destruction left upon the ancient church, we should find that Time had had much less hand in them than men and especially professional men.

In the first place, to adduce only some capital examples, there are assuredly few more beautiful specimens of architecture than that façade, where the three porches with their pointed arches; the plinth embroidered and fretted with twenty-eight royal niches; the immense central mullioned window, flanked by its two lateral windows, like the priest by the deacon and the sub-deacon; the lofty and light gallery of open-work arcades supporting a heavy platform upon its slender pillars; lastly, the two dark and massive towers with their slated penthouses—harmonious parts of a magnificent whole, placed one above another in five gigantic stages—present themselves to the eye in a crowd yet without confusion, with their innumerable details of statuary, sculpture, and carving, powerfully contributing to the tranquil grandeur of the whole—a vast symphony of stone, if we may be allowed the expression; the colossal product of the combination of all the force of the age, in which the fancy of the workman, chastened by the genius of the artist, is seen starting forth in a hundred forms upon every stone: in short, a sort of human creation, mighty and fertile like the divine creation, from which it seems to have borrowed the twofold character of variety and eternity.

What we here say of the façade must be said of the whole church; and what we say of the cathedral of Paris must be said of all the churches of Christendom in the middle ages. But to return to the façade of Notre-Dame such as it appears to us at present, when we piously go there to admire the solemn and gorgeous cathedral, which, to use the language of the chroniclers, "by its vastness struck terror into the spectator."

That façade, as we now see it, has lost three important accessories: in the first place, the flight of eleven steps, which raised it above the level of the ground; in the next, the lower range of statues which filled the niches of the three porches, and the upper range of twenty-eight more ancient sovereigns of France which adorned the gallery of the first story, commencing with Childebert and ending with Philip Augustus, holding in his hand "the imperial globe."

Time, raising by a slow and irresistible progress the level of the city, occasioned the removal of the steps; but if this rising tide of the pavement of Paris has swallowed up, one after another, those eleven steps which added to the majestic height of the edifice, Time has given to the church more perhaps than it has taken away: for it is Time that has imparted to the façade that sombre hue of antiquity which makes the old age of buildings the period of their greatest beauty.

But who has thrown down the two ranges of statues?—who has left the niches empty?—who has inserted that new and bastard pointed arch in the middle of the beautiful central porch?—who has dared to set up that tasteless and heavy door of wood, carved in the style of Louis XV., beside the arabesques of Biscornette?—The men, the architects, the artists, of our days.

And, if we step within the edifice, who has thrown down that colossal St. Christopher, proverbial among statues for the same reason as the great hall of the Palace among halls, and the steeple of Strasburg among steeples? who has brutally swept away those myriads of statues which peopled all the intercolumniations of the nave and the choir, kneeling, standing, on horseback, men, women, children, kings, bishops, soldiers, of stone, marble, gold, silver, copper, and even wax? Not Time most assuredly.

And who has substituted to the old Gothic altar,

splendidly encumbered with shrines and reliquaries, that heavy sarcophagus of marble with its cherubs and its clouds, looking for all the world like a stray specimen of the Val de Grace or the Invalids? who has stupidly inserted that clumsy anachronism of stone in the Carlovingian pavement of Hercandus? Is it not Louis XIV. fulfilling the vow of Louis XIII.?

And who has put cold white glass instead of those deeply coloured panes, which caused the astonished eyes of our ancestors to pause between the rose of the great porch and the pointed arches of the chancel? What would a sub-chorister of the sixteenth century say on beholding the yellow plaster with which our Vandal archbishops have bedaubed their cathedral? He would recollect that this was the colour with which the executioner washed over the houses of criminals; he would recollect the hotel of the Petit-Bourbon, thus beplastered with yellow on account of the treason of the Constable, "and a yellow of so good quality," saith Sauval, "and so well laid on, that more than a century hath not yet faded its colour;" he would imagine that the sacred fane has become infamous, and flee from it as fast as he could.

And if we go up into the cathedral without pausing over the thousand barbarisms of all kinds, what has been done with that charming little belfry, which stood over the point of intersection of the transept, and which, neither less light nor less bold than its neighbour the steeple of the Holy Chapel (likewise destroyed) rose, light, elegant, and sonorous, into the air, overtopping the towers? It was amputated (1787) by an architect of taste, who deemed it sufficient to cover the wound with that large plaster of lead, which looks, for all the world, like the lid of a saucepan.

It is thus that the wonderful art of the middle ages has been treated in almost every country, especially in France. In its ruins we may distinguish three kinds of injuries, which have affected it in different degrees: in the first place Time, which has here and there chapped and every where worn its surface; in the next, revolutions, political and religious, which, blind and furious by nature, have rushed tumultuously upon it, stripped it of its rich garb of sculptures and carvings, broken its open work and its chains of arabesques and fanciful figures, torn down its statues, sometimes on account of their mitres, at others on account of their crowns; lastly, the fashions, more and more silly and grotesque, which since the splendid deviations of the regeneration have succeeded each other in the necessary decline of architecture. The fashions have in fact done more mischief than revolutions. They have cut into the quick; they have attacked the osseous system of the art; they have hacked, hewn, mangled, murdered, the building, in the form as well as in the symbol, in its logic not less than in its beauty. And then, they have *renewed*—a presumption from which at least time and revolutions have been exempt. In the name of *good taste*, forsooth, they have impudently clapped upon the wounds of Gothic architecture their paltry gewgaws of a day, their ribands of marble, their pompoons of metal, a downright leprosy of eggs, volutes, spirals, draperies, garlands, fringes, flames of stone, clouds of bronze, plethoric cupids, chubby cherubs, which begins to eat into the face of art in the oratory of Catherine de' Medicis, and puts it to death two centuries later, writhing and grinning in the boudoir of the Dubarry.

Thus, to sum up the points to which we have directed attention, three kinds of ravages now-a-days disfigure Gothic architecture: wrinkles and warts on the epidermis—these are the work of Time; wounds, contusions, fractures, from brutal violence—these are the work of revolutions from Luther to Mirabeau; mutilations, amputations, dislocations of members, *restorations*—this is the barbarous Greek and Roman work of professors, according to Vitruvius and Vignole. That magnificent art which the Vandals produced academies have murdered. With Time and revolutions, whose ravages are at any rate marked by impartiality and grandeur, has been associated a host of architects, duly bred, duly patented, and duly sworn, despoiling with the discernment of bad taste, substituting the chicories of Louis XV. to the Gothic lace-work, for the greater glory of the Parthenon. This is truly the ass's kick to the expiring lion; the old oak throwing out its leafy crown, to be bitten, gnawed, and torn by caterpillars.

How widely different this from the period when Robert Cenalis, comparing Notre-Dame at Paris with the famous temple of Diana at Ephesus, "so highly extolled by the ancient heathen," pronounced the

Gallican cathedral "more excellent in length, breadth, height, and structure."

Notre-Dame, however, is not what may be called a complete building, nor does it belong to any definite class. It is not a Roman church, neither is it a Gothic church. Notre-Dame has not, like the abbey of Tournus, the heavy, massive squareness, the cold nakedness, the majestic simplicity, of edifices which have the circular arch for their generative principle. It is not, like the cathedral of Bourges, the magnificent, light, multiform, efflorescent, highly decorated production of the pointed arch. It cannot be classed among that ancient family of churches, gloomy, mysterious, low, and crushed as it were by the circular arch; quite hieroglyphic, sacerdotal, symbolical; exhibiting in their decorations more lozenges and zigzags than flowers, more flowers than animals, more animals than human figures; the work not so much of the architect as of the bishop; the first transformation of the art, impressed all over with theocratic and military discipline, commencing in the Lower Empire and terminating with William the Conqueror. Neither can our cathedral be placed in that other family of churches, light, lofty, rich in painted glass and sculptures; sharp in form, bold in attitude; free, capricious, unruly, as works of art; the second transformation of architecture, no longer hieroglyphic, unchangeable, and sacerdotal, but artistical, progressive, and popular, beginning with the return from the Crusades and ending with Louis XI. Notre-Dame is not of pure

Roman extraction like the former, neither is it of pure Arab extraction, like the latter.

It is a transition edifice. The Saxon architect had set up the first pillars of the nave, when the pointed style, brought back from the Crusades, seated itself like a conqueror upon those broad Roman capitals designed to support circular arches only. The pointed style, thenceforward mistress, constructed the rest of the church; but, unpractised and timid at its outset, it displays a breadth, a flatness, and dares not yet shoot up into steeples and pinnacles, as it has since done in so many wonderful cathedrals. You would say that it is affected by the vicinity of the heavy Roman pillars.

For the rest, those edifices of the transition from the Roman to the Gothic style are not less valuable as studies than the pure types of either. They express a shade of the art which would be lost but for them—the engrafting of the pointed upon the circular style.

Notre-Dame at Paris is a particularly curious specimen of this variety. Every face, every stone, of the venerable structure is a page not only of the history of the country, but also of the history of art and science. Thus, to glance merely at the principal details, while the little Porte Rouge attains almost to the limits of the Gothic delicacy of the fifteenth century, the pillars of the nave, by their bulk and heaviness, carry you back to the date of the Carlovingian abbey of St. Germain des Prés. You would imagine that there were six centuries between that door-way and those pillars. There are none, down to the alchymists themselves, but find in the symbols of the grand porch a satisfactory compendium of their science, of which the church of St. Jacques de la Boucherie was so complete an hieroglyphic. Thus the Roman abbey and the philosophical church, Gothic art and Saxon art, the heavy round pillar, which reminds you of Gregory VII., papal unity and schism, St. Germain des Prés and St. Jacques de la Boucherie—are all blended, combined, amalgamated, in Notre-Dame. This central mother-church is a sort of chimæra among the ancient churches of Paris; it has the head of one, the limbs of another, the trunk of a third, and something of them all.

These hybrid structures, as we have observed, are not the less interesting to the artist, the antiquary, and the historian. They shew how far architecture is a primitive art, inasmuch as they demonstrate (what is also demonstrated by the Cyclopean remains, the pyramids of Egypt, the gigantic Hindoo pagodas) that the grandest productions of architecture are not so much individual as social works, rather the offspring of nations in labour than the inventions of genius; the deposit left by a people; the accumulations formed by ages; the residuum of the successive evaporations of human society—in short, a species of formations. Every wave of time superinduces its alluvion, every generation deposits its stratum upon the structure, every individual brings his stone. Such is the process of the beavers, such that of the bees, such that of men. The great emblem of architecture, Babel, is a bee-hive.

Great edifices, like great mountains, are the work of

ages. It is frequently the case that art changes while they are still in progress. The new art takes the structure as it finds it, incrusts itself upon it, assimilates itself to it, proceeds with it according to its own fancy, and completes it if it can. The thing is accomplished without disturbance, without effort, without reaction, agreeably to a natural and quiet law. Certes, there is matter for very thick books, and often for the universal history of mankind, in those successive inoculations of various styles at various heights upon the same structure. The man, the artist, the individual, are lost in these vast masses without any author's name; while human skill is condensed and concentrated in them. Time is the architect, the nation is the mason.

To confine our view here to Christian European architecture, that younger sister of the grand style of the East, it appears to us like an immense formation divided into three totally distinct zones laid one upon another: the Roman* zone, the Gothic zone, and the zone of the revival, which we would fain call the Greco-Roman. The Roman stratum, which is the most ancient and the lowest, is occupied by the circular arch, which again appears, supported by the Greek column, in the modern and uppermost stratum of the revival. The pointed style is between both. The edifices belonging

---

* This is the same that is likewise called, according to countries, climates, and species, Lombard, Saxon, and Byzantine. These four are parallel and kindred varieties, each having its peculiar character, but all derived from the same principle,—the circular arch.

exclusively to one of these three strata are absolutely distinct, one, and complete. Such are the abbey of Jumièges, the cathedral of Rheims, the Holy Cross at Orleans. But the three zones blend and amalgamate at their borders, like the colours in the solar spectrum. Hence the complex structures, the transition edifices. The one is Roman at the foot, Gothic in the middle, Greco-Roman at the top. The reason is that it was six centuries in building. This variety is rare; the castle of Etampes is a specimen of it. But the edifices composed of two formations are frequent. Such is Notre-Dame at Paris, a building in the pointed style, the first pillars of which belong to the Roman zone, like the porch of St. Denis, and the nave of St. Germain des Prés. Such too is the charming semi-gothic capitular hall of Bocherville, exhibiting the Roman stratum up to half its height. Such is the cathedral of Rouen, which would be entirely Gothic, were it not for the extremity of its central steeple, which penetrates into the zone of the revival.*

For the rest, all these shades, all these differences, affect only the surface of edifices; it is but art which has changed its skin. The constitution itself of the Christian church is not affected by them. There is always the same internal arrangement, the same logical disposition of parts. Be the sculptured and embroidered outside of a cathedral what it may, we invariably find underneath

* It was precisely this part of the steeple, which was of wood, that was destroyed by the fire of heaven in 1823.

at least the germ and rudiment of the Roman basilica. It uniformly expands itself upon the ground according to the same law. There are without deviation two naves, intersecting each other in the form of a cross, and the upper extremity of which rounded into an apsis, forms the chancel; and two ailes for processions and for chapels, a sort of lateral walking-places, into which the principal nave disgorges itself by the intercolumniations. These points being settled, the number of the chapels, porches, towers, pinnacles, is varied to infinity, according to the caprice of the age, the nation, and the art. Accommodation for the exercises of religion once provided and secured, architecture does just what it pleases. As for statues, painted windows, mullions, arabesques, open work, capitals, basso-relievos—it combines all these devices agreeably to the system which best suits itself. Hence the prodigious external variety in those edifices within which reside such order and unity. The trunk of the tree is unchangeable, the foliage capricious.

CHARLES BAUDELAIRE
(1821–1867)

Generations of devoted readers have proclaimed Charles Baudelaire France's greatest poet. A melancholic dandy with expensive tastes and, accordingly, crushing debts, his reputation is largely built on one collection of poems, *Les Fleurs du mal* (literally *The Flowers of Evil*), which he worked on continuously in one form or another from 1840 until the end of his life. In verse after polished verse, Baudelaire reflects on beauty and death, evil and exoticism, dejection and ecstasy. These ideas and ideals, like his poems and thought, were almost always refracted through his vision of Paris, where Baudelaire was born and died, and where he witnessed his beloved city advancing towards a frightening but thrilling modernity. This poem, among his most famous, laments the shifting face of that cherished cityscape while at the same time remaining fascinated by the change itself.

The Swan

Andromache, I think of you! The stream,
The poor, sad mirror where in bygone days
Shone all the majesty of your widowed grief,
The lying Simoïs flooded by your tears,
Made all my fertile memory blossom forth
As I passed by the new-built Carrousel.
Old Paris is no more (a town, alas,
Changes more quickly than man's heart may change);
Yet in my mind I still can see the booths;
The heaps of brick and rough-hewn capitals;
The grass; the stones all over-green with moss;
The *débris*, and the square-set heaps of tiles.
There a menagerie was once outspread;
And there I saw, one morning at the hour
When toil awakes beneath the cold, clear sky,
And the road roars upon the silent air,
A swan who had escaped his cage, and walked
On the dry pavement with his webby feet,
And trailed his spotless plumage on the ground.
And near a waterless stream the piteous swan
Opened his beak, and bathing in the dust
His nervous wings, he cried (his heart the while
Filled with a vision of his own fair lake):
"O water, when then wilt thou come in rain?
Lightning, when wilt thou glitter?"

Sometimes yet

I see the hapless bird—strange, fatal myth—
Like him that Ovid writes of, lifting up
Unto the cruelly blue, ironic heavens,
With stretched, convulsive neck a thirsty face,
As though he sent reproaches up to God!

II.

Paris may change; my melancholy is fixed.
New palaces, and scaffoldings, and blocks,
And suburbs old, are symbols all to me
Whose memories are as heavy as a stone.
And so, before the Louvre, to vex my soul,
The image came of my majestic swan
With his mad gestures, foolish and sublime,
As of an exile whom one great desire
Gnaws with no truce. And then I thought of you,
Andromache! torn from your hero's arms;
Beneath the hand of Pyrrhus in his pride;
Bent o'er an empty tomb in ecstasy;
Widow of Hector—wife of Helenus!
And of the negress, wan and phthisical,
Tramping the mud, and with her haggard eyes
Seeking beyond the mighty walls of fog
The absent palm-trees of proud Africa;
Of all who lose that which they never find;
Of all who drink of tears; all whom grey grief
Gives suck to as the kindly wolf gave suck;
Of meagre orphans who like blossoms fade.
And one old Memory like a crying horn

Sounds through the forest where my soul is lost . . .
I think of sailors on some isle forgotten;
Of captives; vanquished . . . and of many more.

OLIVER WENDELL HOLMES SR.
(1809–1894)

Born in Cambridge, Massachusetts, but based for much of his life in Boston, Holmes was a polymath who excelled as a lecturer, poet, doctor and inventor. Today, his reputation is surpassed by that of his son, Oliver Wendell Holmes Jr., who went on to become a justice of the US Supreme Court and one of the most influential legal scholars in American history. Holmes Sr., however, was regarded by his contemporaries as one of America's outstanding intellectuals and was widely admired for his witty, relaxed style that mixed gentle humour with penetrating insights into contemporary life. In this extract, based on his experiences studying medicine in Paris, he gives a haunting account of how the French capital can leave an unexpected mark on people's minds.

from The Autocrat of the Breakfast Table

I used very often, when coming home from my morning's work at one of the public institutions of Paris, to step in at the dear old church of St Etienne du Mont. The tomb of St Genevieve, surrounded by burning candles and votive tablets, was there; the mural tablet of Jacobus Benignus Winslow was there; there was a noble organ with carved figures; the pulpit was borne on the oaken shoulders of a stooping Samson; and there was a marvellous staircase like a coil of lace. These things I mention from memory, but not all of them together impressed me so much as an inscription on a small slab of marble fixed in one of the walls. It told how this church of St Stephen was repaired and beautified in the year 16**, and how, during the celebration of its re-opening, two girls of the parish (*filles de la paroisse*) fell from the gallery, carrying a part of the balustrade with them, to the pavement, but by a miracle escaped uninjured. Two young girls, nameless, but real presences to my imagination, as much as when they came fluttering down on the tiles with a cry that outscreamed the sharpest treble in the Te Deum. (Look at Carlyle's article on Boswell, and see how he speaks of the poor young woman Johnson talked with in the streets one evening.) All the crowd gone but these two "filles de la paroisse,"—gone as utterly as the dresses they wore, as the shoes that were on their feet, as the bread and meat that were in the market on that day.

Not the great historical events, but the personal incidents that call up single sharp pictures of some human being in its pang or struggle, reach us most nearly.

Guillaume Apollinaire
(1880–1918)

Born in Rome, Italy, Wilhelm Albert Włodzimierz Apolinary Kostrowicki moved to Paris in 1900, where he adopted the name Guillaume Apollinaire and set about becoming an artist. He quickly proved a popular figure among the most exciting painters and writers of his day: Modigliani and Picasso made portraits of him, he discussed best poetic practice with André Breton and, as an art critic and theorist, Apollinaire is often credited with coining the terms Cubism and Surrealism. Meanwhile, his own experiments in poetry – many of which artfully arranged words to create striking images on the page – had a significant impact on the course of twentieth-century experimental literature. In this never-before-translated extract, Apollinaire offers a characteristically idiosyncratic description of the Paris neighbourhood Auteuil, with a wistful eye for what the past carries with it.

from Le Flâneur des Deux Rives

People can never give up anything without regret, and even the places, things, and individuals that have made them unhappiest cannot be surrendered without pain.

And so in 1912 it was not without bitterness that I left you, far-flung Auteuil, charming district of my great sorrows. I wasn't to return until 1916, to be trepanned at the villa Molière.

★

When I first moved to Auteuil in 1909, the rue Raynouard still looked as it did in Balzac's time. It's really quite ugly nowadays. There's still the rue Berton, of course, lit by petrol lamps, but that will doubtless soon change, too.

It's an old street, situated between the neighbourhoods of Passy and Auteuil. It would have disappeared completely were it not for the war, or at least become unrecognisable. The municipality had decided to alter its general look, and to widen it for motor traffic. In doing so, they would have destroyed one of the most picturesque parts of Paris.

It was originally a route that, from the banks of the Seine, led across vineyards to the tops of the Passy hills. The street's appearance has hardly changed since the time when, fleeing some unwelcome visitor, Balzac would take the horse-drawn *patache* from Saint-Cloud to Paris.

The passer-by who, from the riverbanks at Passy, notices the rue Berton sees nothing more than a poorly-maintained road, riddled with ruts and stones and hemmed in by crumbling walls; to the left, the fence of a splendid park and, to the right, a plot of land reserved by its owners for diverse and curious ends. One section is used for a garden; another has a vegetable plot; and from a large door that gives on to the waterside, a wide sand path leads to a large theatre made of wood. Called the Joan of Arc auditorium, it's an unexpected monument for such a place. Tattered posters show that, in 1914, *The Passion of our Lord Jesus Christ* was put on there. The actors were perhaps from a fashionable crowd, and you might have encountered in one of the salons in Auteuil Christ himself; meanwhile, some stock-exchange baron and Christian convert might have performed to perfection that thankless role of Judas the saintly Canaanite, who began his career in finance, went on to the apostolate, and finished as a traitor.

But should the passer-by enter the rue Berton, he will be struck by the walls that are overloaded with inscriptions of all sorts – or *graffiti*, to put it like an antiques dealer. He will thus ascertain that "Lili from Auteuil loves Totor from the *Point du Jour*". And that, to mark her love, she traced an arrow-pierced heart and the date, 1884. Alas! Poor Lili, all the years gone by since this sign of love must have healed that wound which ran through your heart.

Other nameless scribes exhibited all the enthusiasm of their souls through this deeply-graven cry: "long live working girls!"

But there are also more tragic exclamations like: "cursed be the 4 June 1903 and he who gave it to us". Graffiti like these, by turns sinister and merry, lead on towards an old building that offers, to the left, a superb carriage entrance flanked by two pavilions with slanting roofs; after which point you arrive at a roundabout, where a gate brings you into a marvellous park that contains a famous nursing home. Here you can find the one thing that ties the rue Berton to Parisian life – but ever so weakly, seeing as the service is so poorly run – a postbox.

A little further, you find some rubble over which sits a plaster dog. This cast is still intact, and I've always seen it in the same place, where it will most likely remain until one day workmen come to change the whole face of the rue Berton. The street then turns at a right angle and, just before the corner, there's another set of railings from which one can see a modern villa set within a cleft in the hillside. The villa looks miserably new on that timeworn street which, from the corner, can be seen in all its aged and unexpected beauty. The street becomes narrow, a stream runs through the middle, and above the walls which bound it hang the dense foliage of Dr Blanche's historic nursing home – luxuriant vegetation that casts cool shade over the old road.

From square to square, posts and marking stones rise up against the walls. Above one of them, someone has placed a marble plaque which marks where in the past lay the boundaries of the Passy and Auteuil seigneuries.

And then you arrive behind Balzac's house. The main entrance is in a building on the rue Raynouard. You have to go down two storeys to get there (owing to the good offices of the late monsieur de Royaumont, curator of the Balzac museum, you might have taken the stairs that Balzac himself took towards the rue Berton, but they have since been sealed off). You can, at least, take another set of stairs that the novelist himself used, and which led him into the courtyard that he would have had to cross to get to the rue Berton.

Then you come to a place where the street widens and becomes residential. There, you can find a house that backs on to the rue Raynouard and that looks over it. A vine climbs all along the house and, in flower boxes, fuchsias grow. A steep and narrow set of stairs brings you to where the rue Raynouard joins the newly constructed road, which used to be the avenue Mercédès but which is today known as the avenue du Colonel-Bonnet, and is now one of the most modern thoroughfares in Paris.

But it's better to follow the rue Berton, which draws its dying breaths between two hideous walls behind which no vegetation can be seen, right up to a crossroads where the old street joins the rue Guillou and the rue Raynouard, in front of an ice factory that shivers day and night with the sound of shaken water.

Those who pass through the rue Berton when it's

at its most beautiful, just before the dawn, can hear a harmonious blackbird give a marvellous concert, accompanied by the music of a thousand other birds. At that hour just before the war twinkled the pale flames of a few petrol lamps that haven't yet been replaced.

The last time I passed through the rue Berton, before the war – already so long ago – I was in the company of René Dalize, Lucien Rolmer, and André Dupont, all of whom were killed on the field of honour.

★

But there are many other charming and curious things in Auteuil . . .

PARIS,
CENTRE OF THE WORLD

LADY MARY WORTLEY MONTAGU
(1689–1762)

Lady Mary Wortley Montagu was well known in her lifetime as a cultivated society wit. After her death, however, she became famous across Europe. Through her husband's diplomatic career, she travelled extensively and lived, for a time, in Ottoman Turkey. Her posthumously published *Turkish Embassy Letters*, based on this experience, earned her a wide readership. They excited the admiration of intellectuals like Voltaire and Edward Gibbon, and have had a lasting historical importance, especially for what they convey about the place of women in the Ottoman Empire. Alongside her cosmopolitan culture, entertaining style and keen awareness of gender imbalances, Montagu was also an early advocate of inoculation against smallpox. In this letter, she wittily describes the wonders of eighteenth-century Versailles and playfully compares the Paris of Louis XV and the regency to London under George I.

from Letters from the Right Honourable Lady Mary Wortley Montagu

To Mrs. T—— [Thistlethwayte].
Paris, Oct. 16, O.S. [1718].

You see I'm just to my word, in writing to you from Paris, where I was very much surprised to meet my sister——[Mar]; I need not add, very much pleased. She as little expected to see me as I her (having not received my late letters); and this meeting would shine under the hand of Mr. De Scudérie; but I shall not imitate his style so far as to tell you how often we embraced; how she enquired by what odd chance I returned from Constantinople; and I answered her by asking what adventure brought her to Paris? To shorten the story, all questions and answers, and exclamations, and compliments, being over, we agreed upon running about together, and have seen Versailles, Trianon, Marli, and St. Cloud. We had an order for the waters to play for our diversion, and I was followed thither by all the English at Paris. I own Versailles appeared to me rather vast than beautiful; and after have [having?] seen the exact proportions of the Italian buildings, I thought the irregularity of it shocking.

The King's cabinet of antiques and medals is, indeed, very richly furnished. Among that collection none pleased me so well as the apotheosis of Germanicus, on a large agate, which is one of the most delicate pieces of the kind that I remember to have seen. I observed some ancient statues of great value. But the nauseous flattery, and tawdry pencil of Le Brun, are equally disgusting in the gallery. I will not pretend to describe to you the great apartment, the vast variety of fountains, the theatre, the grove of Esop's fables, &c., all which you may read very amply particularised in some of the French authors that have been paid for those descriptions. Trianon, in its littleness, pleased me better than Versailles; Marli, better than either of them; and St. Cloud, best of all; having the advantage of the Seine running at the bottom of the gardens, the great cascade, &c. You may find in the foresaid books, if you have any curiosity to know, the exact number of the statues, and how many feet they cast up the water.

We saw the King's pictures in the magnificent house of the Duke d'Antin, who has the care of preserving them till his Majesty is of age. There are not many, but of the best hands. I looked with great pleasure on the archangel of Raphael, where the sentiments of superior beings are as well expressed as in Milton. You won't forgive me if I say nothing of the Thuilleries, much finer than our Mall; and the Cours, more agreeable than our Hyde Park, the high trees giving shade in the hottest season. At the Louvre I had the opportunity of seeing the King, accompanied by the Duke Regent. He is tall and well-shaped, but has not the air of holding the crown so many years as his grandfather. And now I am speaking of the court, I must say I saw nothing in

France that delighted me so much as to see an Englishman (at least a Briton) absolute in Paris; I mean Mr. L——, who treats their dukes and peers extremely *de haut en bas*, and is treated by them with the utmost submission and respect.—Poor souls!—This reflection on their abject slavery puts me in mind of the *Place des Victoires*; but I will not take up your time and my own with such descriptions, which are too numerous.

In general, I think Paris has the advantage of London, in the neat pavement of the streets, and the regular lighting of them at nights, the proportion of the streets, the houses all built of stone, and most of those belonging to people of quality, being beautified by gardens. But we certainly may boast of a town very near twice as large; and when I have said that, I know nothing else we surpass it in. I shall not continue here long; if you have any thing to command me during my short stay, write soon, and I shall take pleasure in obeying you.

I am, &c. &c.

HELEN MARIA WILLIAMS
(1759–1827)

Born to a Scottish mother and a Welsh father, Williams spent her early life in England, where she earned a degree of fame in the 1780s for her stirring, sentimental poetry – so much so, in fact, that while still a schoolboy, William Wordsworth took for the subject of his first published poem 'on seeing Miss Helen Maria Williams weep at a tale of distress'. In 1790, Williams moved to France. There, she defended Revolutionary principles, hosted a salon that welcomed notable guests including Mary Wollstonecraft and Thomas Paine and, during the Reign of Terror, spent time in prison. Eventually, she established herself as one of the foremost interpreters of France to English readers. She wrote about French customs and history, translated French fiction and became a naturalized French citizen in 1818, before dying in Paris at the age of sixty-eight. In this extract, she writes movingly about the most famous cemetery in the world, Paris's Père Lachaise.

from Letters on the Events Which Have Passed in France Since the Restoration in 1815

This cemetery has no parallel in any capital of Europe. Placed in the most picturesque situation, its vast extent, the magnificent view it commands, its undulating soil covered with verdure, and shaded by trees, and its beautiful monuments, attract the curiosity of strangers, who admire the purity of taste that prevails in these monuments, which are all modern. This inclosure contains no mouldering sepulchres; every tomb bears a recent date, and is filled with contemporary life. But while the traveller carelessly reads the inscription on the storied urn, and passes on, those who, like me, have long inhabited Paris, wander to that spot with far other emotions. These tombs contain the objects of our tenderest and most sacred affections; those with whom we have passed through the storms of life at an epoch when they beat most pitiless; those whom we have folded to the heart in the agonies of separation; who fixed on us that look which is the last communication of the dying, long after the lips have lost their utterance. Nothing can be more affecting than the sight of this cemetery *le jour des morts*. On that day, sacred to the dead, the Catholics hasten hither in crowds, and, kneeling at the grave of the departed, pray for the repose of their souls. This tender superstition, that soothes the bitterness of

sorrow, is more to be envied than deplored. The prot-
estants bring offerings of fresh flowers, selecting
perhaps those to which some recollection of the heart
have given a predilection. The groves are all carefully
planted with shrubs; that spot where my mother reposes
is encircled with Scotch firs, that seem to blend the
associations of country with the sorrows of affection. At
Paris we all know the place of our repose; we have all
some grave near which we have chosen our last
shelter—we have all said to those who may survive us,
"O lay me, ye that see the light, near the rock of my
rest!"—How soothing a contrast we find in this sad yet
cherished privilege, which those times which I too well
remember, when the dead were thrown into one
common gulf, over which no prayer was uttered, and no
memorial was left.

WILLIAM WELLS BROWN
(1814–1884)

Born into slavery near Lexington, Kentucky, Brown spent much of his early life on the Missouri River, where his slavers put him to work on steamboats. After escaping in 1834, he became a vigorous abolitionist, using his knowledge of the river to help fugitive slaves to freedom. Brown was also an unflagging advocate of education. He famously said of himself: 'He who escapes from slavery at the age of twenty years, without any education, as did the writer of this letter, must read when others are asleep, if he would catch up with the rest of the world.' His own stringent efforts at self-improvement eventually led him to become a popular writer and lecturer. In this extract, written during a years-long sojourn in Europe – prompted, in part, by the 1850 Fugitive Slaves Act, which might have put him in danger on his return home – Brown writes with constant wonder about strolling through Paris streets that are marked by so much history and stained by so much blood.

from Three Years in Europe

*The Tuileries—Place de la Concorde—The Egyptian
Obelisk—Palais Royal—Residence of Robespierre—A Visit
to the Room in which Charlotte Corday killed Marat—
Church de Notre Dame—Palais de Justice—Hotel des
Invalids—National Assembly—The Elysee.*

PARIS, August 28.

Yesterday morning I started at an early hour for the Palace of the Tuileries. A show of my card of membership of the Congress (which had carried me through so many of the public buildings) was enough to gain me immediate admission. The attack of the mob on the palace, on the 20th of June, 1792, the massacre of the Swiss guard on the 10th of August of the same year, the attack by the people in July 1830, together with the recent flight of king Louis Philippe and family, made me anxious to visit the old pile.

We were taken from room to room, until the entire building had been inspected. In front of the Tuileries, are a most magnificent garden and grounds. These were all laid out by Louis XIV, and are left nearly as they were during that monarch's reign. Above fifty acres surrounded by an iron rail fence, fronts the Place de la Concorde, and affords a place of promenade for the Parisians. I walked the pleasing grounds, and saw hundreds of well dressed persons walking under the shade of the great chestnuts, or sitting on chairs which were kept to let at two sous a piece. Near by is the Place de Carrousel, noted for its historical remembrances. Many incidents connected with the several revolutions occurred here, and it is pointed out as the place where Napoleon reviewed that formidable army of his before its departure for Russia.

From the Tuileries, I took a stroll through the Place de la Concorde, which has connected with it so many acts of cruelty, that it made me shudder as I passed over its grounds. As if to take from one's mind the old associations of this place, the French have erected on it, or rather given a place to, the celebrated obelisk of Luxor, which now is the chief attraction on the grounds. The obelisk was brought from Egypt at an enormous expense; for which purpose a ship was built, and several hundred men employed above three years in its removal. It is formed of the finest red syenite, and covered on each side with three lines of hieroglyphic inscriptions, commemorative of Sesostris—the middle lines being the most deeply cut and most carefully finished; and the characters altogether number more than 1600. The obelisk is of a single stone, is 72 feet in height, weighs 500,000 lbs., and stands on a block of granite that weighs 250,000 lbs. He who can read Latin will see that the monument tells its own story, but to me its characters were all blank.

It would be tedious to follow the history of this old and venerated stone, which was taken from the quarry 1550 years before the birth of Christ; placed in Thebes;

its removal; the journey to the Nile, and down the Nile; thence to Cherbourg, and lastly its arrival in Paris on the 23d of December, 1833—just one year before I escaped from slavery. The obelisk was raised on the spot where it now stands, on the 25th of October, 1836, in the presence of Louis Philippe and amid the greetings of 160,000 persons.

Having missed my dinner, I crossed over to the Palais Royal, to a dining saloon, and can assure you that a better dinner may be had there for five francs, than can be got in New York for twice that sum, and especially if the person who wants the dinner is a coloured man. I found no prejudice against my complexion in the Palais Royal.

Many of the rooms in this once abode of Royalty, are most splendidly furnished, and decorated with valuable pictures. The likenesses of Madame de Stael, J. J. Rousseau, Cromwell, and Francis I., are among them.

*

After several unsuccessful attempts to-day, in company with R. D. Webb, Esq., to seek out the house where once resided the notorious Robespierre, I was fortunate enough to find it, but not until I had lost the company of my friend. The house is No. 396, Rue St. Honore, opposite the Church of the Assumption. It stands back, and is reached by entering a court. During the first revolution it was occupied by M. Duplay, with whom Robespierre lodged. The room used by the great man of the revolution, was pointed out to me. It is small, and the ceiling low, with two windows looking out upon the court. The pin upon which the blue coat once hung, is still in the wall. While standing there, I could almost imagine that I saw the great "Incorruptible," sitting at the small table composing those speeches which gave him so much power and influence in the Convention and the Clubs.

Here, the disciple of Rousseau sat and planned how he should outdo his enemies and hold on to his friends. From this room he went forth, followed by his dog Brunt, to take his solitary walk in a favourite and neighbouring field, or to the fiery discussions of the National Convention. In the same street, is the house in which Madame Roland—one of Robespierre's victims—resided.

A view of the residence of one of the master spirits of the French revolution inclined me to search out more, and therefore I proceeded to the old town, and after winding through several small streets—some of them so narrow as not to admit more than one cab at a time—I found myself in the Rue de L'Ecole de Medecine, and standing in front of house No. 20. This was the residence, during the early days of the revolution, of that bloodthirsty demon in human form, Marat.

I said to a butcher, whose shop was underneath, that I wanted to see La Chambre de Marat. He called out to the woman of the house to know if I could be admitted, and the reply was, that the room was used as a sleeping apartment, and could not be seen.

As this was private property, my blue card of membership to the Congress was not available. But after slipping a franc into the old lady's hand, I was informed that the room was now ready. We entered a court and ascended a flight of stairs, the entrance to which is on the right; then crossing to the left, we were shown into a moderate-sized room on the first floor, with two windows looking out upon a yard. Here it was where the "Friend of the People" (as he styled himself,) sat and wrote those articles that appeared daily in his journal, urging the people to "hang the rich upon lamp posts." The place where the bath stood, in which he was bathing at the time he was killed by Charlotte Corday, was pointed out to us; and even something representing an old stain of blood was shown as the place where he was laid when taken out of the bath. The window, behind whose curtains the heroine hid, after she had plunged the dagger into the heart of the man whom she thought was the cause of the shedding of so much blood by the guillotine, was pointed out with a seeming degree of pride by the old woman.

With my Guide Book in hand, I again went forth to "hunt after new fancies."

*

After walking over the ground where the guillotine once stood, cutting off its hundred and fifty heads per day, and then visiting the place where some of the chief movers in that sanguinary revolution once lived, I felt little disposed to sleep, when the time for it had arrived. However, I was out this morning at an early hour, and on the Champs Elysees; and again took a walk over the place where the guillotine stood, when its fatal blade was sending so many unprepared spirits into eternity. When standing here, you have the Palace of the Tuileries on one side, the arch on the other; on a third, the classic Madeleine; and on the fourth, the National Assembly. It caused my blood to chill, the idea of being on the identical spot where the heads of Louis XVI. and his Queen, after being cut off, were held up to satisfy the blood-thirsty curiosity of the two hundred thousand persons that were assembled on the Place de la Revolution. Here Royal blood flowed as it never did before or since. The heads of patricians and plebians, were thrown into the same basket, without any regard to birth or station Here Robespierre and Danton had stood again and again, and looked their victims in the face as they ascended the scaffold; and here, these same men had to mount the very scaffold that they had erected for others. I wandered up the Seine, till I found myself looking at the statue of Henry the IV. over the principal entrance of the Hotel de Ville. When we take into account the connection of the Hotel de Ville with the different revolutions, we must come to the conclusion, that it is one of the most remarkable buildings in Paris. The room was pointed out where Robespierre held his counsels, and from the windows of which he could look out upon the Place de Greve, where the guillotine stood before its removal to the Place de la

Concorde. The room is large, with gilded hangings, splendid old-fashioned chandeliers, and a chimney-piece with fine antiquated carvings, that give it a venerable appearance. Here Robespierre not only presided at the counsels that sent hundreds to the guillotine; but from this same spot, he, with his brother St. Just and others, were dragged before the Committee of Public Safety, and thence to the guillotine, and justice and revenge satisfied.

MARIE BASHKIRTSEFF
(1858–1884)

The daughter of Russian nobility, Marie Bashkirtseff spent an itinerant childhood between Germany, the French Riviera, Italy and Paris. As a young woman, she hoped to establish herself as a singer in the French capital. Misdiagnosed tuberculosis damaged her voice, ending that dream. She became a painter instead. Gifted, it seems, in everything she turned her hand to, her paintings were soon accepted into the prestigious Salon. Her talent was just becoming recognized when she died at the age of twenty-five. Today, her reputation rests on the extraordinary journal she kept from adolescence to the end of her life. In these extracts, which are by turns loving and furious, tender and dismissive, romantic and cynical, Bashkirtseff reveals her deep ambivalence towards Paris and Parisian life, as well as her talent for introspection and arresting literary style.

from The Journal of Marie Bashkirtseff

Paris.—At last I have found what I wished for without knowing it. To live means Paris! . . . Paris means to live. I made a martyr of myself because I didn't know what I wanted. Now that I see more clearly, I know what I want. Move from Nice to Paris, furnish a flat, and have horses just as at Nice; to be introduced to society by the ambassador of Russia; this, this it is I want. How happy one is when one knows what one wants! There's something, however, which tortures me; I think I am plain. It's horrible!

We have been to the photographer Valéry, 9, Rue de Londres, and I saw the photograph of G——. How beautiful she is! But in ten years she will be old; in ten years I shall be grown up; I might be handsome if I were taller. I was taken eight times. The photographer said, "If it succeeds this time I shall be satisfied." We left without knowing how it had turned out.

After our last walk in town we arrived in time to take our departure.

A thunderstorm burst overhead; the lightning was terrible. Sometimes it struck the ground in the distance, leaving a silvery furrow in the sky as narrow as a Roman candle.

Paris, Tuesday, August 24th.—I hope to be introduced into society, that society for which I call loudly and on both knees—for it's life, it's happiness. I begin to live and to try and realise my dreams of being celebrated. I am already known to many people. I look at myself in the glass and think myself pretty. What do I want more? O God, in giving me a little beauty (I say little from modesty), it is still more than I deserve, coming from Thee. I feel I am beautiful, and I fancy I shall succeed in everything. The world is full of smiles for me, and I am happy, happy, happy!

The noise of Paris, this hotel as big as a town, with people always walking, talking, reading, smoking, staring, makes me awfully giddy. I love Paris and my heart beats. I want to live faster; yes, faster, faster . . . . "I never saw such a fever of life," D—— said, looking at me. Yes, I fear this desire to live by steam may be the forerunner of a short life. Who knows? Come now, I am growing melancholy. No, I don't want melancholy . . . .

Wednesday, July 5th.—Yesterday, at two o'clock, I left Nice with my aunt and my maid Amelia. Chocolat has hurt his feet, and will be sent on in a couple of days.

Mamma was crying over my departure for three days before I left, so I have been very gentle and affectionate with her.

We reached Paris at half-past one. It must be admitted that if Paris is not the most beautiful of towns, she is, at any rate, the most winning and charming.

Has not Paris also the history of greatness, decay, revolution, glory, and terror? And yet all pales before Rome, for Rome was the mother of all the other nations.

Rome swallowed up Greece, the nursery of civilisation, art, heroes, and poets. As to architecture, sculpture, or thought, which has since been developed, is it aught but imitation of the ancients?

With us there is no originality except in what is mediæval. Oh, why, why is it that the world is *effete*? Is it that the spirit of man has already done all that it is capable of doing?

Wednesday, September 27th.—[. . .] The first touch of cold has forced me to put on my winter furs. Put away as they had been, they kept the scent which they had at Rome; this scent, these furs . . .

Have you ever noticed that you only need a perfume, a sound, a colour, to transport you in fancy to any place whatever? . . . To pass the winter at Paris? Oh no! . . .

Thursday, September 28th.—I am bored till I cry; I want to go away; I am unhappy here. I am losing my time, my life; I am wretched, I am getting mouldy, I suffer, I am *set on edge*. Ah, that's the phrase!

Paris, Saturday, July 7th.—I think I can fairly say that I have become more reasonable, though very recently, and I see things in a tolerably clear light; and have got over many illusions and many vexations.

We only learn true wisdom by personal experience.

Sunday, July 15th.—I am bored to death; so much so indeed that I think there is nothing in the world which can amuse or interest me. I wish for nothing! I want nothing! Ay, I should very much like not to be ashamed of sinking into stupidity. In short, to be able to live without doing anything, or thinking of anything, like a plant, without any remorse of conscience.

Captain B—— has spent the evening with us, and we

talked together; but I am fairly out of conceit with my conversational efforts since I have read what Mme. de Staël says about foreigners imitating the brilliancy of the French. According to her, one must hide in one's hole, and never dare to come in contact with the sublime genius of the French.

Reading, drawing, music, and *ennui, ennui, ennui!* Some living thing is necessary besides occupation and relaxation; and I am bored.

I am not bored because I am a marriageable young lady. No; you have too good an opinion of me to believe that. But I am bored because my life is cross-grained, and because I am bored!

Paris is killing me! It is a café, a well-managed hotel, a bazaar. Well, I can only hope that in the winter, what with the opera, the Bois, and my studies, I shall get used to it.

Friday, April 12*th.*—Yesterday Julian met Robert Fleury at the café, and Robert Fleury said I was a really interesting and surprising pupil, and that he hoped much from my future.

I begin to believe I have a true passion for my art, which reassures and consoles me. I want nothing else, and I am too disgusted with everything to think of anything else.

If it were not for that uneasiness, that fear, I should be happy.

It is quite fine—real spring-time. One feels it as much as one ever can in Paris, where even in the most charming of woods, under the trees, which seem most mysterious and full of poetry, one is sure to find a waiter, with his white apron turned up, and a glass of beer in his hand.

Sunday, October 20th.—I ordered the carriage for nine o'clock, and, accompanied by my maid of honour, Mlle. Elsnitz, I went to see Saint Philippe, Saint Thomas d'Aquin, and Notre Dame. I ascended to the top, and I went to see the bells, just like an English girl. Well! There is a Paris I adore and that is old Paris, and I could be happy there, but only by avoiding the boulevards, the Champs Elysées, all the new and fine quarters, which I abominate, and which irritate me. But over there in the Faubourg Saint Germain you feel quite differently.

We saw the École des Beaux-Arts. It is enough to make one cry.

Why cannot I go and study there? Where can any one get such thorough teaching as there? I went to see the Exhibition of the Prix de Rome. The second prize was won by one of Julian's pupils. Julian is much pleased. If ever I am rich I will found a School of Art for women.

Sunday, December 14th.—Bertha called for me, and, accompanied by Bojidar, we went on foot to explore the Quartier Latin, Place Saint-Sulpice, Rue Mouffetard, Rue de Nevers, the Morgue, Rue des Anglais, &c.

We took the tramway for a quarter of an hour, and then we began walking again; this lasted from three to seven o'clock. There is nothing so adorable as old Paris; it reminds me of Rome and Dumas' novels, and Notre

Dame de Paris with Quasimodo, and a heap of delightful and ancient things.

We have bought some chestnuts at a street corner, and we then spent twenty minutes at a sockseller's, where we spent nearly nine francs, and then at another's, who nearly abused us for beating her down:—"What, Madame, you make a fuss over seven francs, and you do not hesitate to give two hundred francs for a fur cloak!"—I was wearing one worth two thousand francs.

Wednesday, October 13th.—I have always hated Paris physically, always, always! Madrid is much more sympathetic, in spite of its irregular streets and poverty-stricken look, when compared with Paris. Look at Paris! its elegance is wearisome; its shops, its cocottes, its bran-new houses, are all dreadfully anti-artistic. Oh Rome! (and Madrid is a little like it). Oh the South! I come from the South; I was born in the Ukraine, and grew up in Nice. I adore the South.

Saturday, November 5th.—I am in Paris! What boundless delight! I counted the hours while shivering in the train. The grey tones of this fine city are very enjoyable after the exciting air and burning sun of Spain, and I think with satisfaction of the art treasures of the Louvre—I who was bored by the mere thought of them.

Julian thought that I would return much later, and most likely in ill-health, and perhaps never return at all. What a sweet thing is sympathy, but above all things painting.

Paris, Thursday, April 20th.—Well, I don't feel as I did after Spain; I am not enchanted at seeing Paris again, only satisfied . . . Besides, I cannot account for any feeling, I am so disturbed about my work. I tremble to think what will be said, and I am crushed by the remembrance of Breslau, who is treated by the public as a full-fledged artist. I went to see Julian yesterday (we reached Paris yesterday morning), and he no longer treats me as a serious worker—brilliant, yes, but no depth, no will; he would have desired more—he had hoped better things. All that, in the course of conversation, made me feel very bad. I am waiting for him to see my work from Nice, and no longer hope for anything good.

Wednesday, June 25th.—Re-read my diaries of 1875, 1876, and 1877. I complain in them of I know not what; I have aspirations towards something indefinite. Every evening I felt sore and discouraged, spending my strength in fury and despair in trying to find *what to do*. Go to Italy? Stop in Paris? Get married? Paint? What was to be done? If I went to Italy I couldn't be in Paris and I wanted to be everywhere at once!! What vigour there was in it all!!!

As a man, I should have conquered Europe. Young girl as I was, I wasted it in excesses of language and silly eccentricities. Oh, misery!

F. Berkeley Smith
(1869–1931)

Frank Berkeley Smith was destined for an unconventional career. One of his ancestors, Francis Hopkinson, was a lawyer, composer and signatory of the Declaration of Independence. His own father, Francis Hopkinson Smith, was at once a popular author, award-winning painter and a talented engineer who built the foundation for the Statue of Liberty. Frank Berkeley Smith followed in their footsteps by trying his hand at many arts. He trained as an architect before becoming a designer and illustrator. He encountered some success in both. It was as a writer, however, that he truly distinguished himself. His travel books on London, Paris and Budapest proved extremely popular and made him something of a minor literary celebrity. Here he writes with amused affection about fine dining in the French capital.

from How Paris Amuses Itself

In no city in the world are there so many and so varied places to dine as in Paris. One can hardly look right or left from any corner of any street and not find restaurants, from little *boîtes,* where a *plat du jour* and a bottle of wine are to be had for a few sous, to those whose cuisine and rare vintages are adapted only to the well-filled purse of an epicure. There are numberless resorts frequented by the vast army of bohemians, some the rendezvous for students and *grisettes,* others for the poets, the pensive, long-haired devotees of the symbolistic school, and kindred souls in the realm of art. There are those patronized by jolly, devil-may-care young doctors, sleepless night-owls, who discuss till graying dawn their latest operations with a complacent sense of superiority over the other half of the human world, who, they are convinced, without their medical aid would be left as helpless as a mass of struggling white bait in a net. And there, too, buried away in the dingy alleys of Montmartre and fringing the ill-reputed neighborhoods of La Butte and the great Halles, are the feeding places of thieves, reeking from the odor of decaying vegetables and bad cheeses, yet, they say, supplied with some of the rarest wines.

It was a famous French sociologist who declared, from extended personal investigations of the private life of the Parisian mendicants, that the best *champagne brut* he had yet encountered he had found on the dinner tables of professional beggars.

Along the lighted streets and boulevards are the great *brasseries* for Munich beer and German dishes, and the richly decorated taverns, some of them in black oak shining in pewter and ornate with medieval decoration and stained glass. These are swarming with eddies from the passing world until long after midnight. Many of these are the habitual rendezvous of journalists, like the Café Navarin. Others, like the Café des Variétés and the Taverne de la Capitale, are the favorite places for actors, and still others for painters and musicians. There is hardly a resort in Paris which has not its distinct clientèle, from the *buvettes* of the *cochers* to Maxime's.

And of soberer kind are the innumerable, perfectly kept establishments created by Duval and imitated by Boulant. They are big places for small purses; everything is of excellent quality, well cooked, and served by respectable women in spotless white caps and aprons.

There are hundreds of other restaurants besides, with *diners* and *déjeuners* at a *prix fixe,* in which a secondary quality of food is turned into a clever imitation of the best, and where the wine is plain and harmless and included with a course dinner *au choix* for two francs fifty and less. On *fête* days and Sundays these well patronized *petits diners de Paris* are crowded with bourgeois folk: clerks with their sweethearts, *commerçants* and their families, economical bachelors, and others, frugal-minded, from out of Paris who have come into the metropolis to spend a long-anticipated holiday.

And in contrast to all these dining places are the smart restaurants, filled with the correct *grand monde* and the chic *demi-monde*—the Café de Madrid, the Maison Anglaise, Paillard, Arménonville, La Rue, Joseph, Ledoyen, Voisin and the Café de Paris. There are serious old places, such as the Tour d'Argent, plain and unadorned, where all the wealth is in the *casserolles* and the cobwebbed bottles. Then, too, there is the ancient Restaurant Foyot, with its clientèle of senators, academicians and military officers, and the Restaurant La Pérouse on the quay of the Seine, where resort savants and magistrates and others less grave—an old-fashioned place with a narrow stairway leading to quaint, low-ceiled *cabinets particuliers* and excellent things simmering over the kitchen fires below stairs and certain rare old Burgundy lining the walls of the cellar.

Just such a place of seclusion and good cooking is the "Père La Thuille" in Montmartre. It is often a pleasure to dine in a room devoid of gilt and tinsel. The Père La Thuille is restful in this respect. The cuisine is perfect and the wine very old.

At one of the tables in the rectangular dining-room a celebrated diva whose bodice glitters in gems is dining with monsieur, the aged director of a gas company. Several empty tables away another elderly gentleman is filling Mademoiselle Fifi's glass of champagne. Half hidden in another corner of the long leather settee a lady with delicate features and frank, intelligent eyes pours forth her soul and the remainder of a bottle to a well-groomed man at her side. The light from the shaded candles shows more clearly his strong fine hands. Now the little finger of his companion touches his seal ring quite unconsciously, as one would give an accent by a gesture to a confession. For a moment he covers her tiny hand with his own. Poor devil! he must return to his regiment to-morrow and, what is still sadder, the lady is married.

The New York Dairy Lunch, with its mirrored and marbled bathroom decoration, its elevating Bible texts, and depressing "sinkers," and its dyspeptic griddle-cakes cooked in the window, would never make a success with Parisians. One of the most doleful sights I have seen in Paris was a sad-looking gentleman in black sitting at a cold marble-topped table of an expensive *patisserie* lunching on a weak cup of tea and a plate of cream-puffs—*Chacun son goût!*

There exist here, however, "Express Bars" along the boulevards, where by dropping two sous in a slot you are permitted to rob the nickel-plated chicken house installed beneath of any of a dozen different articles, from a *baba au rhum* to a glass of beer. But Parisians stop at these places very much as they would to hear a phonograph, or as French children stop for their *goûter* at four o'clock in the cake shops, or as men and women of all classes drop in for the celebrated fruits in spirits dispensed at the famous solid silver bar of La Mère Moreau.

The French never hurry over dinner. The pleasure of dining must not be spoiled by haste. It is an hour which nothing postpones. If anything serious is to be decided upon, Parisians dine first and then think the matter over. Perhaps after all they are right, for are we not at our best in heart and spirit when we have dined wisely? Anger, hatred, even the green monster jealousy, fade away with the progress of a good dinner.

Into the Restaurant Weber comes an old *bon-vivant* growling. He stands for a brief moment surveying the tables, chooses one of the few unoccupied ones and plants himself savagely in front of the snow-white cloth. "The devil!" he mutters to himself. "She'll get my letter to-morrow. *Bon Dieu!* to think I have been imbecile enough to trust her!"

"Has monsieur le comte ordered?" interrupted quietly the *maître d'hôtel* Léon.

The count glowers over the menu.

"Some *filets de hareng saurs*"

"*Parfaitement, monsieur*," replies Léon, and he repeats the order to a waiter.

There follows a pause, during which the count's irate eye (the one not occupied with his monocle) wanders absently over the list.

"Perhaps monsieur would like an excellent purée of peas to follow?" Léon naïvely suggests.

"*Bon!*" gruffly accepts the comte. "And a *homard*, and a roast partridge with a good salad, and a bottle of Veuve Clicquot, '93," adds the count.

"*Bien, monsieur*, I will season the salad myself." And Léon, with an authoritative gesture, claps his hands twice, stirring into increased activity the already alert waiters, gives a final touch to the appointments of the count's table, and hurries off to attend to another dinner, a jolly party of four who need no further cheering up.

"She has the innocent eyes of a child when she lies!" mutters the count, returning to his thoughts.

But the tiny *filets de hareng*, with their tang of the sea, sharpen his appetite, and the wine quiets his nerves and refreshes his brain, and the purée warms him and the lobster steaming in its thick, spicy sauce cheers him. The hatred within him is growing less. That lump of jealousy buried so deep half an hour ago has so diminished that, when the fat little partridge arrives, garnished and sunk in its nest of fresh watercress, this gives the fatal *coup* to ill humor. Again the champagne is rattled out of its cooler. Léon, whose watchful eye is everywhere and whose intuition tells him when a patron wishes to talk, now comes to the count's table.

The count has by this time become the soul of good humor. He compliments Léon on the dinner and Léon compliments him on his taste in selection of viands, and so they talk on until Léon goes himself for a special liqueur.

The count gazes peacefully on those about him and admires, with the critical eye of a connoisseur of beauty, the pretty woman at the corner table. Silent waiters lay the fresh cloth and bring him an extensive choice of Havanas. All these final accessories have little by little taken away the remnants of his ill feeling. He puffs reminiscently at his cigar. His very spirit of revenge seems to have been steamed, sautéed and grilled out of him. Now he takes from his waistcoat pocket a thin gold watch—the one he bought at a round sum in Geneva years ago and which has been faithfully ticking away the seconds of his turbulent life so long that he has come to regard it somewhat with awe, as one would the change from his last dollar.

The delicate hands have crept to nine o'clock and two tiny bells within strike the hour. The count writes upon his visiting card a short line, seals it in its envelope, calls the *chasseur* and, giving him the note, directs: "Stop on your way at Véton's for the red roses."

Ah, mesdames et messieurs, how many of your little troubles have been settled by the doctor with the *cordon bleu* and the shining saucepans!

PARIS, LOVE, LOVERS,
AND THE LONELY

HONORÉ DE BALZAC
(1799–1850)

Born into a family where hard work was expected, Balzac toiled over his books with a feverish passion. He would confine himself to a sparsely furnished room where, dressed in a large cloak like a monk's cassock and fuelled by heroic quantities of coffee, he wrote through the night. The result – his vast fictional edifice, *The Human Comedy* – helped change the course of literature. It moved fiction away from abstract settings and fixed social situations to a close attention on the concrete facts of an unfolding modernity. His other obsessions ended less happily: the get-rich-quick schemes that invariably failed, the heavy foods in which he overindulged, the pretensions to aristocracy that made him appear slightly ridiculous to even his most passionate admirers. But Balzac himself didn't seem to care. By his own admission, the crowning achievements of his life were his *Human Comedy* and his marriage to a Polish noblewoman, Ewelina Hańska, who first contacted the author as a devoted anonymous reader. Best known today for long page-turners like *Lost Illusions*, this great fresco painter was also an incomparable miniaturist, as one of Balzac's biggest fans, Marcel Proust, put it. In this short story, Balzac writes teasingly about the foibles of Parisian *savants*.

from A Street of Paris and its Inhabitant

PHYSIOGNOMY OF THE STREET

Paris has curved streets, streets that are serpentine. It counts, perhaps, only the Rue Boudreau in the Chaussée d'Antin and the Rue Duguay-Trouin near the Luxembourg as streets shaped exactly like a T-square. The Rue Duguay-Trouin extends one of its two arms to the Rue d'Assas and the other to the Rue de Fleurus.

In 1827 the Rue Duguay-Trouin was paved neither on one side nor on the other; it was lighted neither at its angle nor at its ends. Perhaps it is not, even to-day, paved or lighted. In truth, this street has so few houses, or the houses are so modest, that one does not see them; the city's forgetfulness of them is explained, then, by their little importance.

Lack of solidity in the soil is a reason for that state of things. The street is situated on a point of the Catacombs so dangerous that a portion of the road disappeared recently, leaving an excavation to the astonished eyes of the scarce inhabitants of that corner of Paris.

A great clamor arose in the newspapers about it. The government corked up the "Fontis"—such is the name of that territorial bankruptcy—and the gardens that border the street, destitute of passers-by, were reassured the more easily because the tax list did not weigh on them.

The arm of the street that extends to the Rue de Fleurus is entirely occupied, at the left, by a wall on the top of which shine broken bottles and iron lances fixed in the plaster—a sort of warning to hands of lovers and of thieves.

In this wall is a door, the famous little garden door, so necessary to dramas and to novels, which is beginning to disappear from Paris.

This door, painted in dark green, having an invisible lock, and on which the tax collector had not yet painted a number; this wall, along which grow thistles and grass with beaded blades; this street, with furrows made by the wheels of wagons; other walls gray and crowned with foliage, are in harmony with the silence that reigns in the Luxembourg, in the convent of the Carmelites, in the gardens of the Rue de Fleurus.

If you went there, you would ask yourself, "Who can possibly live here?"

Who? Wait and see.

II

Silhouette of the Inhabitant

One day, about three in the afternoon, that door was opened. Out of it came a little old man, fat, provided with an abdomen heavy and projecting which obliges him to make many sacrifices. He has to wear trousers excessively wide, not to be troubled in walking. He has renounced, long ago, the use of boots and trouser straps. He wears shoes. His shoes were hardly polished.

The waistcoat, incessantly impelled to the upper part of the gastric cavities by that great abdomen, and depressed by the weight of two thoracic bumps that would make the happiness of a thin woman, offers to the pleasantries of the passers-by a perfect resemblance to a napkin rolled on the knees of a guest absorbed in discussion at dessert.

The legs are thin, the arm is long, one of the hands is gloved only on most solemn occasions and the other hand ignores absolutely the advantage of a second skin.

That personage avoids the alms and the pity that his venerable green frock coat invites, by wearing the red ribbon at his button-hole. This proves the utility of the Order of the Legion of Honor which has been contested too much in the past ten years, the new Knights of the Order say.

The battered hat, in a constant state of horror in the places where a reddish fuzz endures, would not be picked up by the rag picker, if the little old man let it fall and left it at a street corner.

Too absent minded to submit to the bother that the wearing of a wig entails, that man of science—he is a man of science—shows, when he makes a bow, a head that, viewed from the top, has the appearance of the Farnese Hercules's knee.

Above each ear, tufts of twisted white hair shine in the sun like the angry silken hairs of a boar at bay. The neck is athletic and recommends itself to the notice of caricaturists by an infinity of wrinkles, of furrows; by a dewlap faded but armed with darts in the fashion of thistles.

The constant state of the beard explains at once why the necktie, always crumpled and rolled by the gestures of a disquiet head, has its own beard, infinitely softer than that of the good old man, and formed of threads scratched from its unfortunate tissue.

Now, if you have divined the torso and the powerful back, you will know the sweet tempered face, somewhat pale, the blue ecstatic eyes and the inquisitive nose of that good old man, when you learn that, in the morning, wearing a silk head kerchief and tightened in a dressing-gown, the illustrious professor—he is a professor—resembled an old woman so much that a young man who came from the depths of Saxony, of Weimar, or of Prussia, expressly to see him, said to him, "Forgive me, Madame!" and withdrew.

This silhouette of one of the most learned and most venerated members of the Institute betrays so well enthusiasm for study and absent-mindedness caused by application to the quest of truth, that you must recognize in it the celebrated Professor Jean Népomucène Apollodore Marmus de Saint-Leu, one of the most admirable men of genius of our time.

MADAME ADOLPHE

When the old man—the professor counted then sixty-two summers—had walked three steps, he turned his head at this question, hurled in an acute tone by a voice that he recognized:

"Have you a handkerchief?"

A woman stood on the step of the garden door and was watching her master with solicitude.

She seemed to be fifty years of age, and her dress indicated that she was one of those servants who are invested with full authority in household affairs.

She was darning stockings.

The man of science came back and said naïvely:

"Yes, Madame Adolphe, I have my handkerchief."

"Have you your spectacles?" she asked.

The man of science felt the side pocket of his waistcoat.

"I have them," he replied.

"Show them to me," she said. "Often you have only the case."

The professor took the case out of his pocket and showed the spectacles with a triumphant air.

"You would do well to keep them on your nose," she said.

M. de Saint-Leu put on his spectacles, after rubbing the glasses with his handkerchief.

Naturally, he thrust the handkerchief under his left arm while he set his spectacles on his nose. Then he walked a few steps towards the Rue de Fleurus and relaxed his hold on the handkerchief, which fell.

"I was sure of it," said Madame Adolphe to herself. She picked up the handkerchief and cried:

"Monsieur! Monsieur!"

"Well!" exclaimed the professor, made indignant by her watchfulness.

"I beg your pardon," he said, receiving the handkerchief.

"Have you money?" asked Madame Adolphe with maternal solicitude.

"I need none," he replied naïvely, explaining thus the lives of all men of science.

"It depends," Madame Adolphe said. "If you go by way of the Pont des Arts you need one sou."

"You are right," replied the man of science, as if he were retracing instructions for a voyage to the North Pole. "I will go through the Luxembourg, the Rue de Seine, the Pont des Arts, the Louvre, the Rue du Coq, the Rue Croix-des-Petits-Champs, the Rue des Fossés-Montmartre. It is the shortest route to the Faubourg Poissonnière."

"It is three o'clock," Madame Adolphe said. "Your sister-in-law dines at six. You have three hours before you—Yes—you'll be there, but you'll be late." She searched her apron pocket for two sous, which she handed to the professor.

"Very well, then," she said to him. "Do not eat too much. You are not a glutton, but you think of other things. You are frugal, but you eat when you are absent-minded as if you had no bread at home. Take care not to make Madame Vernet, your sister-in-law, wait. If you make her wait, you will never be permitted again to go there alone, and it will be shameful for you."

Madame Adolphe returned to the threshold of the little door and from there watched her master. She had to cry to him, "To the right! To the right!" for he was turning toward the Rue Notre-Dame-des-Champs.

"And yet he is a man of science, people say," she muttered to herself. "How did he ever manage to get married? I'll ask Madame when I dress her hair."

IV

Inconvenience of Quays Where are Book Stalls

At four o'clock, Professor Marmus was at the end of the Rue de Seine, under the arcades of the Institute. Those who know him will admit that he had done nobly, since he had taken only one hour to go through the Luxembourg and down the Rue de Seine.

There a lamentable voice, the voice of a child, plucked from the good man the two sous that Madame Adolphe had given to him. When he reached the Pont des Arts he remembered that he had to pay toll and turned back suddenly to beg for a sou from the child.

The little rascal had gone to break the coin, in order to give only one sou to his mother. She was walking up and down the Rue Mazarine with her baby at her breast.

It became necessary for the professor to turn his

back on the veteran soldier who guards against the possibility of a Parisian passing over the bridge without paying toll.

Two roads were open to him: the Pont Neuf and the Pont Royal. Curiosity attracted the man of science to the Pont Royal. Curiosity makes one lose more time in Paris than anywhere else.

How may one walk without looking at those little oblong boxes, wide as the stones of the parapet, that all along the quays stimulate book lovers with posters saying, "Four Sous—Six Sous—Ten Sous—Twelve Sous—Thirty Sous?" These catacombs of glory have devoured many hours that belonged to the poets, to the philosophers and to the men of science of Paris.

Great is the number of ten-sous pieces spent in the four-sous stalls!

The professor saw a pamphlet by Vicq-d'Azyr, a complete Charles Bonnet in the edition of Fauche Borel, and an essay on Malus.

"And such then is the sum of our achievements," he said to himself. "Malus! A genius arrested in his course when he had almost captured the empire of light! But we have had Fresnel. Fresnel has done excellent things!—Oh, they will recognize some day that light is only a mode of substance."

The professor held the notice on Malus. He turned its pages. He had known Malus. He recalled to himself and recited the names of all the Maluses. Then he returned to Malus, to his dear Malus, for they had entered the Institute together at the return to Paris of the expedition to Egypt. Ah! It was then the Institute of France and not a mass of disunited Academies.

"The Emperor had preserved," said Marmus to himself, "the saintly idea of the Convention. I remember," he muttered aloud, "what he said to me when I was presented to him as a member of the Institute. Napoleon the First said, 'Marmus, I am the Emperor of the French, but you are the King of the infinitely little and you will organize them as I have organized the Empire.' Ah, he was a very great man and a man of wit! The French appreciated this too late."

The professor replaced Malus and the essay on him in the ten-sous stall, without remarking how often hope had been lit and extinguished alternately in the gray eyes of an old woman seated on a stool in an angle of the quay.

"He was there," Marmus said, pointing to the Tuileries on the opposite bank of the river. "I saw him reviewing his sublime troops! I saw him thin, ardent as the sands of Egypt; but, as soon as he became Emperor, he grew fat and good natured, for all fat men are excellent—this is why Sinard is thin, he is a gall-making machine. But would Napoleon have supported my theory?"

V

First Course

It was the hour at which they went to the dinner table in the house of Marmus's sister-in-law. The professor walked slowly toward the Chamber of Deputies, asking himself if his theory might have had Napoleon's support. He could no longer judge Napoleon save from that point of view. Did Napoleon's genius coincide with that of Marmus in regard to the assimilation of things engendered by an attraction perpetual and continuous?

<h1 style="text-align:center">VI</h1>

SECOND COURSE

No, Baron Sinard was a worshipper of power. He would have gone to the Emperor and told him that my theory was the inspiration of an atheist. And Napoleon, who has done a great deal of religious sermonizing for political reasons, would have persecuted me. He had no love for ideas. He was a courtier of facts! Moreover, in Napoleon's time, it would not have been possible for me to communicate freely with Germany. Would they have lent me their aid–Wytheimler, Grosthuys, Scheele, Stambach, Wagner?

"To make men of science agree—men of science agree!—the Emperor should have made peace; in time of peace, perhaps, he would have taken an interest in my quarrel with Sinard! Sinard, my friend, my pupil, become my antagonist, my enemy! He, a man of genius—

"Yes, he is a man of genius. I do justice to him in the face of all the world."

At this moment the professor could talk aloud without trouble to himself or to the passers-by. He was near the Chamber of Deputies, the session was closed, all Paris was at dinner—except the man of science.

Marmus was haranguing the statues which, it must be conceded, are similar to all audiences. In France there is not an audience that is not prohibited from giving marks of approval or disapproval. Otherwise, there is not an audience that would not turn orator.

At the Iena bridge Marmus had a pain in the stomach. He heard the hoarse voice of a cab driver. Marmus thought that he was ill and let himself be ushered into the cab. He made himself comfortable in it.

When the driver asked, "Where?" Marmus replied quietly:

"Home."

"Where is your home, Monsieur?" asked the driver.

"Number three," Marmus replied.

"What street?" asked the driver.

"Ah, you are right, my friend. But this is extraordinary," he said, taking the driver into his confidence. "I have been so busy comparing the hyoides and the caracoides—yes, that's it. I will catch Sinard in the act. At the next session of the Institute he will have to yield to evidence."

The driver wrapped his ragged cloak around him. Resignedly, he was saying to himself, "I have seen many odd folks, but this one—" He heard the word "Institute."

"The Institute, Monsieur?" he asked.

"Yes, my friend, the Institute," replied Marmus.

"Well he wears the red ribbon," said the driver to

himself. "Perhaps he has something to do with the Institute."

The professor, infinitely more comfortable in his cab than on the sidewalk, devoted himself entirely to solving the problem that went against his theory and would not surrender—the rascal! The cab stops at the Institute; the janitor sees the Academician and bows to him respectfully. The cab driver, his suspicions dispelled, talks with the janitor of the Institute while the illustrious professor goes—at eight in the evening—to the Académie des Sciences.

The cab driver tells the janitor where he found his fare.

"At the Iena bridge," repeats the janitor. "M. Marmus was coming back from Passy. He had dined, doubtless, with M. Planchette, one of his friends of the Academy."

"He couldn't tell me his address," says the cab driver.

"He lives in the Rue Duguay-Trouin, Number three," says the janitor.

"What a neighborhood!" exclaims the driver.

"My friend," asks of the janitor the professor who had found the door shut, "is there no meeting of the Academy to-day?"

"To-day!" exclaims the janitor. "At this hour!"

"What is the time?" asks the man of science.

"About eight o'clock," the janitor replies.

"It is late" comments M. Marmus. "Take me home, driver."

The driver goes through the quays, the Rue du Bac, falls into a tangle of wagons, returns by the Rue de Grenelle, the Croix-Rouge, the Rue Cassette, then he makes a mistake. He tries to find the Rue d'Assas, in the Rue Honoré-Chevalier, in the Rue Madame, in all the impossible streets and, swearing that if he had known he would not have come so far for a hundred sous, disembarks the professor in the Rue Duguay-Trouin.

The cab driver claims an hour, for the police ordinances, that defend consumers of time in cabs from the stratagems of cab drivers, had not yet posted the walls of Paris with their protecting articles that settle in advance all difficulties.

"Very well, my friend," says M. Marmus to the cab driver. "Pay him," M. Marmus says to Madame Adolphe. "I do not feel well, my child."

"Monsieur, what did I tell you?" she exclaimed. "You have eaten too much. While you were away, I said to myself, 'It is Mme. Vernet's birthday. They will urge him at table and he will come back sick.' Well, go to bed. I will make camomile tea for you."

VII
DESSERT

The professor walked through the garden into a pavilion at one of its corners, where he lived alone in order not to be disturbed by his wife.

He went up the stairway leading to his little room,

and complained so much of his pains in the stomach that Madame Adolphe filled him with camomile tea.

"Ah, here is a carriage! It is Madame returning in great anxiety, I am sure," said Madame Adolphe, giving to the professor his sixth cup of camomile tea. "Now, sir, I hope that you will be able to drink it without me. Do not let it fall all over your bed. You know how Madame would laugh. You are very happy to have a little wife who is so amiable and so joyful."

"Say nothing to her, my child," exclaimed the professor, whose features expressed a sort of childish fear.

The truly great man is always more or less a child.

VIII
THIS SHOWS THAT THE WIFE OF A MAN OF SCIENCE IS VERY UNHAPPY

"Well, good-bye. Return in the cab, it is paid for," Madame Marmus was saying when Madame Adolphe arrived at the door.

The cab had already turned around the corner. Madame Adolphe, not having seen Madame Marmus's escort, said to herself:

"Poor Madame! He must be her nephew."

Madame Marmus, a little woman, lithe, graceful, mirthful, was divinely dressed and in a fashion too young for her age, counting her twenty-five years as a wife. Nevertheless, she wore well a gown with small pink stripes, a cape embroidered and edged with lace, boots pretty as the wings of a butterfly. She carried in her hand a pink hat with peach flowers.

"You see, Madame Adolphe," she said, "my hair is all uncurled. I told you that in this hot weather it should be dressed in bandeaux."

"Madame," the servant replied, "Monsieur is very sick. You let him eat too much."

"What could I do?" Madame Marmus replied. "He was at one end of the table and I at the other. He returned without me, as his habit is! Poor little man! I will go to him as soon as I change my dress."

Madame Adolphe returns to the pavilion to propose an emetic, and scolds the professor for not having returned with Madame Marmus.

"Since you wished to come in a cab, you might have spared me the expense of the one that Madame Marmus took. The charge for your cab was an hour. Did you stop anywhere?"

"At the Institute," he replied.

"At the Institute! Where did you take the cab?" she asked.

"In front of a bridge, I think," he replied.

"Was it still daylight?" she asked.

"Almost," he said.

"Then you did not go to Madame Vernet's!" exclaimed Madame Adolphe.

"Why did you not come to Madame Vernet's?" asked his wife.

Madame Marmus, having come to the door on the tips of her toes, had heard Madame Adolphe's exclamation. She did not wish to see Madame Adolphe's astonishment. Surely Madame Adolphe could not have forgotten the assurance with which the professor's wife had placed him in imagination at Madame Vernet's table.

"My dear child, I do not know," said the professor in a repentant tone.

"Then you have not dined," said Madame Marmus, whose attitude remained that of the purest innocence.

"With what could he have dined, Madame? He had two sous," said Madame Adolphe, looking at Madame Marmus with an accusing air.

"Ah, I am truly to be pitied, my poor Madame Adolphe," said Madame Marmus. "This sort of thing has been going on for twenty years, and I am not yet accustomed to it. Six days after our wedding, we were going out of our room one morning to take breakfast. M. Marmus hears the drum of the Polytechnic School pupils of whom he was the professor. He quits me to go and see them pass. I was nineteen years of age and when I pouted, you cannot guess what he said to me. He said, 'These young people are the flower and the glory of France!' This is how my marriage began. You can judge of the rest."

"Oh, Monsieur, is it possible?" asked Madame Adolphe with an indignant air.

"I have cornered Sinard!" exclaimed M. Marmus triumphantly.

"Oh, he would let himself die!" exclaimed Madame Adolphe.

"Get something for him to eat," said Madame Marmus. "He would let himself do anything. Ah, my good Madame Adolphe, a man of science, you see, is a man who knows nothing—of life."

The malady was cured by a cataplasm of Italian cheese that the man of science ate without knowing what he was eating, for he held Sinard in a corner—

"Poor Madame," said the kind Madame Adolphe, "I pity you. He was really so absent-minded as that!"

And Madame Adolphe forgot the strange avowal of her mistress.

EUGÈNE FRANÇOIS VIDOCQ
(1775–1857)

A career criminal turned police informant, Vidocq rose from felonious infamy and low-level double-crossings to head a major section of the French police, eventually going on to found what was perhaps the world's first private detective agency. Today, he is also thought to be one of the founders of modern criminology. His contemporaries, however, saw Vidocq as a perfect paradox. His double career on both sides of the law may have inspired Jean Valjean *and* Javert in Hugo's *Les Misérables*, as well as Balzac's diabolical criminal mastermind Vautrin, along with countless other fictional figures. Vidocq was also a memoirist and author in his own right (though much of his work was likely penned with the help of a ghost-writer). Here, he writes with a connoisseur's eye about some of the finer aspects of Parisian delinquency.

from Jean Monette

At the time when I first became commissary of police, my arrondissement was in that part of Paris which includes the Rue St. Antoine—a street which has a great number of courts, alleys, and culs-de-sac issuing from it in all directions. The houses in these alleys and courts are, for the most part, inhabited by wretches wavering betwixt the last shade of poverty and actual starvation, ready to take part in any disturbance, or assist in any act of rapine or violence.

In one of these alleys, there lived at that time a man named Jean Monette, who was tolerably well stricken in years, but still a hearty man. He was a widower, and, with an only daughter, occupied a floor, au quatrième, in one of the courts; people said he had been in business and grown rich, but that he had not the heart to spend his money, which year after year accumulated, and would make a splendid fortune for his daughter at his death. With this advantage, Emma, who was really a handsome girl, did not want for suitors, and thought that, being an heiress, she might wait till she really felt a reciprocal passion for some one, and not throw herself away upon the first tolerable match that presented itself. It was on a Sunday, the first in the month of June, that Emma had, as an especial treat, obtained sufficient money from her father for an excursion with some friends to see the fountains of Versailles.

It was a beautiful day, and the basin was thronged around with thousands and thousands of persons, looking, from the variety of their dresses, more like the colors of a splendid rainbow than aught besides; and when, at four o'clock, Triton and his satellites threw up their immense volumes of water, all was wonder, astonishment, and delight; but none were more delighted than Emma, to whom the scene was quite new.

And, then, it was so pleasant to have found a gentleman who could explain everything and everybody; point out the duke of this, and the count that, and the other lions of Paris; besides, such an agreeable and well-dressed man; it was really quite condescending in him to notice them! And then, toward evening, he would insist they should all go home together in a fiacre, and that he alone should pay all the expenses, and when, with a gentle pressure of the hand and a low whisper, he begged her to say where he might come and throw himself at her feet, she thought her feelings were different to what they had ever been before. But how could she give her address—tell so dashing a man that she lived in such a place? No, she could not do that, but she would meet him at the Jardin d'Eté next Sunday evening, and dance with no one else all night.

She met him on the Sunday, and again and again, until her father began to suspect, from her frequent absence of an evening—which was formerly an unusual circumstance with her—that something must be wrong. The old man loved his money, but he loved his daughter more. She was the only link in life that kept together the chain of his affections. He had been passionately fond of his wife, and when she died, Emma had filled up the void in his heart. They were all, save his money, that he had ever loved. The world had cried out against him as a hard-hearted, rapacious man, and he, in return, despised the world.

He was, therefore, much grieved at her conduct, and questioned Emma as to where her frequent visits led her, but could only obtain for answer that she was not aware she had been absent so much as to give him uneasiness. This was unsatisfactory, and so confirmed the old man in his suspicions that he determined to have his daughter watched.

This he effected through the means of an ancien ami, then in the profession of what he called an "inspector," though his enemies (and all men have such) called him a mouchard, or spy. However, by whatever name he called himself, or others called him, he understood his business, and so effectually watched the young lady that he discovered her frequent absences to be for the purpose of meeting a man who, after walking some distance with her, managed, despite the inspector's boasted abilities, to give him the slip.

This naturally puzzled him, and so it would any man in his situation. Fancy the feelings of one of the government's employees in the argus line of business, a man renowned for his success in almost all the arduous and intricate affairs that had been committed to his care, to find himself baffled in a paltry private intrigue, and one which he had merely undertaken for the sake of friendship!

For a second time, he tried the plan of fancying himself to be well paid, thinking this would stimulate his dormant energies, knowing well that a thing done for friendship's sake is always badly done; but even here he failed. He watched them to a certain corner, but, before he could get around it, they were nowhere to be seen. This was not to be borne. It was setting him at defiance. Should he call in the assistance of a brother in the line? No, that would be to acknowledge himself beaten, and the disgrace he could not bear—his honor was concerned, and he would achieve it single handed; but, then, it was very perplexing.

The man, to his experienced eye, seemed not, as he had done to Emma, a dashing gentleman, but more like a foul bird in fine feathers. Something must be wrong, and he must find it out—but, then, again came that confounded question, how?

He would go and consult old Monette—he could, perhaps, suggest something; and, musing on the strangeness of the adventure, he walked slowly toward the house of the old man to hold a council with him on the situation.

On the road, his attention was attracted by a disturbance in the street, and mingling with the crowd, in hope of seizing some of his enemies exercising their illegal functions on whom the whole weight of his official vengeance might fall, he for the time forgot his adventure. The crowd had been drawn together by a difference of opinion between two gentlemen of the vehicular profession, respecting some right of way, and, after all the usual expressions of esteem common on such occasions had been exhausted, one of them drove off, leaving the other at least master of the field, if he had not got the expected job.

The crowd began to disperse, and with them also was going our friend, the detective, when, on turning round, he came in contact with Mlle. Monette, leaning on the arm of her mysterious lover. The light from a lamp above his head shone immediately on the face of Emma and her admirer, showing them both as clear as noonday, so that when his glance turned from the lady to the gentleman, and he obtained a full view of his face, he expressed his joy at the discovery by a loud "Whew!" which, though a short sound and soon pronounced, meant a great deal.

For first, it meant that he had made a great discovery; secondly, that he was not now astonished because he had not succeeded before in his watchfulness; thirdly—but perhaps the two mentioned may be sufficient; for, turning sharply round, he made the greatest haste to reach Monette and inform him, this time, of the result of his espionage.

After a long prelude, stating how fortunate Monette was to have such a friend as himself, a man who knew everybody and everything, he proceeded to inform him of the pleasing intelligence that his daughter was in the habit of meeting, and going to some place (he forgot to say where) with the most desperate and abandoned character in Paris—one who was so extremely dexterous in all his schemes that the police, though perfectly aware of his intentions, had not been able to fix upon him the commission of any one of his criminal acts, for he changed his appearance so often as to set at naught all the assiduous exertions of the Corps des Espions.

The unhappy father received from his friend at parting the assurance that they would catch him yet, and give him an invitation to pass the rest of his days in the seclusion of a prison.

On Emma's return, he told her the information he had received, wisely withholding the means from which his knowledge came, saying that he knew she had that moment parted from a man who would lead her to the brink of destruction, and then cast her off like a child's broken plaything. He begged, nay, he besought her, with tears in his eyes, to promise she would never again see him. Emma was thunderstruck, not only at the accuracy of her father's information, but at hearing such a character of one whom she had painted as perfection's self; and, calling to her aid those never-failing woman's arguments, a copious flood of tears, fell on her father's neck and promised never again to see her admirer and, if possible, to banish all thoughts of him from her mind.

"My child," said the old man, "I believe you from my heart—I believe you. I love you, but the world says I am rich—why, I know not. You know I live in a dangerous neighborhood, and all my care will be necessary to prevent my losing either my child or my reputed wealth;

therefore, to avoid all accidents, I will take care you do not leave this house for the next six months to come, and in that time your lover will have forgotten you, or what will amount to the same thing, you will have forgotten him; but I am much mistaken if the man's intentions are not to rob me of my money, rather than my child."

The old man kept his word, and Emma was not allowed for several days to leave the rooms on the fourth floor.

She tried, during the time, if it were possible to forget the object of her affections, and thought if she could but see him once more, to bid him a long and last farewell, she might in time wear out his remembrance from her heart; but in order to do that, she must see him once more; and having made up her mind that this interview would be an essential requisite to the desired end, she took counsel with herself how it was to be accomplished. There was only one great obstacle presenting itself to her view, which was that "she couldn't get out."

Now women's invention never fails them, when they have set their hearts upon any desired object; and it occurred to her, that although she could not get out, yet it was not quite so apparent that he could not get in; and this point being settled, it was no very difficult matter to persuade the old woman who occasionally assisted her in the household arrangements, to be the bearer of a short note, purporting to say that her father having been unwell for the last few days, usually retired early to rest, and that if her dear Despreau would come about eleven o'clock on the following evening, her father would be asleep, and she would be on the watch for a signal, which was to be three gentle taps on the door.

The old woman executed her commission so well that she brought back an answer vowing eternal fidelity, and promising a punctual attendance at the rendezvous. Nor was it likely that he meant to fail—seeing it was the object he had had for months in view, and he reasoned with himself that if he once got there, he would make such good use of his time as to render a second visit perfectly unnecessary.

Therefore it would be a pity to disappoint any one, and he immediately communicated his plans to two of his confederates, promising them a good share of the booty, and also the girl herself, if either of them felt that way inclined, as a reward for their assistance.

His plans were very well managed, and would have gone on exceedingly well, but for one small accident which happened through the officious interference of the inspector, who, the moment he had discovered who the Lothario was, had taken all the steps he could to catch him, and gain the honor of having caught so accomplished a gentleman. He rightly judged that it would not be long before he would pay a visit to Monette's rooms, and the letters, before their delivery by the old woman, had been read by him, and met with his full approbation.

I was much pleased on being informed by the inspector that he wanted my assistance, one evening, to apprehend the celebrated Despreau, who had planned a robbery near the Rue St. Antoine, and make me acquainted with nearly all the circumstances. So, about half past ten o'clock, I posted myself with the inspector and four men where I could see Despreau pass, and at eleven o'clock, punctual to the moment, he and his two associates began to ascend the stairs.

The two confederates were to wait some time, when he was to come to the door on some pretext and let them in.

After the lapse of half an hour they were let in, when we ascended after them, and the inspector, having a duplicate key, we let ourselves gently in, standing in the passage, so as to prevent our being seen; in a few minutes we heard a loud shriek from Emma, and old Monette's voice most vociferously crying "Murder!" and "Thieves!" On entering the rooms, we perceived that the poor girl was lying on the ground, while one of the men was endeavoring to stifle her cries by either gagging or suffocating her, though in the way he was doing it, the latter would have soon been the case.

The old man had been dragged from his bed, and Despreau stood over him with a knife, swearing that unless he showed him the place where his money and valuables were deposited, it should be the last hour of his existence.

Despreau, on seeing us, seemed inclined to make a most desperate resistance, but not being seconded by his associates, submitted to be pinioned, expressing his regret that we had not come half an hour later, when we might have been saved the trouble.

Despreau was shortly after tried for the offense, which was too clearly proved to admit of any doubt. He was sentenced to the galleys for life, and is now at Brest, undergoing his sentence. Emma, soon afterward, married a respectable man, and old Monette behaved on the occasion much more liberally than was expected.

GUY DE MAUPASSANT
(1850–1893)

The literary-minded son of wealthy Norman bourgeois, Maupassant had the early good luck of falling under the protection of one of the world's great novelists, Gustave Flaubert. The author of *Madame Bovary* helped train Maupassant's eye and instilled in him a passion for rigorously controlled expression, a hatred of hypocrisy and a ferocious commitment to his art. These served as the foundation for the nearly 300 short stories that Maupassant penned in his relatively brief lifetime and that have since earned him worldwide fame as a master of the swift, cutting yarn. In this characteristic tale, Maupassant shows off his gleeful eye for bitter ironies by describing a provincial Frenchwoman who, starved of excitement and filled with clichéd ideas about Parisian life, embarks on a romantic adventure.

An Adventure in Paris

Is there any stronger feeling than curiosity in a woman? Oh! Fancy seeing, knowing, touching what one has dreamt about! What would a woman not do for that? When once a woman's eager curiosity is aroused, she will be guilty of any folly, commit any imprudence, venture upon anything, and recoil from nothing. I am speaking of women who are really women, who are endowed with that triple-bottomed disposition, which appears to be reasonable and cold on the surface, but whose three secret compartments are filled. The first, with female uneasiness, which is always in a state of flutter; the next, with sly tricks which are colored in imitation of good faith, with those sophistical and formidable tricks of apparently devout women; and the last, with all those charming, improper acts, with that delightful deceit, exquisite perfidy, and all those wayward qualities, which drive lovers who are stupidly credulous, to suicide; but which delight others.

The woman whose adventure I am about to relate, was a little person from the provinces, who had been insipidly chaste till then. Her life, which was apparently so calm, was spent at home, with a busy husband and two children, whom she brought up like an irreproachable woman. But her heart beat with unsatisfied curiosity, and some unknown longing. She was continually thinking of Paris, and read the fashionable papers eagerly. The accounts of parties, of the dresses and various entertainments, excited her longing; but, above all, she was strangely agitated by those paragraphs which were full of double meaning, by those veils which were half raised by clever phrases, and which gave her a glimpse of culpable and ravishing delights, and from her country home, she saw Paris in an apotheosis of magnificent and corrupt luxury.

And during the long nights, when she dreamt, lulled by the regular snores of her husband, who was sleeping on his back by her side, with a silk handkerchief tied round his head, she saw in her sleep those well-known men whose names appeared on the first page of the newspapers as great stars in the dark skies; and she pictured to herself their life of continual excitement, of constant debauches, of orgies such as they indulged in in ancient Rome, which were horridly voluptuous, with refinements of sensuality which were so complicated that she could not even picture them to herself.

The boulevards seemed to her to be a kind of abyss of human passions, and there could be no doubt that the houses there concealed mysteries of prodigious love. But she felt that she was growing old, and this, without having known life, except in those regular, horridly monotonous, every-day occupations, which constitute the happiness of the home. She was still pretty, for she was well preserved in her tranquil existence, like some winter fruit in a closed cupboard; but she was agitated and devoured by her secret ardor. She used to ask herself whether she should die without having experienced any of those damning, intoxicating joys, without having plunged once, just once into that flood of Parisian voluptuousness.

By dint of much perseverance, she paved the way for a journey to Paris, found a pretext, got some relations to invite her, and as her husband could not go with her, she went alone, and as soon as she arrived, she invented a reason for remaining for two days, or rather for two nights, if necessary, as she told him that she had met some friends who lived a little way out of town.

And then she set out on a voyage of discovery. She went up and down the boulevards, without seeing anything except roving and numbered vice. She looked into the large *cafés,* and read the *Agony Column* of the *Figaro,* which every morning seemed to her like a tocsin, a summons to love. But nothing put her on the track of those orgies of actors and actresses; nothing revealed to her those temples of debauchery which she imagined opened at some magic word, like the cave in the *Arabian Nights,* or those catacombs in Rome, where the mysteries of a persecuted religion were secretly celebrated.

Her relations, who were quite middle-class people, could not introduce her to any of those well-known men with whose names her head was full, and in despair she was thinking of returning, when chance came to her aid. One day, as she was going along the *Rue de la Chaussée d'Antin,* she stopped to look into a shop full of those colored Japanese knick-knacks, which strike the eye on account of their color. She was looking at the little ivory buffoons, the tall vases of flaming enamel, and the curious bronzes, when she heard the shopkeeper dilating, with many bows, on the value of an enormous, pot-bellied, comical figure, which was quite unique, he said, to a little, bald-headed, gray-bearded man.

Every moment, the shopkeeper repeated his customer's name, which was a celebrated one, in a voice like a trumpet. The other customers, young women and well-dressed gentlemen, gave a swift and furtive, but respectful glance at the celebrated writer, who was looking admiringly at the china figure. They were both equally ugly, as ugly as two brothers who had sprung from the same mother.

"I will let you have it for a thousand francs, Monsieur Varin, and that is exactly what it cost me. I should ask anybody else fifteen hundred, but I think a great deal of literary and artistic customers, and have special prices for them. They all come to me, Monsieur Varin. Yesterday, Monsieur Busnach bought a large, antique goblet of me, and the other day I sold two candelabra like this (is it not handsome?) to Monsieur Alexander Dumas. If Monsieur Zola were to see that Japanese figure, he would buy it immediately, Monsieur Varin."

The author hesitated in perplexity, as he wanted to have the figure, but the price was above him, and he thought no more about her looking at him than if he had been alone in the desert. She came in trembling, with her eyes fixed shamelessly upon him, and she did not even ask herself whether he were good-looking, elegant or young. It was Jean Varin himself, Jean Varin.

After a long struggle, and painful hesitation, he put the figure down onto the table. "No, it is too dear," he said. The shopkeeper's eloquence redoubled. "Oh! Monsieur Varin, too dear? It is worth two thousand francs, if it is worth a sou." But the man of letters replied sadly, still looking at the figure with the enameled eyes: "I do not say it is not; but it is too dear for me." And thereupon, she, seized by a kind of mad audacity, came forward and said: "What shall you charge me for the figure?" The shopkeeper, in surprise, replied: "Fifteen hundred francs, Madame." "I will take it."

The writer, who had not even noticed her till that moment, turned round suddenly; he looked at her from head to foot, with half-closed eyes, observantly, and then he took in the details, as a connoisseur. She was charming, suddenly animated by that flame which had hitherto been dormant in her. And then, a woman who gives fifteen hundred francs for a knick-knack is not to be met with every day.

But she was overcome by a feeling of delightful delicacy, and turning to him, she said in a trembling voice: "Excuse me, Monsieur; no doubt I have been rather hasty, as perhaps you had not finally made up your mind." He, however, only bowed, and said: "Indeed, I had, Madame." And she, filled with emotion, continued: "Well, Monsieur, if either to-day, or at any other time, you change your mind, you can have this Japanese figure. I only bought it because you seemed to like it."

He was visibly flattered, and smiled. "I should much like to find out how you know who I am?" he said. Then she told him how she admired him, and became quite eloquent as she quoted his works, and while they were talking he rested his arms on a table, and fixed his bright eyes upon her, trying to make out who and what she really was. But the shopkeeper, who was pleased to have that living puff of his goods, called out, from the other end of the shop: "Just look at this, Monsieur Varin; is it not beautiful?"

And then everyone looked round, and she almost trembled with pleasure at being seen talking so intimately with such a well-known man.

At last, however, intoxicated, as it were, by her feelings, she grew bold, like a general does, who is going to give the order for an assault. "Monsieur," she said, "will you do me a great, a very great pleasure? Allow me to offer you this funny Japanese figure, as a keepsake from a woman who admires you passionately, and whom you have seen for ten minutes."

Of course he refused, and she persisted, but still he resisted her offer, at which he was much amused, and at which he laughed heartily; but that only made her more obstinate, and she said: "Very well, then, I shall take it to your house immediately. Where do you live?"

He refused to give her his address, but she got it from the shopkeeper, and when she had paid for her purchase, she ran out to take a cab. The writer went after her, as he did not wish to accept a present for which he could not possibly account. He reached her just as she was jumping into the vehicle, and getting in after her, he almost fell onto her, and then tumbled onto the bottom of the cab as it started. He picked himself up, however, and sat down by her side, feeling very much annoyed.

It was no good for him to insist and to beg her; she showed herself intractable, and when they got to the door, she stated her conditions. "I will undertake not to leave this with you," she said, "if you will promise to do all I want to-day." And the whole affair seemed so funny to him that he agreed. "What do you generally do at this time?" she asked him; and after hesitating for a few moments, he replied: "I generally go for a walk." "Very well, then, we will go to the *Bois de Boulogne!*" she said, in a resolute voice, and they started.

He was obliged to tell her the names of all the well-known women, pure or impure, with every detail about them; their life, their habits, their private affairs, and their vices; and when it was getting dusk, she said to him: "What do you do every day at this time?" "I have some absinthe," he replied, with a laugh. "Very well, then, Monsieur," she went on, seriously, "let us go and have some absinthe."

They went into a large *café* on the boulevard which he frequented, and where he met some of his colleagues, whom he introduced to her. She was half mad with pleasure, and she kept saying to herself: "At last! At last!" But time went on, and she observed that she supposed it must be about his dinner time, and she suggested that they should go and dine. When they left *Bignon's,* after dinner, she wanted to know what he did in the evening, and looking at her fixedly, he replied:

"That depends; sometimes I go to the theater." "Very well, then, Monsieur; let us go to the theater."

They went to the Vaudeville with an order, thanks to him, and, to her great pride, the whole house saw her sitting by his side, in the balcony stalls.

When the play was over, he gallantly kissed her hand, and said: "It only remains for me to thank you for this delightful day . . ." But she interrupted him: "What do you do at this time, every night?" "Why . . . why . . . I go home." She began to laugh, a little tremulous laugh. "Very well, Monsieur . . . let us go to your rooms."

They did not say anything more. She shivered occasionally, from head to foot, feeling inclined to stay, and inclined to run away, but with a fixed determination, after all, to see it out to the end. She was so excited that she had to hold onto the baluster as she went upstairs, and he came up behind her, with a wax match in his hand.

As soon as they were in the room, she undressed herself quickly, and retired without saying a word, and then she waited for him, cowering against the wall. But she was as simple as it was possible for a provincial lawyer's wife to be, and he was more exacting than a pascha with three tails, and so they did not at all understand each other. At last, however, he went to sleep, and the night passed, and the silence was only disturbed by the *tick-tack* of the clock, and she, lying motionless, thought of her conjugal nights; and by the light of the Chinese lantern, she looked, nearly heart-broken, at the little fat man lying on his back, whose round stomach raised up the bed-clothes like a balloon filled with gas. He snored with the noise of a wheezy organ pipe, with prolonged snorts and comic chokings. His few hairs profited by his sleep, to stand up in a very strange way, as if they were tired of having been fastened for so long to that pate, whose bareness they were trying to cover, and a small stream of saliva was running out of one corner of his half-open mouth.

At last the daylight appeared through the drawn blinds; so she got up and dressed herself without making any noise, and she had already half opened the door, when she made the lock creak, and he woke up and rubbed his eyes. He was some moments before he quite came to himself, and then, when he remembered all that had happened, he said: "What! Are you going already?" She remained standing, in some confusion, and then she said, in a hesitating voice: "Yes, of course; it is morning . . ."

Then he sat up, and said: "Look here, I have something to ask you, in my turn." And as she did not reply, he went on: "You have surprised me most confoundedly since yesterday. Be open, and tell me why you did it all, for upon my word I cannot understand it in the least." She went close up to him, blushing like as if she had been a virgin, and said: "I wanted to know . . . what . . . what vice . . . really was, . . . and . . . well . . . well, it is not at all funny."

And she ran out of the room, and downstairs into the street.

A number of sweepers were busy in the streets,

brushing the pavements, the roadway, and sweeping everything on one side. With the same regular motion, the motion of mowers in a meadow, they pushed the mud in front of them in a semi-circle, and she met them in every street, like dancing puppets, walking automatically with their swaying motion. And it seemed to her as if something had been swept out of her; as if her over-excited dreams had been pushed into the gutter, or into the drain, and so she went home, out of breath, and very cold, and all that she could remember was the sensation of the motion of those brooms sweeping the streets of Paris in the early morning.

As soon as she got into her room, she threw herself onto her bed and cried.

MARK TWAIN
(1835–1910)

When the young Samuel Clemens left home in rural Missouri to seek his fortune, he was equipped with little more than a wicked sense of humour, a taste for trouble-making and vague literary ambitions. He spent the following years wandering the US, working in printing shops, as a riverboat pilot and, later, as a reporter, before eventually taking up the *nom de plume* Mark Twain. (Borrowed, as it happens, from another literary-minded riverboat pilot roving the Mississippi.) Clemens soon found celebrity through his comic short stories and witty travelogues. Later, he became an American literary icon, known for his classic, voice-driven novels about Tom Sawyer and Huckleberry Finn. In this extract, drawn from one of his most successful books of travel writing, Twain gives his own irreverent take on the story of Heloïse and Abelard, whose passionate correspondence had been known and admired for centuries.

The Story of Abelard and Heloise

Heloise was born seven hundred and sixty-six years ago. She may have had parents. There is no telling. She lived with her uncle Fulbert, a canon of the cathedral of Paris. I do not know what a canon of a cathedral is, but that is what he was. He was nothing more than a sort of a mountain howitzer, likely, because they had no heavy artillery in those days. Suffice it, then, that Heloise lived with her uncle the howitzer, and was happy.—She spent the most of her childhood in the convent of Argenteuil—never heard of Argenteuil before, but suppose there was really such a place. She then returned to her uncle, the old gun, or son of a gun, as the case may be, and he taught her to write and speak Latin, which was the language of literature and polite society at that period.

Just at this time, Pierre Abelard, who had already made himself widely famous as a rhetorician, came to found a school of rhetoric in Paris. The originality of his principles, his eloquence, and his great physical strength and beauty created a profound sensation. He saw Heloise, and was captivated by her blooming youth, her beauty and her charming disposition. He wrote to her; she answered. He wrote again, she answered again. He was now in love. He longed to know her—to speak to her face to face.

His school was near Fulbert's house. He asked

Fulbert to allow him to call. The good old swivel saw here a rare opportunity: his niece, whom he so much loved, would absorb knowledge from this man, and it would not cost him a cent. Such was Fulbert—penurious.

Fulbert's first name is not mentioned by any author, which is unfortunate. However, George W. Fulbert will answer for him as well as any other. We will let him go at that. He asked Abelard to teach her.

Abelard was glad enough of the opportunity. He came often and staid long. A letter of his shows in its very first sentence that he came under that friendly roof like a cold-hearted villain as he was, with the deliberate intention of debauching a confiding, innocent girl. This is the letter:

"I can not cease to be astonished at the simplicity of Fulbert; I was as much surprised as if he had placed a lamb in the power of a hungry wolf. Heloise and I, under pretext of study, gave ourselves up wholly to love, and the solitude that love seeks our studies procured for us. Books were open before us, but we spoke oftener of love than philosophy, and kisses came more readily from our lips than words."

And so, exulting over an honorable confidence which to his degraded instinct was a ludicrous "simplicity," this unmanly Abelard seduced the niece of the man whose guest he was. Paris found it out. Fulbert was told of it—told often—but refused to believe it. He could not comprehend how a man could be so depraved as to use the sacred protection and security of hospitality as a means for the commission of such a crime as that. But when he heard the rowdies in the streets singing the love-songs of Abelard to Heloise, the case was too plain—love-songs come not properly within the teachings of rhetoric and philosophy.

He drove Abelard from his house. Abelard returned secretly and carried Heloise away to Palais, in Brittany, his native country. Here, shortly afterward, she bore a son, who, from his rare beauty, was surnamed Astrolabe—William G. The girl's flight enraged Fulbert, and he longed for vengeance, but feared to strike lest retaliation visit Heloise—for he still loved her tenderly. At length Abelard offered to marry Heloise—but on a shameful condition: that the marriage should be kept secret from the world, to the end that (while her good name remained a wreck, as before,) his priestly reputation might be kept untarnished. It was like that miscreant. Fulbert saw his opportunity and consented. He would see the parties married, and then violate the confidence of the man who had taught him that trick; he would divulge the secret and so remove somewhat of the obloquy that attached to his niece's fame. But the niece suspected his scheme. She refused the marriage, at first; she said Fulbert would betray the secret to save her, and besides, she did not wish to drag down a lover who was so gifted, so honored by the world, and who had such a splendid career before him. It was noble, self-sacrificing love, and characteristic of the pure-souled Heloise, but it was not good sense.

But she was overruled, and the private marriage took

place. Now for Fulbert! The heart so wounded should be healed at last; the proud spirit so tortured should find rest again; the humbled head should be lifted up once more. He proclaimed the marriage in the high places of the city, and rejoiced that dishonor had departed from his house. But lo! Abelard denied the marriage! Heloise denied it! The people, knowing the former circumstances, might have believed Fulbert, had only Abelard denied it, but when the person chiefly interested—the girl herself—denied it, they laughed despairing Fulbert to scorn.

The poor canon of the cathedral of Paris was spiked again. The last hope of repairing the wrong that had been done his house was gone. What next? Human nature suggested revenge. He compassed it. The historian says:

"Ruffians, hired by Fulbert, fell upon Abelard by night, and inflicted upon him a terrible and nameless mutilation."

I am seeking the last resting place of those "ruffians." When I find it I shall shed some tears on it, and stack up some bouquets and immortelles, and cart away from it some gravel whereby to remember that howsoever blotted by crime their lives may have been, these ruffians did one just deed, at any rate, albeit it was not warranted by the strict letter of the law.

Heloise entered a convent and gave good-bye to the world and its pleasures for all time. For twelve years she never heard of Abelard—never even heard his name mentioned. She had become prioress of Argenteuil, and led a life of complete seclusion. She happened one day to see a letter written by him, in which he narrated his own history. She cried over it, and wrote him. He answered, addressing her as his "sister in Christ." They continued to correspond, she in the unweighed language of unwavering affection, he in the chilly phraseology of the polished rhetorician. She poured out her heart in passionate, disjointed sentences; he replied with finished essays, divided deliberately into heads and sub-heads, premises and argument. She showered upon him the tenderest epithets that love could devise, he addressed her from the North Pole of his frozen heart as the "Spouse of Christ!" The abandoned villain!

On account of her too easy government of her nuns, some disreputable irregularities were discovered among them, and the Abbot of St. Denis broke up her establishment. Abelard was the official head of the monastery of St. Gildas de Ruys, at that time, and when he heard of her homeless condition a sentiment of pity was aroused in his breast (it is a wonder the unfamiliar emotion did not blow his head off,) and he placed her and her troop in the little oratory of the Paraclete, a religious establishment which he had founded. She had many privations and sufferings to undergo at first, but her worth and her gentle disposition won influential friends for her, and she built up a wealthy and flourishing nunnery. She became a great favorite with the heads of the church, and also the people, though she seldom appeared in public. She rapidly advanced in esteem, in good report and in usefulness, and Abelard as rapidly lost ground. The Pope so honored her that he made her the head of her order. Abelard, a man of splendid talents, and ranking as the first debater of his time, became timid, irresolute, and distrustful of his powers. He only needed a great misfortune to topple him from the high position he held in the world of intellectual excellence, and it came. Urged by kings and princes to meet the subtle St. Bernard in debate and crush him, he stood up in the presence of a royal and illustrious assemblage, and when his antagonist had finished he looked about him, and stammered a commencement; but his courage failed him, the cunning of his tongue was gone: with his speech unspoken, he trembled and sat down, a disgraced and vanquished champion.

He died a nobody, and was buried at Cluny, A. D., 1144. They removed his body to the Paraclete afterward, and when Heloise died, twenty years later, they buried her with him, in accordance with her last wish. He died at the ripe age of 64, and she at 63. After the bodies had remained entombed three hundred years, they were removed once more. They were removed again in 1800, and finally, seventeen years afterward, they were taken up and transferred to Père la Chaise, where they will remain in peace and quiet until it comes time for them to get up and move again.

SIDONIE-GABRIELLE COLETTE
(1873–1954)

An outstanding stylist and penetrating observer, Colette's early works appeared under her first husband's pen name, 'Willy'. Her husband kept almost all the earnings from these successful early novels, leaving Colette in poverty and ill health following an inevitable divorce. She supported herself in a variety of ways, most notably through journalism. She kept writing fiction, using her exceptional literary talents to tell painful stories that frequently centre on gender inequalities. Forever marked by her childhood in Burgundy, her work often points to the colossal divide between rural communities and life in the capital. In *Claudine in Paris* – Colette's second novel written as 'Willy' – she describes with sparkling playful wit what little of the spring season one can find in the manicured gardens of Paris.

from Claudine in Paris

Aunt Wilhelmina came to see me and I was not in. Mélie told me she talked with Papa and was annoyed to find that I had gone out alone. Undoubtedly she had no idea how many students from the Beaux-Arts there were in that quarter.

I had gone out to look at the leaves. Alas! Green leaves; they come out quickly here! Back in Montigny, at the most there would be that green mist on the hawthorn bushes with which their tender green shoots enshroud them. In the Luxembourg Gardens I wanted to eat the leaf shoots, but they crunched between my teeth because they were covered with coal dust. And never, never do I smell the scent of decayed leaves and reedy pools, nor the faint tang in a breeze that has blown over woods where charcoal is burning. Back there the first violets are up; I can see them! The border, near the garden wall, the one that faces west, is full of little stunted violets, ugly and weak-looking, but with a miraculous scent. How sad I am! The dampness and stuffiness of this Paris spring makes me feel like a poor animal caged in a menagerie. They sell primroses and yellow daisies by the cartload. The daisy-balls that I make from force of habit only amuse Fanchette who, in spite of her fat tummy, is still active and manipulates them cleverly with one of her paws shaped like a spoon. I'm in a pretty bad state of mind. Fortunately my body is all right. It pleases me to discover this frequently when in my wooden tub of hot water. It's flexible, tall, not very fat, but with good enough muscles not to seem too thin.

Though I have no trees to climb, I insist on keeping my flexibility. I stand on my right foot in my tub and lean back as far as I can, lifting the left leg very high, using my right hand to balance with, and clasping the back of my neck with my left hand. That seems easy. Just try it once. I fell out on to the floor once and, since I wasn't dried, my behind made a round wet spot on the floor. Fanchette stared at me coldly from the bed, full of scorn for my awkwardness and for the incredible mania I had for sitting in water. But I triumphed with other exercises: the feet placed alternatively behind the neck, or making yourself into a bow with the head and the calves bending upwards. Mélie was all admiration but warned me against too many gymnastics.

"You'll spoil the picture."

After these intimate diversions I generally fell back into my mood of apathy and enervation: hands too hot or too cold, eyes shining but tired. My face looked like an angry cat's, but I don't say it was ugly, though it easily could have been, with its cap of curls. What was lacking? . . . I would know only too soon, and it would be humiliating.

The result, at the moment, of all this is an unexpected passion for Francis Jammes, because that preposterous poet understands the country, animals, old-fashioned gardens, and the gravity of the stupid little things of daily life.

PARIS, CITY OF POETS AND POETRY

WILLA CATHER
(1873–1947)

Born in Back Creek, Virginia, but raised in rural Nebraska, Cather was indelibly marked by the Great Plains that stretch out across that state. After a university education in Lincoln, she moved to Pittsburgh and then New York, where she eventually found fame for her diamond-hard novels that often centre on the American frontier, winning the Pulitzer Prize for *One of Ours* (1922). She was also, in her early career, a poet and an avid traveller. In these brief verses, drawn from her debut work *April Twilights* (1903), Cather lyrically describes an idealized Paris as it might have appeared to her at the turn of the twentieth century.

Paris

Behind the arch of glory sets the day;
The river lies in curves of silver light,
The Fields Elysian glitter in a spray
Of golden dust; the gilded dome is bright,
The towers of Notre Dame cut clean and gray
The evening sky, and pale from left to right
A hundred bridges leap from either quay.
Pillared with pride, the city of delight
Sits like an empress by her silver Seine,
Heavy with jewels, all her splendid dower
Flashing upon her, won from shore and main
By shock of combat, sacked from town and tower.
Wherever men have builded hall or fane
Red war hath gleaned for her and men have slain
To deck her loveliness. I feel again
That joy which brings her art to faultless flower,
That passion of her kings, who, reign on reign,
Arrayed her star by star with pride and power.

ELIZABETH BARRETT BROWNING
(1806–1861)

Beleaguered by chronic pain and ill health throughout her life, Elizabeth Barrett Browning nonetheless produced one of the most striking and original poetic works of the nineteenth century, *Aurora Leigh* (1856), an epic feminist novel written in blank verse. By the time she wrote it she was already famous and admired, most notably by the poet Robert Browning, with whom she conducted a deeply romantic clandestine correspondence. The couple eventually married in secret and moved to Florence, Italy, where Elizabeth died in 1861. In this extract, drawn from *Aurora Leigh*, she captures with sharp poetic brilliance a broad sweep of Parisian life.

from Aurora Leigh

So, I mused
Up and down, up and down, the terraced streets,
The glittering boulevards, the white colonnades
Of fair fantastic Paris who wears boughs
Like plumes, as if man made them,—tossing up
Her fountains in the sunshine from the squares,
As dice i' the game of beauty, sure to win;
Or as she blew the down-balls of her dreams,
And only waited for their falling back,
To breathe up more, and count her festive hours.
The city swims in verdure, beautiful
As Venice on the waters, the sea-swan.
What bosky gardens, dropped in close-walled courts,
As plums in ladies' laps, who start and laugh:
What miles of streets that run on after trees,
Still carrying the necessary shops,
Those open caskets, with the jewels seen!
And trade is art, and art's philosophy,
In Paris. There's a silk, for instance, there,
As worth an artist's study for the folds,
As that bronze opposite! nay, the bronze has faults;
Art's here too artful,—conscious as a maid,
Who leans to mark her shadow on the wall
Until she lose a 'vantage in her step.
Yet Art walks forward, and knows where to walk:
The artists also, are idealists,

Too absolute for nature, logical
To austerity in the application of
The special theory: not a soul content
To paint a crooked pollard and an ass,
As the English will, because they find it so,
And like it somehow.—Ah, the old Tuileries
Is pulling its high cap down on its eyes,
Confounded, conscience-stricken, and amazed
By the apparition of a new fair face
In those devouring mirrors. Through the grate,
Within the gardens, what a heap of babes,
Swept up like leaves beneath the chesnut-trees,
From every street and alley of the town,
By the ghosts perhaps, that blow too bleak this way
A-looking for their heads! Dear pretty babes;
I'll wish them luck to have their ball-play out
Before the next change comes.—And, farther on,
What statues, poised upon their columns fine,
As if to stand a moment were a feat,
Against that blue! What squares! what breathing-room
For a nation that runs fast,—ay, runs against
The dentist's teeth at the corner, in pale rows,
Which grin at progress in an epigram.

ALAN SEEGER
(1888–1916)

'I have a rendezvous with death': so wrote the young Seeger with painful foresight. A talented and earnest young poet, he was also a committed Francophile with an authentic passion for Paris. He was living in the city when, in 1914, war broke out in Europe. His love for France led him to enlist in the French Foreign Legion. Two years later, he died of his wounds at the Battle of the Somme. In this lovely poem, 'Paris I', Seeger celebrates with characteristic lyricism his bright beloved city.

Paris I

First, London, for its myriads; for its height,
Manhattan heaped in towering stalagmite;
But Paris for the smoothness of the paths
That lead the heart unto the heart's delight . . .
Fair loiterer on the threshold of those days
When there's no lovelier prize the world displays
Than, having beauty and your twenty years,
You have the means to conquer and the ways,
And coming where the cross-roads separate
And down each vista glories and wonders wait,
Crowning each path with pinnacles so fair
You know not which to choose, and hesitate—
Oh, go to Paris . . . In the midday gloom
Of some old quarter take a little room
That looks off over Paris and its towers
From Saint-Gervais round to the Emperor's Tomb,—
So high that you can hear a mating dove
Croon down the chimney from the roof above,
See Notre-Dame and know how sweet it is
To wake between Our Lady and our love.
And have a little balcony to bring
Fair plants to fill with verdure and blossoming,
That sparrows seek, to feed from pretty hands,
And swallows circle over in the Spring.
There of an evening you shall sit at ease
In the sweet month of flowering chestnut-trees,

There with your little darling in your arms,
Your pretty dark-eyed Manon or Louise.
And looking out over the domes and towers
That chime the fleeting quarters and the hours,
While the bright clouds banked eastward back of them
Blush in the sunset, pink as hawthorn flowers,
You cannot fail to think, as I have done,
Some of life's ends attained, so you be one
Who measures life's attainment by the hours
That Joy has rescued from oblivion.

AMY LOWELL
(1874–1925)

To many of her contemporaries, Amy Lowell was an oddball spinster of Boston Brahmin stock who liked to smoke cigars, wore a pince-nez and fancied herself a poet. As a young woman, she enjoyed the life of a leisured socialite. Eventually, though, she fell under the spell of poetry. From her late twenties on, she devoted herself to the art with characteristic restless energy. She used her enterprising nature and considerable personal wealth to bring a wider readership to challenging modern poets like Ezra Pound and H.D. Pound, in return, saw her as an uninspired interloper who appropriated other people's innovations. Lowell was, however, a prolific and intelligent poet in her own right, whose wide reading and numerous voyages helped her craft an intriguing body of work, including this deft and witty Parisian piece.

Two Travellers in the Place Vendôme

REIGN OF LOUIS PHILIPPE

A great tall column spearing at the sky
With a little man on top. Goodness! Tell me why?
He looks a silly thing enough to stand up there
 so high.

What a strange fellow, like a soldier in a play,
Tight-fitting coat with the tails cut away,
High-crowned hat which the brims overlay.

Two-horned hat makes an outline like a bow.
Must have a sword, I can see the light glow
Between a dark line and his leg. Vertigo

I get gazing up at him, a pygmy flashed with sun.
A weathercock or scarecrow or both things in one?
As bright as a jewelled crown hung above a throne.

Say, what is the use of him if he doesn't turn?
Just put up to glitter there, like a torch to burn,
A sort of sacrificial show in a lofty urn?

But why a little soldier in an obsolete dress?
I'd rather see a Goddess with a spear, I confess.
Something allegorical and fine. Why, yes—

I cannot take my eyes from him. I don't know why
  at all.
I've looked so long the whole thing swims. I feel
  he ought to fall.
Foreshortened there among the clouds he's pitifully
  small.

What do you say? There used to be an Emperor
  standing there,
With flowing robes and laurel crown. Really? Yet I
  declare
Those spiral battles round the shaft don't seem just
  his affair.

A togaed, laurelled man's I mean. Now this chap
  seems to feel
As though he owned those soldiers. Whew! How he
  makes one reel,
Swinging round above his circling armies in a wheel.

Sweeping round the sky in an orbit like the sun's,
Flashing sparks like cannon-balls from his own long
  guns.
Perhaps my sight is tired, but that figure simply stuns.

How low the houses seem, and all the people are mere
  flies.
That fellow pokes his hat up till it scratches on the
  skies.
Impudent! Audacious! But, by Jove, he blinds the eyes!

Sara Teasdale
(1884–1933)

Author of seven books of verse and recipient of what would later become the Pulitzer Prize for poetry, Sara Teasdale spent a cossetted youth in St. Louis, Missouri, before growing to artistic maturity in Chicago. Her rare lyrical gifts accompanied her to New York, where disillusionment, depression and suicide awaited. But during her brief life, the uncommon musicality of her verses and the frequently autobiographical nature of her work won Teasdale critical admiration and a degree of popularity. In 'Paris in Spring', the lightest and most joyous of the poems included here, Teasdale's lines effervesce with the easy lyrical vigour that marked her best work.

Paris in Spring

The city's all a-shining
  Beneath a fickle sun,
A gay young wind's a-blowing,
  The little shower is done.
But the rain-drops still are clinging
  And falling one by one—
Oh, it's Paris, it's Paris,
  And spring-time has begun.

I know the Bois is twinkling
  In a sort of hazy sheen,
And down the Champs the gray old arch
  Stands cold and still between.
But the walk is flecked with sunlight
  Where the great acacias lean,
Oh, it's Paris, it's Paris,
  And the leaves are growing green.

The sun's gone in, the sparkle's dead,
  There falls a dash of rain,
But who would care when such an air
  Comes blowing up the Seine?
And still Ninette sits sewing
  Beside her window-pane,
When it's Paris, it's Paris,
  And spring-time's come again.

INJUSTICE, REVOLUTION, WAR

Madame De Sévigné
(Marie De Rabutin-Chantal, Marquise De Sévigné)
(1626–1696)

Venerated in her native France as one of the nation's great prose stylists, Madame de Sévigné never published a single book in her lifetime. Her fame rests instead on the decades-long correspondence she kept with her daughter who, following a brilliant marriage, became Madame de Grignan. Brimming with fascinating anecdotes that are by turns scabrous and moving, raucous and sensitive, Madame de Sévigné's letters are everywhere animated by a sparkling wit, a keen consciousness of drama and a crushing sense of irony. Occasionally criticized as an inveterate gossip, in this letter she shows her serious side by recounting, in gory detail, a death sentence carried out under the *ancien régime*.

from The Letters of Madame de Sévigné to her Daughter and Friends

PARIS, FRIDAY, FEB. 23, 1680.

Indeed, my child, this has been a very pretty week for the Grignans; should Providence favour the elder brother in proportion as it has the younger, we might soon expect to see him in a charming situation. In the mean time, I think it no disagreeable thing to have brothers in such favour. The chevalier had scarcely returned thanks for his pension of a thousand crowns, when he was chosen, out of eight or ten persons of quality and merit, to be an attendant upon the dauphin, with a salary of two thousand crowns; so here are appointments to the value of nine thousand livres a year, in the space of three days. He immediately went back to St. Germain with his second acknowledgements, for it seems he had been appointed in his absence, while he was here in Paris. His personal merit has greatly contributed to this choice: his distinguished reputation, his strict honour and probity, and the regularity of his conduct, have been remarked; and it is the general opinion, that his majesty could not have made a better choice. There are but eight persons named yet, Dangeau, d'Antin, Clermont, Sainte-Maure, Matignon,

Chiverni, Florensac, and Grignan*. The last is universally approved. Permit me, then, to pay my compliments of congratulation to M. de Grignan, the coadjutor, and yourself.

My son sets out to-morrow; he has read the reproaches you make him; possibly the charms of the court he wishes to leave, and where he has so handsome an establishment, will make him change his opinion. We have prevailed on him not to be in a hurry, but to wait quietly till he meets with the temptation of a greater sum than he gave.

You have given me a specimen of M. de Grignan's joy by my own, in hearing that you are better. As your complaints are no longer continual, I am in great hopes, that, by taking care of yourself, using a milk diet, and giving up writing, you will in the end restore my daughter to me as lovely as ever.

I am charmed with Montgobert's sincerity: had she always written me word you were well, I should never have given credit to her: she has managed the whole business to a miracle, and has won my heart by her candour; so natural is it for us to love not to be deceived. May Heaven preserve you, my dear, in this prosperous state! which gives us all such flattering hopes. But to return to the Grignans, for we seem to have forgotten them. Nothing else is talked of here. Nothing but complimenting passes in this house; one has scarcely done

* These were afterwards reduced to six, viz. Mess. Dangeau, d'Antin, Saint-Maure, Chiverni, Florensac, and Grignan.

when another begins. I have not seen either of them since the chevalier has been made a lady of honour, as M. de Rochefoucault calls it. He will write you all the news much better than I can possibly do. It is supposed that madame de Soubise will not be one of the travelling party. See how long my letter is growing!—Well, I will only mention La Voisin's affair; and conclude.

She was not burnt on Wednesday, as I wrote you word; the sentence was not executed till yesterday. She knew her fate on the Monday, a very extraordinary circumstance! In the evening, she said to those who guarded her, "What! no medianoche!" She ate with them at midnight out of whim, for it was no fast-day, drank plentifully of wine, and sung several drinking songs. On Monday she received the question ordinary and extraordinary. She had now dined, and slept nearly eight hours. She was confronted while under the torture with mesdames de Dreux and Le Feron, and several more. Her answers have not yet transpired, but every one expects to hear strange things. She supped in the evening, and, lacerated and disjointed as she was, gave a loose to her excess, to the disgust of every one present. They endeavoured to make her sensible of her ill conduct, and that she would be much better employed in thinking of God, and singing devout hymns, than such songs; upon which she sung a psalm or two in mockery, and then fell asleep. Wednesday was spent in the like confronting, drinking, and singing; she absolutely refused to let a confessor come near her. In short, on the Thursday, that is, yesterday, they denied her all kinds of food, excepting only a little broth, of which she complained greatly, seeming to be apprehensive that she should not have strength to carry her through the business of the day.

She came from Vincennes to Paris in a coach; she seemed embarrassed, and as if she wished to conceal what she felt. They would have had her confess, but she would not hear of it. At five o'clock she was bound and set on the sledge, dressed in white, with taper in her hand. She was extremely red in the face, and was seen to push away the confessor and the crucifix with great violence. Madame de Chaulnes, madame de Sully, the countess (de Fiesque), myself, and several others, saw her pass by the hôtel de Sully. When she came to the church of Notre-Dame, she refused to pronounce the amende-honorable; and at the Grêve, she struggled with all her might to prevent their taking her out of the sledge: she was, however, dragged out by main force, and made to sit down on the pile, to which she was bound by iron chains, and then covered over with straw; she swore prodigiously, and pushed away the straw five or six times; but at length the fire increased, she sunk out of sight, and her ashes are by this time floating in the air. This is the end of madame Voisin, celebrated for her crimes and her impiety. One of the judges, to whom my son happened to mention his surprise at persons' being burnt alive, in a slow fire, made answer, "My dear sir, there are some indulgences granted to the women in favour of their sex." "How, pray sir? are they strangled?" "No, sir, they are covered with faggots, and the executioner tears off their heads with iron hooks." So you see, my child, this is not so dreadful as we have been told it was. How do you find yourself after this little story? It made my blood run cold in my veins. One of the wretches that were hanged the other day had begged her life of M. Louvois, promising to make considerable discoveries, but was refused. "Very well," replied she, "I promise you no torments shall make me speak." Upon this she was put to the torture, and so severely, that she was very near dying under it, as one of her accomplices had just done. A physician stood by to feel her pulse all the while—but mum for that. This woman then suffered all this without uttering a word. At the place of execution, just before she was placed on the pile, she cried out that she had something to say; when silence being commanded, she presented herself heroically, and exclaimed, "Gentlemen, pray be so good as to present my respects to M. de Louvois, and tell him that I have kept my word. Come, friend, make an end of your work." She was dispatched immediately. What say you to this kind of heroism? I could tell you a thousand such stories, were it possible to crowd them all into a letter.

I have given you this as a sample of the agreeable topics that form our present conversations, while you are carousing, dancing, and feasting. I should be very glad to hear some particulars of your entertainments. I know you do nothing else during the holidays, and you are in the right to make hay while the sun shines, for Lent is at hand, which will put an end to all.

Jules Michelet
(1798–1874)

The colossus of French historical writing, Michelet, more than anyone, transformed the discipline of history in his native land. He refashioned it for an age that was less welcoming than ever to the old clerical or monarchical pieties, and anxiously in pursuit of durable republican ideals. Part of what made Michelet popular in the first place – an impassioned and deliberately partial approach to history – has since fallen out of favour. But he is still admired today for his undeniable narrative gifts and his rich percussive style, which tends towards the oratorical and relentlessly builds suspense. In the following piece, drawn from one of his landmark multi-volume historical works, Michelet rolls through events like an enraged Biblical prophet recounting the birth of modern France, focusing on a foundational scene from the French Revolution: the taking of the Bastille.

from The History of the French Revolution

Versailles, with an organised government, a king, ministers, a general, and an army, was all hesitation, doubt, uncertainty, and in a state of the most complete moral anarchy.

Paris, all commotion, destitute of every legal authority, and in the utmost confusion, attained, on the 14th of July, what is morally the highest degree of order,—unanimity of feeling.

On the 13th, Paris thought only of defending itself; on the 14th, it attacked.

On the evening of the 13th, some doubt still existed, but none remained in the morning. The evening had been stormy, agitated by a whirlwind of ungovernable frenzy. The morning was still and serene,—an awful calm.

With daylight, one idea dawned upon Paris, and all were illumined with the same ray of hope. A light broke upon every mind, and the same voice thrilled through every heart: "Go! and thou shalt take the Bastille!" That was impossible, unreasonable, preposterous. And yet everybody believed it. And the thing was done.

The Bastille, though an old fortress, was nevertheless impregnable, unless besieged for several days and with an abundance of artillery. The people had, in that crisis, neither the time nor the means to make a regular siege.

Had they done so, the Bastille had no cause for fear, having enough provisions to wait for succour so near at hand, and an immense supply of ammunition. Its walls, ten feet thick at the top of the towers, and thirty or forty at the base, might long laugh at cannon-balls; and its batteries firing down upon Paris, could, in the mean-time, demolish the whole of the Marais and the Faubourg Saint-Antoine. Its towers, pierced with windows and loop-holes, protected by double and triple gratings, enabled the garrison, in full security, to make a dreadful carnage of its assailants.

The attack on the Bastille was by no means reasonable. It was an act of faith.

Nobody proposed; but all believed, and all acted. Along the streets, the quays, the bridges, and the boulevards, the crowd shouted to the crowd: "To the Bastille! The Bastille!" And the tolling of the tocsin thundered in every ear: "*à la Bastille!*"

On the 14th, about midnight, seven shots were fired at the sentinels upon the towers.—Alarm!—The governor ascends with staff, remains half-an-hour, listening to the distant murmuring of the town; finding all quiet he descends.

The next morning many people were about, and, from time to time, young men (from the Palais Royal, or others) were calling out that they must give them arms. They pay no attention to them. They hear and introduce the pacific deputation of the Hôtel-de-Ville, which, about ten o'clock, intreats the governor to withdraw his cannon, promising that if he does not fire, he shall not be attacked. He, willingly, accepts, having no orders to fire, and highly delighted, obliges the envoys to breakfast with him.

As they were leaving, a man arrives who speaks in a very different tone.

A violent, bold man, unacquainted with human respect, fearless and pitiless, knowing neither obstacle nor delay, and bearing in his breast the passionate genius of the Revolution—he came to summon the Bastille.

Terror accompanied him. The Bastille was afraid; the governor, without knowing why, was troubled and stammered.

That man was Thuriot, a monster of ferocity, one of the race of Danton. We meet with him twice, in the beginning and at the end. And twice his words are deadly; he destroys the Bastille, and he kills Robespierre.

He was not to pass the bridge; the governor would not allow it; and yet he passed. From the first court, he marches to a second; another refusal; but he passes on, and crosses the second ditch by the draw-bridge. Behold him now in front of the enormous iron gate by which the third court was shut. This seemed a monstrous well rather than a court, its eight towers united together, forming its inside walls. Those frightful gigantic towers did not look towards the court, nor had they a single window. At their feet, in their shadow, was the prisoners' only walk. Lost at the bottom of the pit, and overwhelmed by those enormous masses, he could contemplate only the stern nudity of the walls. On one side only, had been placed a clock, between two figures of captives in chains, as if to fetter time itself, and make the slow succession of hours still more burdensome.

There were the loaded cannon, the garrison, and the staff. Thuriot was daunted by nothing. "Sir," said he to the governor, "I summon you, in the name of the people, in the name of honour, and of our native land, to withdraw your cannon, and surrender the Bastille."—Then, turning towards the garrison, he repeated the same words.

The cannon were drawn back and masked, but still pointed. The view from that height of a hundred and forty feet was immense and startling; the streets and openings full of people, and all the garden of the arsenal crowded with armed men. But, on the other side, a black mass was advancing. It was the faubourg Saint Antoine.

The governor turned pale. He grasped Thuriot by the arm: "What have you done? You abuse your privilege as an envoy! You have betrayed me!"

They were both standing on the brink, and De Launey had a sentinel on the tower. Everybody in the Bastille was bound by oath to the governor; in his fortress, he was king and the law. He was still able to avenge himself.

But, on the contrary, it was Thuriot who made him afraid: "Sir," said he, "one word more, and I swear to you that one of us two shall be hurled headlong into the moat!"

At the same moment, the sentinel approached, as

frightened as the governor, and, addressing Thuriot: "Pray, Sir," said he, "show yourself; there is no time to lose; they are marching forward. Not seeing you, they will attack us." He leaned over through the battlements; and the people seeing him alive, and standing boldly upon the tower, uttered deafening shouts of joy and approbation.

Thuriot descended with the governor, again crossed through the court, and addressing the garrison once more: "I am going to give my report," said he; "I hope the people will not refuse to furnish a citizen guard to keep the Bastille with you."

The people expected to enter the Bastille as soon as Thuriot came forth. When they saw him depart, to make his report to the Hôtel-de-Ville, they took him for a traitor, and threatened him. Their impatience was growing into fury. The crowd seized on three Invalids, and wanted to tear them to pieces. They also seized on a young lady whom they believed to be the governor's daughter, and some wanted to burn her, if he refused to surrender. Others dragged her from them.

What will become of us, said they, if the Bastille be not taken before night?

Several strange singular means were proposed to the electors for taking the fortress. A carpenter advised the erection of a Roman catapult, in wood-work, to hurl stones against the walls. The commanders of the town said it was necessary to attack in a regular way, and open a trench. During this long and useless debate, a letter at that moment intercepted, was brought in and read; it was from Besenval to de Launey, commanding him to hold out to the last extremity.

To appreciate the value of time at that momentous crisis, and understand the dread felt at any delay, we must know that there were false alarms every instant. It was supposed that the court, informed at two o'clock of the attack on the Bastille, which had begun at noon, would take that opportunity of pouring down its Swiss and German troops upon Paris. Again, would those at the Military School pass the day in inaction? That was unlikely. What Besenval says about the little reliance he could place on his troops seems like an excuse. The Swiss showed themselves very firm at the Bastille, as appeared from the carnage; the German dragoons had, on the 12th, fired several times, and killed some of the French Guards; the latter had killed several dragoons; a spirit of mutual hatred ensured fidelity.

In the faubourg Saint Honoré, the paving-stones were dug up, the attack being expected every moment; La Villette was in the same state, and a regiment really came and occupied it, but too late.

Every appearance of dilatoriness appeared treason. The provost's shuffling conduct caused him to be suspected, as well as the electors. The exasperated crowd perceived it was losing time with them. An old man exclaimed: "Friends, why do we remain with these traitors? Let us rather hasten to the Bastille!" They all vanished. The electors, thunder-struck, found themselves alone. One of them goes out, but returns with a livid, spectral countenance: "You have not two minutes to live," says he, "if you remain here. La Grève is filled by a furious crowd. Here they are coming." They did not, however, attempt to fly; and that saved their lives.

All the fury of the people was now concentrated on the provost. The envoys of the different districts came successively to accuse him of treachery to his face. A part of the electors, finding themselves compromised with the people, by his imprudence and falsehood, turned round and accused him. Others, the good old Dussaulx (the translator of Juvenal), and the intrepid Fauchet endeavoured to defend him, innocent or guilty, and to save him from death. Being forced by the people to remove from their bureau into the grand hall of Saint Jean, they surrounded him, and Fauchet sat down by his side. The terrors of death were impressed on his countenance. "I saw him," says Dussaulx, "chewing his last mouthful of bread; it stuck in his teeth, and he kept it in his mouth two hours before he could swallow it." Surrounded with papers, letters, and people who came to speak to him on business, and amid shouts of death, he strove hard to reply with affability. The crowds of the Palais Royal and from the district of Saint Roch, being the most inveterate, Fauchet hastened to them to pray for pardon. The district body was assembled in the church of Saint Roch; twice did Fauchet ascend the pulpit, praying, weeping, and uttering the fervent language which his noble heart dictated in that hour of need; his robe, torn to tatters by the bullets of the Bastille, was eloquent also; it prayed for the people, for the honour of that great day, and that the cradle of liberty might be left pure and undefiled.

The provost and the electors remained in the hall of Saint Jean, between life and death, guns being levelled at them several times. All those who were present, says Dussaulx, were like savages; sometimes they would listen and look on in silence; sometimes a terrible murmur, like distant thunder, arose from the crowd. Many spoke and shouted; but the greater number seemed astounded by the novelty of the sight. The uproar, the exclamations, the news, the alarms, the intercepted letters, the discoveries, true or false, so many secrets revealed, so many men brought before the tribunal, perplexed the mind and reason. One of the electors exclaimed: "Is not doomsday come?" So dizzy, so confounded was the crowd, that they had forgotten everything, even the provost and the Bastille.

It was half-past five when a shout arose from La Grève. An immense noise, like the growling of distant thunder, resounds nearer and nearer, rushing on with the rapidity and roaring of a tempest. The Bastille is taken.

[. . .] the benches are thrown down, and the barrier driven upon the bureau, the bureau upon the president.

All were armed in a fantastical manner; some almost naked, others dressed in every colour. One man was borne aloft upon their shoulders and crowned with laurel; it was Elie, with all the spoils and prisoners around him. At the head, amid all that din, which would have drowned a clap of thunder, advanced a young man full of meditation and religion; he carried suspended and pierced with his bayonet a vile, a thrice-accursed object,—the regulations of the Bastille.

The keys too were carried,—those monstrous, vile, ignoble keys, worn out by centuries and the sufferings of men. Chance or Providence directed that they should be intrusted to a man who knew them but too well,—a former prisoner. The National Assembly placed them in its Archives; the old machine of tyrants thus lying beside the laws that had destroyed them. We still keep possession of those keys, in the iron safe of the Archives of France. Oh! would that the same iron-chest might contain the keys of all the Bastilles in the world!

Correctly speaking, the Bastille was not taken; it surrendered. Troubled by a bad conscience it went mad, and lost all presence of mind.

Some wanted to surrender; others went on firing, especially the Swiss, who, for five hours, pointed out, aimed at, and brought down whomsoever they pleased, without any danger or even the chance of being hurt in return. They killed eighty-three men and wounded eighty-eight. Twenty of the slain were poor fathers of families, who left wives and children to die of hunger.

Shame for such cowardly warfare, and the horror of shedding French blood, which but little affected the Swiss, at length caused the Invalids to drop their arms. At four o'clock the subaltern officers begged and prayed De Launey to put an end to this massacre. He knew what he deserved; obliged to die one way or other, he had, for a moment, the horribly ferocious idea of blowing up the citadel: he would have destroyed one-third of Paris. His hundred and thirty-five barrels of gunpowder would have blown the Bastille into the air, and shattered or buried the whole faubourg, all the Marais, and the whole of the quartier of the Arsenal. He seized a match from a cannon. Two subaltern officers prevented the crime; they crossed their bayonets, and barred his passage to the magazines. He then made a show of killing himself, and seized a knife, which they snatched from him.

He had lost his senses and could give no orders.* When the French Guards had ranged their cannon and fired (according to some), the captain of the Swiss saw plainly that it was necessary to come to terms; he wrote and passed a note,** in which he asked to be allowed to go forth with the honours of war. Refused. Next, that his life should be spared. Hullin and Elie promised it. The difficulty was to perform their promise. To prevent a revenge accumulating for ages, and now incensed by so many murders perpetrated by the Bastille, was beyond the power of man. An authority of an hour's existence, that had but just come from La Grève, and was known only to the two small bands of the vanguard, was not adequate to keep in order the hundred thousand men behind.

* Even in the morning, according to Thuriot's testimony. See the *Procès-verbal des électeurs*.
** To fetch it, a plank was placed on the moat. The first who ventured, fell; the second (Arné?—or Maillard?) was more lucky and brought back the note.

The crowd was enraged, blind, drunk with the very sense of their danger. And yet they killed but one man in the fortress. They spared their enemies the Swiss, whom their smock-frocks caused to pass for servants or prisoners; but they ill-treated and wounded their friends the Invalids. They wished to have annihilated the Bastille; they pelted and broke to pieces the two captives of the dial; they ran up to the top of the towers to spurn the cannon; several attacked the stones, and tore their hands in dragging them away. They hastened to the dungeons to deliver the prisoners: two had become mad. One, frightened by the noise, wanted to defend himself, and was quite astonished when those who had battered down his door threw themselves into his arms and bathed him with their tears. Another, whose beard reached to his waist, inquired about the health of Louis XV., believing him to be still reigning. To those who asked him his name, he replied that he was called the Major of Immensity.

The conquerors were not yet at the end of their labours: in the Rue Saint Antoine they had to fight a battle of a different kind. On approaching La Grève, they came successfully on crowds of men, who, having been unable to take any part in the fight, wanted at all events to do something, were it merely to massacre the prisoners. One was killed at the Rue des Tournelles, and another on the quay. Women, with dishevelled hair, came rushing forward, and recognizing their husbands among the slain, left them to fly upon their assassins;

one of them, foaming at the mouth, ran about asking everybody for a knife.

De Launey was conducted and supported in that extreme danger by two men of extraordinary courage and strength, Hullin, and another. The latter went with him as far as the Petit Antoine, but was there torn from his side by the rush of the crowd. Hullin held fast. To lead his man from that spot to La Grève, which is so near, was more than the twelve labours of Hercules. No longer knowing how to act, and perceiving that they knew De Launey only by his being alone without a hat, he conceived the heroic idea of putting his own upon his head; and, from that moment, he received the blows intended for the governor.* At length, he passed the Arcade Saint Jean; if he could but get him on the flight of steps, and push him towards the stairs, all was over.

---

* The royalist tradition which aspires to the difficult task of inspiring interest for the least interesting of men, has pretended that De Launey, still more heroic than Hullin, gave him his hat back again, wishing rather to die than expose him. The same tradition attributes the honour of a similar deed to Berthier, the intendant of Paris. Lastly, they relate that the major of the Bastille, on being recognized and defended at La Grève, by one of his former prisoners, whom he had treated with kindness, dismissed him, saying: "You will ruin yourself without saving me." This last story, being authentic, very probably gave rise to the two others. As for De Launey and Berthier, there is nothing in their previous conduct to incline us to believe in the heroism of their last moments. The silence of Michaud, the biographer, in the article *De Launey*, drawn up from information furnished by that family, sufficiently shows that they did not believe in that tradition.

The crowd saw that very plainly, and accordingly made a desperate onset. The Herculean strength hitherto displayed by Hullin no longer served him here. Stifled by the pressure of the crowd around him, as in the crushing fold of an enormous boa, he lost his footing, was hurled to and fro, and thrown upon the pavement. Twice he regained his feet. The second time he beheld aloft the head of De Launey at the end of a pike.

Another scene was passing in the hall of Saint Jean. The prisoners were there, in great danger of death. The people were especially inveterate towards three Invalids, whom they supposed to have been the cannoneers of the Bastille. One was wounded; De la Salle, the commandant, by incredible efforts, and proclaiming loudly his title of commandant, at last managed to save him; whilst he was leading him out, the two others were dragged out and hung up to the lamp at the corner of the Vannerie, facing the Hôtel-de-Ville.

All this great commotion, which seemed to have caused Flesselles to be forgotten, was nevertheless what caused his destruction. His implacable accusers of the Palais Royal, few in number, but discontented to see the crowd occupied with any other business, kept close to the bureau, menacing him, and summoning him to follow them. At length he yielded: whether the long expectation of death appeared to him worse than death itself, or that he hoped to escape in the universal preoccupation about the great event of the day. "Well! gentlemen," said he, "let us go to the Palais Royal." He had not reached the quay before a young man shot him through the head with a pistol bullet.

The dense multitude crowding the hall did not wish for bloodshed; according to an eye-witness, they were stupefied on beholding it. They stared gaping at that strange, prodigious, grotesque, and maddening spectacle. Arms of the middle ages and of every age were mingled together; centuries had come back again. Elie, standing on a table, with a helmet on his brow, and a sword hacked in three places, in his hand, seemed a Roman warrior. He was entirely surrounded by prisoners, and pleading for them. The French Guards demanded the pardon of the prisoners as their reward.

At that moment, a man, followed by his wife, is brought or rather carried in; it was the Prince de Montbarrey, an ancient minister, arrested at the barrier. The lady fainted; her husband was thrown upon the bureau, held down by the arms of twelve men, and bent double. The poor man, in that strange posture, explained that he had not been minister for a long time, and that his son had taken a prominent part in the revolution of his province. De la Salle, the commandant, spoke for him, and exposed himself to great danger. Meanwhile, the people relented a little, and for a moment let go their hold. De la Salle, a very powerful man, caught him up, and carried him off. This trial of strength pleased the people, and was received with applause.

At the same moment, the brave and excellent Elie found means to put an end at once to every intention of trial or condemnation. He perceived the children of the Bastille, and began to shout: "Pardon! for the children, pardon!"

Then you might have seen sunburnt faces and hands blackened with gunpowder, washed with big tears, falling like heavy drops of rain after a shower. Justice and vengeance were thought of no longer. The tribunal was broken up; for Elie had conquered the conquerors of the Bastille. They made the prisoners swear fidelity to the nation, and led them away; the Invalids marched off in peace to their Hôtel; the French Guards took charge of the Swiss, placed them in safety within their ranks, conducting them to their own barracks, and gave them lodging and food.

What was most admirable, the widows showed themselves equally magnanimous. Though needy, and burdened with children, they were unwilling to receive alone a small sum allotted to them; they shared it with the widow of a poor Invalid who had prevented the Bastille from being blown up, but was killed by mistake. The wife of the besieged was thus adopted, as it were, by those of the besiegers.

GUSTAVE FLAUBERT
(1821–1880)

Born in the mid-sized city of Rouen, Flaubert went to study law in Paris as a young man. He never settled in the capital and, after a severe epileptic episode, abandoned his studies and returned to his native Normandy, where he spent the rest of his life devoted to literature. A notoriously slow worker, his painstaking efforts sent him pacing around his house, reading his drafts in a booming voice, seeking to eradicate assonances and repetitions, searching always for the *mot juste*, the single word that was good and right to use. It sometimes took him months to finish a few pages. With Flaubert's meticulously crafted debut, *Madame Bovary* (1856) – now recognized as one of the world's great literary masterpieces – the effort is widely believed to have paid off. In this excerpt, drawn from Flaubert's Paris-set novel *Sentimental Education*, he describes the confusion and excitement that greeted the Revolution of 1848.

from Sentimental Education

He was abruptly roused from sleep by the noise of a discharge of musketry; and, in spite of Rosanette's entreaties, Frederick was fully determined to go and see what was happening. He hurried down to the Champs-Elysées, from which shots were being fired. At the corner of the Rue Saint-Honoré some men in blouses ran past him, exclaiming:

"No! not that way! to the Palais-Royal!"

Frederick followed them. The grating of the Convent of the Assumption had been torn away. A little further on he noticed three paving-stones in the middle of the street, the beginning of a barricade, no doubt; then fragments of bottles and bundles of iron-wire, to obstruct the cavalry; and, at the same moment, there rushed suddenly out of a lane a tall young man of pale complexion, with his black hair flowing over his shoulders, and with a sort of pea-coloured swaddling-cloth thrown round him. In his hand he held a long military musket, and he dashed along on the tips of his slippers with the air of a somnambulist and with the nimbleness of a tiger. At intervals a detonation could be heard.

On the evening of the day before, the spectacle of the wagon containing five corpses picked up from amongst those that were lying on the Boulevard des Capucines had charged the disposition of the people; and, while at the Tuileries the aides-de-camp succeeded each other, and M. Molé, having set about the composition of a new Cabinet, did not come back, and M. Thiers was making efforts to constitute another, and while the King was cavilling and hesitating, and finally assigned the post of commander-in-chief to Bugeaud in order to prevent him from making use of it, the insurrection was organising itself in a formidable manner, as if it were directed by a single arm.

Men endowed with a kind of frantic eloquence were engaged in haranguing the populace at the street-corners, others were in the churches ringing the tocsin as loudly as ever they could. Lead was cast for bullets, cartridges were rolled about. The trees on the boulevards, the urinals, the benches, the gratings, the gas-burners, everything was torn off and thrown down. Paris, that morning, was covered with barricades. The resistance which was offered was of short duration, so that at eight o'clock the people, by voluntary surrender or by force, had got possession of five barracks, nearly all the municipal buildings, the most favourable strategic points. Of its own accord, without any effort, the Monarchy was melting away in rapid dissolution, and now an attack was made on the guard-house of the Château d'Eau, in order to liberate fifty prisoners, who were not there.

Frederick was forced to stop at the entrance to the square. It was filled with groups of armed men. The Rue Saint-Thomas and the Rue Fromanteau were occupied by companies of the Line. The Rue de Valois was choked up by an enormous barricade. The smoke which fluttered about at the top of it partly opened. Men kept running overhead, making violent gestures; they vanished from sight; then the firing was again renewed. It was answered from the guard-house without anyone being seen inside. Its windows, protected by oaken window-shutters, were pierced with loop-holes; and the monument with its two storys, its two wings, its fountain on the first floor and its little door in the centre, was beginning to be speckled with white spots under the shock of the bullets. The three steps in front of it remained unoccupied.

At Frederick's side a man in a Greek cap, with a cartridge-box over his knitted vest, was holding a dispute with a woman with a Madras neckerchief round her shoulders. She said to him:

"Come back now! Come back!"

"Leave me alone!" replied the husband. "You can easily mind the porter's lodge by yourself. I ask, citizen, is this fair? I have on every occasion done my duty—in 1830, in '32, in '34, and in '39! To-day they're fighting again. I must fight! Go away!"

And the porter's wife ended by yielding to his remonstrances and to those of a National Guard near them—a man of forty, whose simple face was adorned with a circle of white beard. He loaded his gun and fired while talking to Frederick, as cool in the midst of the outbreak as a horticulturist in his garden. A young lad with a packing-cloth thrown over him was trying to coax this man to give him a few caps, so that he might make use of a gun he had, a fine fowling-piece which a "gentleman" had made him a present of.

"Catch on behind my back," said the good man, "and keep yourself from being seen, or you'll get yourself killed!"

The drums beat for the charge. Sharp cries, hurrahs of triumph burst forth. A continual ebbing to and fro made the multitude sway backward and forward. Frederick, caught between two thick masses of people, did not move an inch, all the time fascinated and exceedingly amused by the scene around him. The wounded who sank to the ground, the dead lying at his feet, did not seem like persons really wounded or really dead. The impression left on his mind was that he was looking on at a show.

In the midst of the surging throng, above the sea of heads, could be seen an old man in a black coat, mounted on a white horse with a velvet saddle. He held in one hand a green bough, in the other a paper, and he kept shaking them persistently; but at length, giving up all hope of obtaining a hearing, he withdrew from the scene.

The soldiers of the Line had gone, and only the municipal troops remained to defend the guard-house. A wave of dauntless spirits dashed up the steps; they were flung down; others came on to replace them, and the gate resounded under blows from iron bars. The municipal guards did not give way. But a wagon, stuffed full of hay, and burning like a gigantic torch, was dragged against the walls. Faggots were speedily brought, then straw, and a barrel of spirits of wine. The fire mounted up to the stones along the wall; the building began to send forth smoke on all sides like the crater of a volcano; and at its summit, between the balustrades of the terrace, huge flames escaped with a harsh noise. The first story of the Palais-Royal was occupied by National Guards. Shots were fired through every window in the square; the bullets whizzed, the water of the fountain, which had burst, was mingled with the blood, forming little pools on the ground. People slipped in the mud over clothes, shakos, and weapons. Frederick felt something soft under his foot. It was the hand of a sergeant in a grey great-coat, lying on his face in the stream that ran along the street. Fresh bands of people were continually coming up, pushing on the combatants at the guard-house. The firing became quicker. The wine-shops were open; people went into them from time to time to smoke a pipe and drink a glass of beer, and then came back again to fight. A lost dog began to howl. This made the people laugh.

Frederick was shaken by the impact of a man falling on his shoulder with a bullet through his back and the death-rattle in his throat. At this shot, perhaps directed against himself, he felt himself stirred up to rage; and he was plunging forward when a National Guard stopped him.

"'Tis useless! the King has just gone! Ah! if you don't believe me, go and see for yourself!"

This assurance calmed Frederick. The Place du Carrousel had a tranquil aspect. The Hôtel de Nantes stood there as fixed as ever; and the houses in the rear; the dome of the Louvre in front, the long gallery of wood at the right, and the waste plot of ground that ran unevenly as far as the sheds of the stall-keepers were, so to speak, steeped in the grey hues of the atmosphere, where indistinct murmurs seemed to mingle with the fog; while, at the opposite side of the square, a stiff light, falling through the parting of the clouds on the façade of the Tuileries, cut out all its windows into white patches. Near the Arc de Triomphe a dead horse lay on the ground. Behind the gratings groups consisting of five or six persons were chatting. The doors leading into the château were open, and the servants at the thresholds allowed the people to enter.

EDITH WHARTON
(1862–1937)

Born to great wealth and high social standing in New York City, Wharton was a bright and sensitive child who grew up to become a literary celebrity and one of the chief chroniclers of America's Gilded Age. Justly admired for her tragic piercing novels that typically focus on the upper echelons of American society, she was also a committed Francophile who spoke French fluently and, later in life, made France her permanent home. When her adopted country was drawn into the First World War, Wharton set about creating what she called a 'propaganda of love', a book that she hoped would win support for the French cause. In this extract, drawn from the first such work, she describes with a novelist's sharp eye the early days of French mobilisation for the Great War.

from Fighting France

It was sunset when we reached the gates of Paris. Under the heights of St. Cloud and Suresnes the reaches of the Seine trembled with the blue-pink lustre of an early Monet. The Bois lay about us in the stillness of a holiday evening, and the lawns of Bagatelle were as fresh as June. Below the Arc de Triomphe, the Champs Elysées sloped downward in a sun-powdered haze to the mist of fountains and the ethereal obelisk; and the currents of summer life ebbed and flowed with a normal beat under the trees of the radiating avenues. The great city, so made for peace and art and all humanest graces, seemed to lie by her river-side like a princess guarded by the watchful giant of the Eiffel Tower.

The next day the air was thundery with rumours. Nobody believed them, everybody repeated them. War? Of course there couldn't be war! The Cabinets, like naughty children, were again dangling their feet over the edge; but the whole incalculable weight of things-as-they-were, of the daily necessary business of living, continued calmly and convincingly to assert itself against the bandying of diplomatic words. Paris went on steadily about her midsummer business of feeding, dressing, and amusing the great army of tourists who were the only invaders she had seen for nearly half a century.

All the while, every one knew that other work was

going on also. The whole fabric of the country's seemingly undisturbed routine was threaded with noiseless invisible currents of preparation, the sense of them was in the calm air as the sense of changing weather is in the balminess of a perfect afternoon. Paris counted the minutes till the evening papers came.

They said little or nothing except what every one was already declaring all over the country. "We don't want war—*mais il faut que cela finisse!*" "This kind of thing has got to stop"; that was the only phrase one heard. If diplomacy could still arrest the war, so much the better: no one in France wanted it. All who spent the first days of August in Paris will testify to the agreement of feeling on that point. But if war had to come, then the country, and every heart in it, was ready.

At the dressmaker's, the next morning, the tired fitters were preparing to leave for their usual holiday. They looked pale and anxious—decidedly, there was a new weight of apprehension in the air. And in the rue Royale, at the corner of the Place de la Concorde, a few people had stopped to look at a little strip of white paper against the wall of the Ministère de la Marine. "General mobilization" they read—and an armed nation knows what that means. But the group about the paper was small and quiet. Passers by read the notice and went on. There were no cheers, no gesticulations: the dramatic sense of the race had already told them that the event was too great to be dramatized. Like a monstrous landslide it had fallen across the path of an orderly laborious nation, disrupting its routine, annihilating its industries, rending families apart, and burying under a heap of senseless ruin the patiently and painfully wrought machinery of civilization . . .

That evening, in a restaurant of the rue Royale, we sat at a table in one of the open windows, abreast with the street, and saw the strange new crowds stream by. In an instant we were being shown what mobilization was—a huge break in the normal flow of traffic, like the sudden rupture of a dyke. The street was flooded by the torrent of people sweeping past us to the various railway stations. All were on foot, and carrying their luggage; for since dawn every cab and taxi and motor-omnibus had disappeared. The War Office had thrown out its drag-net and caught them all in. The crowd that passed our window was chiefly composed of conscripts, the *mobilisables* of the first day, who were on the way to the station accompanied by their families and friends; but among them were little clusters of bewildered tourists, labouring along with bags and bundles, and watching their luggage pushed before them on hand-carts—puzzled inarticulate waifs caught in the cross-tides racing to a maelstrom.

In the restaurant, the befrogged and red-coated band poured out patriotic music, and the intervals between the courses that so few waiters were left to serve were broken by the ever-recurring obligation to stand up for the Marseillaise, to stand up for God Save the King, to stand up for the Russian National Anthem, to stand up again for the Marseillaise. "*Et dire que ce sont des*

Hongrois qui jouent tout cela!" a humourist remarked from the pavement.

As the evening wore on and the crowd about our window thickened, the loiterers outside began to join in the war-songs. "*Allons, debout!*"—and the loyal round begins again. "La chanson du départ!" is a frequent demand; and the chorus of spectators chimes in roundly. A sort of quiet humour was the note of the street. Down the rue Royale, toward the Madeleine, the bands of other restaurants were attracting other throngs, and martial refrains were strung along the Boulevard like its garlands of arc-lights. It was a night of singing and acclamations, not boisterous, but gallant and determined. It was Paris *badauderie* at its best.

Meanwhile, beyond the fringe of idlers the steady stream of conscripts still poured along. Wives and families trudged beside them, carrying all kinds of odd improvised bags and bundles. The impression disengaging itself from all this superficial confusion was that of a cheerful steadiness of spirit. The faces ceaselessly streaming by were serious but not sad; nor was there any air of bewilderment—the stare of driven cattle. All these lads and young men seemed to know what they were about and why they were about it. The youngest of them looked suddenly grown up and responsible: they understood their stake in the job, and accepted it.

The next day the army of midsummer travel was immobilized to let the other army move. No more wild rushes to the station, no more bribing of concierges, vain quests for invisible cabs, haggard hours of waiting in the queue at Cook's. No train stirred except to carry soldiers, and the civilians who had not bribed and jammed their way into a cranny of the thronged carriages leaving the first night could only creep back through the hot streets to their hotels and wait. Back they went, disappointed yet half-relieved, to the resounding emptiness of porterless halls, waiterless restaurants, motionless lifts: to the queer disjointed life of fashionable hotels suddenly reduced to the intimacies and make-shift of a Latin Quarter *pension*. Meanwhile it was strange to watch the gradual paralysis of the city. As the motors, taxis, cabs and vans had vanished from the streets, so the lively little steamers had left the Seine. The canal-boats too were gone, or lay motionless: loading and unloading had ceased. Every great architectural opening framed an emptiness; all the endless avenues stretched away to desert distances. In the parks and gardens no one raked the paths or trimmed the borders. The fountains slept in their basins, the worried sparrows fluttered unfed, and vague dogs, shaken out of their daily habits, roamed unquietly, looking for familiar eyes. Paris, so intensely conscious yet so strangely entranced, seemed to have had *curare* injected into all her veins.

The next day—the 2nd of August—from the terrace of the Hôtel de Crillon one looked down on a first faint stir of returning life. Now and then a taxi-cab or a private motor crossed the Place de la Concorde, carrying soldiers to the stations. Other conscripts, in detachments, tramped by on foot with bags and banners. One detachment stopped before the black-veiled statue of Strasbourg and laid a garland at her feet. In ordinary times this demonstration would at once have attracted a crowd; but at the very moment when it might have been expected to provoke a patriotic outburst it excited no more attention than if one of the soldiers had turned aside to give a penny to a beggar. The people crossing the square did not even stop to look. The meaning of this apparent indifference was obvious. When an armed nation mobilizes, everybody is busy, and busy in a definite and pressing way. It is not only the fighters that mobilize: those who stay behind must do the same. For each French household, for each individual man or woman in France, war means a complete reorganization of life. The detachment of conscripts, unnoticed, paid their tribute to the Cause and passed on . . .

Looked back on from these sterner months those early days in Paris, in their setting of grave architecture and summer skies, wear the light of the ideal and the abstract. The sudden flaming up of national life, the abeyance of every small and mean preoccupation, cleared the moral air as the streets had been cleared, and made the spectator feel as though he were reading a great poem on War rather than facing its realities.

Something of this sense of exaltation seemed to penetrate the throngs who streamed up and down the Boulevards till late into the night. All wheeled traffic had ceased, except that of the rare taxi-cabs impressed to carry conscripts to the stations; and the middle of the Boulevards was as thronged with foot-passengers as an

Italian market-place on a Sunday morning. The vast tide swayed up and down at a slow pace, breaking now and then to make room for one of the volunteer "legions" which were forming at every corner: Italian, Roumanian, South American, North American, each headed by its national flag and hailed with cheering as it passed. But even the cheers were sober: Paris was not to be shaken out of her self-imposed serenity. One felt something nobly conscious and voluntary in the mood of this quiet multitude. Yet it was a mixed throng, made up of every class, from the scum of the Exterior Boulevards to the cream of the fashionable restaurants. These people, only two days ago, had been leading a thousand different lives, in indifference or in antagonism to each other, as alien as enemies across a frontier: now workers and idlers, thieves, beggars, saints, poets, drabs and sharpers, genuine people and showy shams, were all bumping up against each other in an instinctive community of emotion. The "people," luckily, predominated; the faces of workers look best in such a crowd, and there were thousands of them, each illuminated and singled out by its magnesium-flash of passion.

I remember especially the steady browed faces of the women; and also the small but significant fact that every one of them had remembered to bring her dog. The biggest of these amiable companions had to take their chance of seeing what they could through the forest of human legs; but every one that was portable was snugly lodged in the bend of an elbow, and from this safe perch scores and scores of small serious muzzles, blunt or sharp, smooth or woolly, brown or grey or white or black or brindled, looked out on the scene with the quiet awareness of the Paris dog. It was certainly a good sign that they had not been forgotten that night.

EXILES, ADVENTURERS, AND THE LOST

GIACOMO CASANOVA
(1725–1798)

History's most famous lover was born in the Republic of Venice but spent his life wandering Europe, encountering kings, queens, popes and cardinals, artists, artisans, prostitutes, inn-keepers, and just about everyone else in between. His revealing and licentious memoirs are written in an idiosyncratic French – he chose the language after exile from Venice – and are by turns self-deprecating and self-aggrandising, provocative and sanctimonious, humorous and tragic. Often outrageous and always entertaining, they remain a vital historical document about eighteenth-century Europe. Here Casanova describes one of his first visits to Paris, and the lessons in Parisian *politesse* he received after vomiting all over himself in a public stagecoach.

from The Memoirs of Jacques Casanova de Seingalt

We left Lyons in the public diligence, and were five days on our road to Paris. Baletti had given notice of his departure to his family: they therefore knew when to expect him. We were eight in the coach and our seats were very uncomfortable, for it was a large oval in shape, so that no one had a corner. If that vehicle had been built in a country where equality was a principle hallowed by the laws, it would not have been a bad illustration. I thought it was absurd, but I was in a foreign country, and I said nothing. Besides, being an Italian, would it have been right for me not to admire everything which was French, and particularly in France?— Example, an oval diligence: I respected the fashion, but I found it detestable, and the singular motion of that vehicle had the same effect upon me as the rolling of a ship in a heavy sea. Yet it was well hung, but the worst jolting would have disturbed me less.

As the diligence undulates in the rapidity of its pace, it has been called a gondola, but I was a judge of gondolas, and I thought that there was no family likeness between the coach and the Venetian boats which, with two hearty rowers, glide along so swiftly and smoothly.

The effect of the movement was that I had to throw up whatever was on my stomach. My travelling companions thought me bad company, but they did not say so. I was in France and among Frenchmen, who know what politeness is. They only remarked that very likely I had eaten too much at my supper, and a Parisian abbé, in order to excuse me, observed that my stomach was weak. A discussion arose.

"Gentlemen," I said, in my vexation, and rather angrily, "you are all wrong, for my stomach is excellent, and I have not had any supper."

Thereupon an elderly man told me, with a voice full of sweetness, that I ought not to say that the gentlemen were wrong, though I might say that they were not right, thus imitating Cicero, who, instead of declaring to the Romans that Catilina and the other conspirators were dead, only said that they had lived.

"Is it not the same thing?"

"I beg your pardon, sir, one way of speaking is polite, the other is not." And after treating me to a long dissertation on politeness, he concluded by saying, with a smile, "I suppose you are an Italian?"

"Yes, I am, but would you oblige me by telling me how you have found it out?"

"Oh! I guessed it from the attention with which you have listened to my long prattle."

Everybody laughed, and, I, much pleased with his eccentricity, began to coax him. He was the tutor of a young boy of twelve or thirteen years who was seated near him. I made him give me during the journey lessons in French politeness, and when we parted he took me apart in a friendly manner, saying that he wished to make me a small present.

"What is it?"

"You must abandon, and, if I may say so, forget, the particle *non*, which you use frequently at random. *Non* is not a French word; instead of that unpleasant monosyllable, say, *Pardon*. *Non* is equal to giving the lie: never say it, or prepare yourself to give and to receive swordstabs every moment."

"I thank you, monsieur, your present is very precious, and I promise you never to say *non* again."

During the first fortnight of my stay in Paris, it seemed to me that I had become the most faulty man alive, for I never ceased begging pardon. I even thought, one evening at the theatre, that I should have a quarrel for having begged somebody's pardon in the wrong place. A young fop, coming to the pit, trod on my foot, and I hastened to say,—

"Your pardon, sir."

"Sir, pardon me yourself."

"No, yourself."

"Yourself!"

"Well, sir, let us pardon and embrace one another!"

The embrace put a stop to the discussion.

One day during the journey, having fallen asleep from fatigue in the inconvenient gondola, someone pushed my arm.

"Ah, sir! look at that mansion!"

"I see it; what of it?"

"Ah! I pray you, do you not find it . . ."

"I find nothing particular; and you?"

"Nothing wonderful, if it were not situated at a distance of forty leagues from Paris. But here! Ah! would my *badauds* of Parisians believe that such a beautiful mansion can be found forty leagues distant from the metropolis? How ignorant a man is when he has never travelled!"

"You are quite right."

That man was a Parisian and a *badaud* to the backbone, like a Gaul in the days of Cæsar.

But if the Parisians are lounging about from morning till night, enjoying everything around them, a foreigner like myself ought to have been a greater *badaud* than they! The difference between us was that, being accustomed to see things such as they are, I was astonished at seeing them often covered with a mask which changed their nature, while their surprise often arose from their suspecting what the mask concealed.

What delighted me, on my arrival in Paris, was the magnificent road made by Louis XV., the cleanliness of the hotels, the excellent fare they give, the quickness of the service, the excellent beds, the modest appearance of the attendant, who generally is the most accomplished girl of the house, and whose decency, modest manners, and neatness, inspire the most shameless libertine with respect. Where is the Italian who is pleased with the effrontery and the insolence of the hotel-waiters in Italy? In my days, people did not know in France what it was to overcharge; it was truly the home of foreigners. True, they had the unpleasantness of often witnessing acts of odious despotism, *lettres de cachet,* etc.; it was the despotism of a king. Since that time the French have the despotism of the people. Is it less obnoxious?

Vernon Lee (Violet Paget)
(1856–1935)

A French-born British writer, Vernon Lee lived an unconventional life dedicated to art and beauty. Raised by English parents in a cosmopolitan society in Florence, she showed a precocious command of literary and art history, as well as a prodigious flair for refined expression. Perhaps justly fearing the prejudice of small-minded contemporary readers, she took on a masculine pen name to ease the path of her writings. She achieved some fame in her lifetime through her uncanny ghost stories, elegant travel books and challenging essays on aesthetics and literary history. She writes here with touching melancholy about passing briefly through Paris.

from Genius Loci

The day after that I was in Paris. How delicate and brilliant! The trees on the boulevards still bright green, and flags hanging everywhere; an open-air, almost Southern, life lasting deep into the bright summer night: the mere ordinary illumination of the Place de la Concorde looking at a distance like an Aladdin's palace; the river, with its red and green lights reflected among the big wharf trees, and the swishing lit-up steamers, giving the impression of a colossal Fête de Nuit.

But even more charming was Paris in the early morning, a morning touched with autumn crispness, as I drove along the quays, alas! to the Gare de Lyon. Such a fresh renovated morning; the air still hazy, and all objects, rippling poplars and shining slate roofs, hazy, vague after the night's refreshment. Water was being sprinkled all along the pavements; the long book boxes on the quays were beginning to be opened; a breeze, to cool the coming day, was rising along the river trough. But, alas, alas! that day was to be spent by me in hurrying away again out of France.

Arnold Bennett
(1867–1931)

Famous enough to have an omelette named after him, Arnold Bennett was adored by countless devoted readers who devoured the regular fruits of his seemingly indefatigable travail. At the same time, he was dismissed by high-minded critics and detested by literary radicals like Virginia Woolf for what they considered his outmoded literary ideals. There was a touch of classism to these critiques. Born into a middle-class family in Staffordshire, Bennett worked his way to London, first as a legal clerk, later as a magazine editor, and finally as a full-time author. He moved to Paris in 1903, where he fell in love with the city and its people – his first wife was French – along with the countless peculiarities that make Paris the city of so many dreams. The following passages describe the spectacle of a Parisian evening which begins, naturally, with French cuisine before going on to the Opera for a Russian ballet.

from Paris Nights and Other Impressions of Places and People

Sylvain's is the only good restaurant in the centre of Paris where you can dine in the open air, that is to say, in the street. Close by, the dark, still mass of the Opéra rises hugely out of the dusk and out of the flitting traffic at its base. Sylvain's is full of diners who have no eyes to see beyond the surfaces of things.

By virtue of a contract made between Sylvain's and the city, the diners are screened off from the street and from the twentieth century by a row of high potted evergreens. Pass within the screen, and you leave behind you the modern epoch. The Third Republic recedes; the Second Empire recedes; Louis-Philippe has never been, nor even Napoleon; the Revolution has not begun to announce itself. You are become suddenly a *grand seigneur*. Every gesture and tone of every member of the *personnel* of Sylvain's implores your excellency with one word:

"Deign!"

It is curious that while a modern shopkeeper who sells you a cigar or an automobile or a quarter of lamb does not think it necessary to make you a noble of the *ancien régime* before commencing business, a shopkeeper who sells you cooked food could not omit this preliminary without losing his self-respect. And it is the more curious since all pre-democratic books of travel are full of the cheek of these particular shopkeepers. Such tales of old travellers could scarcely be credited, in spite of their unison, were it not that the ancient tradition of rapacious insolence still survives in wild and barbaric spots like the cathedral cities of England.

Your excellency, attended by his gentlemen-in-waiting (who apparently never eat, never want to eat), in the intervals of the ceremonious collation will gaze with interest at the Opéra, final legacy of the Empire to the Republic. A great nation owes it to itself to possess a splendid opera-palace. Art must be fostered. The gracious amenities of life must be maintained. And this is the State's affair. The State has seen to it. The most gorgeous building in Paris is not the legislative chamber, nor the hall of the University, nor the clearing-house of charity. It is the Opéra. The State has paid for it, and the State pays every year for its maintenance. That is, the peasant chiefly pays. There is not a peasant in the farthest corner of France who may not go to bed at dark comforted by the thought that the Opéra in Paris is just opening its cavalry-sentinelled doors, and lighting its fifteen thousand electric candles, and that he is helping to support all that. Paris does not pay; the *habitués* of the Opéra do not pay; the yawning tourists do not pay; the grandiose classes do not pay. It is the nation, as a nation, that accepts the burden, because the encouragement of art is a national duty. (Moreover, visiting monarchs have to be diverted.) Of one sort or another, from the tenor to the vendor of programmes, there are twelve hundred priests and priestesses of art in the superb building. A few may be artists. But it is absolutely certain that all are bureaucrats.

The Opéra is the Circumlocution Office. The Opéra is a State department. More, it is probably the most characteristic of all the State departments, and the most stubbornly reactionary. The nominal director, instead of being omnipotent and godlike, is only a poor human being whose actions are the resultant of ten thousand forces that do not fear him. The Opéra is above all the theatre of secret influences. Every mystery of its enormous and wasteful inefficiency can be explained either by the operation of the secret influence or by the operation of the bureaucratic mind. If the most tedious operas are played the most often, if the stage is held by singers who cannot sing, if original artists have no chance there, if the blight of a flaccid perfunctoriness is upon nearly all the performances, if astute mothers can sell the virginity of their dancing daughters to powerful purchasers in the wings, the reason is a reason of State. The Opéra is the splendid prey of the high officers of State. If such a one wants an evening's entertainment, or a mistress, or to get rid of a mistress, the Opéra is there, at his disposition. The *foyer de la danse* is the most wonderful seraglio in the western world, and it is reserved to the Government and to subscribers. Thus is art fostered, and for this does the peasant pay.

Nevertheless the Opéra is a beautiful and impressive sight in the late, warm dusk of June. Against the deep purple sky the monument stands up like a mountain; and through its innumerable windows—holes in the floor of heaven—can be glimpsed yellow clusters of candelabra and perspectives of marble pillars and frescoed walls. And at the foot of the gigantic *façade* little brightly coloured figures are running up the steps and disappearing eagerly within: they are the world of fashion, and they know that they are correct and that the Opéra is the Opéra.

George Orwell
(1903–1950)

Before he was George Orwell – literary firebrand in love with lucidity, anti-totalitarian campaigner and a steadfast believer in democratic socialism, ferocious journalist and legendary author of *Animal Farm* (1946) and *Nineteen Eighty-Four* (1949) – Eric Arthur Blair was a young man in search of material for future books. Working as an Imperial policeman in colonial Burma led to *Burmese Days* (1934). But before that was *Down and Out in Paris and London* (1933), Orwell's debut and the book for which he selected his now legendary pen name. Inspired by his experiences 'tramping' in London and working as a *plongeur* (or dishwasher) in Paris, Orwell's slim classic is a bruising, vivid description of grinding poverty, daily humiliation and minor consolations in the French capital's Latin Quarter. Here he recounts the gruelling invisible work that takes place in a Parisian restaurant kitchen.

from Down and Out in Paris and London

The *patron* had engaged me as kitchen *plongeur*; that is, my job was to wash up, keep the kitchen clean, prepare vegetables, make tea, coffee and sandwiches, do the simpler cooking, and run errands. The terms were, as usual, five hundred francs a month and food, but I had no free day and no fixed working hours. At the Hotel X. I had seen catering at its best, with unlimited money and good organisation. Now, at the Auberge, I learned how things are done in a thoroughly bad restaurant. It is worth describing, for there are hundreds of similar restaurants in Paris, and every visitor feeds in one of them occasionally.

I should add, by the way, that the Auberge was not the ordinary cheap eating-house frequented by students and workmen. We did not provide an adequate meal at less than twenty-five francs, and we were picturesque and artistic, which sent up our social standing. There were the indecent pictures in the bar, and the Norman decorations—sham beams on the walls, electric lights done up as candlesticks, "peasant" pottery, even a mounting-block at the door—and the *patron* and the head waiter were Russian officers, and many of the customers titled Russian refugees. In short, we were decidedly chic.

Nevertheless, the conditions behind the kitchen door

were suitable for a pigsty. For this is what our service arrangements were like:

The kitchen measured fifteen feet long by eight broad, and half this space was taken up by the stoves and tables. All the pots had to be kept on shelves out of reach, and there was only room for one dustbin. This dustbin used to be crammed full by midday, and the floor was normally an inch deep in a compost of trampled food.

For firing we had nothing but three gas-stoves, without ovens, and all joints had to be sent out to the bakery.

There was no larder. Our substitute for one was a half-roofed shed in the yard, with a tree growing in the middle of it. The meat, vegetables and so forth lay there on the bare earth, raided by rats and cats.

There was no hot water laid on. Water for washing up had to be heated in pans, and, as there was no room for these on the stoves when meals were cooking, most of the plates had to be washed in cold water. This, with soft soap and the hard Paris water, meant scraping the grease off with bits of newspaper.

We were so short of saucepans that I had to wash each one as soon as it was done with, instead of leaving them till the evening. This alone wasted probably an hour a day.

Owing to some scamping of expense in the installation, the electric light usually fused at eight in the evening. The *patron* would only allow us three candles in the kitchen, and the cook said three were unlucky, so we had only two.

Our coffee-grinder was borrowed from a *bistro* near by, and our dustbin and brooms from the concierge. After the first week a quantity of linen did not come back from the wash, as the bill was not paid. We were in trouble with the inspector of labour, who had discovered that the staff included no Frenchmen; he had several private interviews with the *patron*, who, I believe, was obliged to bribe him. The electric company was still dunning us, and when the duns found that we would buy them off with *apéritifs*, they came every morning. We were in debt at the grocery, and credit would have been stopped, only the grocer's wife (a moustachio'd woman of sixty) had taken a fancy to Jules, who was sent every morning to cajole her. Similarly I had to waste an hour every day haggling over vegetables in the Rue du Commerce, to save a few centimes.

These are the results of starting a restaurant on insufficient capital. And in these conditions the cook and I were expected to serve thirty or forty meals a day, and would later on be serving a hundred. From the first day it was too much for us. The cook's working hours were from eight in the morning till midnight, and mine from seven in the morning till half past twelve the next morning—seventeen and a half hours, almost without a break. We never had time to sit down till five in the afternoon, and even then there was no seat except the top of the dustbin. Boris, who lived near by and had not to catch the last Metro home, worked from eight in the morning till two the next morning—eighteen hours a day, seven days a week. Such hours, though not usual, are nothing extraordinary in Paris.

Life settled at once into a routine that made the Hotel X. seem like a holiday. Every morning at six I drove myself out of bed, did not shave, sometimes washed, hurried up to the Place d'Italie and fought for a place on the Metro. By seven I was in the desolation of the cold, filthy kitchen, with the potato skins and bones and fishtails littered on the floor, and a pile of plates, stuck together in their grease, waiting from overnight. I could not start on the plates yet, because the water was cold, and I had to fetch milk and make coffee, for the others arrived at eight and expected to find coffee ready. Also, there were always several copper saucepans to clean. Those copper saucepans are the bane of a *plongeur's* life. They have to be scoured with sand and bunches of chain, ten minutes to each one, and then polished on the outside with Brasso. Fortunately the art of making them has been lost and they are gradually vanishing from French kitchens, though one can still buy them second-hand.

When I had begun on the plates the cook would take me away from the plates to begin skinning onions, and when I had begun on the onions the *patron* would arrive and send me out to buy cabbages. When I came back with the cabbages the *patron's* wife would tell me to go to some shop half a mile away and buy a pot of rouge; by the time I came back there would be more vegetables waiting, and the plates were still not done. In this way our incompetence piled one job on another throughout the day, everything in arrears.

Till ten, things went comparatively easily, though we were working fast, and no one lost his temper. The cook would find time to talk about her artistic nature, and say did I not think Tolstoi was *épatant*, and sing in a fine soprano voice as she minced beef on the board. But at ten the waiters began clamouring for their lunch, which they had early, and at eleven the first customers would be arriving. Suddenly everything became hurry and bad temper. There was not the same furious rushing and yelling as at the Hotel X., but an atmosphere of muddle, petty spite and exasperation. Discomfort was at the bottom of it. It was unbearably cramped in the kitchen, and dishes had to be put on the floor, and one had to be thinking constantly about not stepping on them. The cook's vast buttocks banged against me as she moved to and fro. A ceaseless, nagging chorus of orders streamed from her:

"Unspeakable idiot! How many times have I told you not to bleed the beetroots? Quick, let me get to the sink! Put those knives away; get on with the potatoes. What have you done with my strainer? Oh, leave those potatoes alone. Didn't I tell you to skim the *bouillon*? Take that can of water off the stove. Never mind the washing up, chop this celery. No, not like that, you fool, like this. There! Look at you letting those peas boil over! Now get to work and scale these herrings. Look, do you call this plate clean? Wipe it on your apron. Put that salad on the floor. That's right, put it where I'm bound to step in it! Look out, that pot's boiling over! Get me down that saucepan. No, the other one. Put this on the grill. Throw those potatoes away. Don't waste time, throw them on the floor. Tread them in. Now throw down some sawdust; this floor's like a skating-rink. Look, you fool, that steak's burning! *Mon Dieu*, why did they send me an idiot for a *plongeur*? Who are you talking to? Do you realise that my aunt was a Russian countess?" etc., etc., etc.

This went on till three o'clock without much variation, except that about eleven the cook usually had a *crise de nerfs* and a flood of tears. From three to five was a fairly slack time for the waiters, but the cook was still busy, and I was working my fastest, for there was a pile of dirty plates waiting, and it was a race to get them done, or partly done, before dinner began. The washing up was doubled by the primitive conditions—a cramped draining-board, tepid water, sodden cloths, and a sink that got blocked once in an hour. By five the cook and I were feeling unsteady on our feet, not having eaten or sat down since seven. We used to collapse, she on the dustbin and I on the floor, drink a bottle of beer, and apologise for some of the things we had said in the morning. Tea was what kept us going. We took care to have a pot always stewing, and drank pints during the day.

At half past five the hurry and quarrelling began again, and now worse than before, because everyone was tired out. The cook had a *crise de nerfs* at six and another at nine; they came on so regularly that one could have told the time by them. She would flop down on the dustbin, begin weeping hysterically, and cry out that never, no, never had she thought to come to such a life as this; her nerves would not stand it; she had studied music at Vienna; she had a bedridden husband to support, etc., etc. At another time one would have been sorry for her, but, tired as we all were, her whimpering voice merely infuriated us. Jules used to stand in the doorway and mimic her weeping. The *patron's* wife nagged, and Boris and Jules quarrelled all day, because Jules shirked his work, and Boris, as head waiter, claimed the larger share of the tips. Only the second day after the restaurant opened, they came to blows in the kitchen over a two-franc tip, and the cook and I had to separate them. The only person who never forgot his manners was the *patron*. He kept the same hours as the rest of us, but he had no work to do, for it was his wife who really managed things. His sole job, besides ordering the supplies, was to stand in the bar smoking cigarettes and looking gentlemanly, and he did that to perfection.

The cook and I generally found time to eat our dinner between ten and eleven o'clock. At midnight the cook would steal a packet of food for her husband, stow it under her clothes, and make off, whimpering that these hours would kill her and she would give notice in the morning. Jules also left at midnight, usually after a dispute with Boris, who had to look after the bar till two. Between twelve and half past I did what I could to finish the washing up. There was no time to attempt doing the work properly, and I used simply to rub the grease off the plates with table-napkins. As for the dirt on the floor, I let it lie, or swept the worst of it out of sight under the stoves.

At half past twelve I would put on my coat and hurry out. The *patron*, bland as ever, would stop me as I went down the alley-way past the bar. "*Mais, mon cher monsieur,* how tired you look! Please do me the favour of accepting this glass of brandy."

He would hand me the glass of brandy as courteously as though I had been a Russian duke instead of a *plongeur*. He treated all of us like this. It was our compensation for working seventeen hours a day.

As a rule the last Metro was almost empty—a great advantage, for one could sit down and sleep for a quarter of an hour. Generally I was in bed by half past one. Sometimes I missed the train and had to sleep on the floor of the restaurant, but it hardly mattered, for I could have slept on cobblestones at that time.

LA VIE D'ARTISTE

OUIDA
(1839–1908)

Born Maria Louise Ramé in Bury St Edmunds, England, Ouida achieved fame first as a writer and then as a pleasure-seeker whose extravagant lifestyle left her overwhelmed with debts. Her many novels, which mixed sharp social commentary with melodramatic plots and sentimental twists, sold well and earned her a small fortune, which she frittered away in a life of luxury across Europe's more expensive hotels and restaurants. Lapsed copyrights, diminishing popularity and waning literary output, combined with her flamboyant tastes, meant that she finished life in relative poverty. This excerpt is drawn from one of her popular short stories in which she gives an idealized version of the artist's life in Paris, where financial matters prove secondary to youth and beauty.

from A Dog of Flanders and Other Stories

And a painter in Paris, even though he starve on a few sous a day, can have so much that is lovely and full of picturesque charm in his daily pursuits: the long, wondrous galleries full of the arts he adores; the "*réalité de l'idéal*" around him in that perfect world; the slow, sweet, studious hours in the calm wherein all that is great in humanity alone survives; the trance—half adoration, half aspiration, at once desire and despair—before the face of the Mona Lisa; then, without, the streets so glad and so gay in the sweet, living sunshine; the quiver of green leaves among gilded balconies; the groups at every turn about the doors; the glow of colour in market-place and peopled square; the quaint gray piles in old historic ways; the stones, from every one of which some voice from the imperishable Past cries out; the green and silent woods, the little leafy villages, the winding waters garden girt; the forest heights, with the city gleaming and golden in the plain;—all these are his.

With these,—and youth,—who shall dare say the painter is not rich,—ay, though his board be empty and his cup be dry?

I had not loved Paris,—I, a little imprisoned rose, caged in a clay pot, and seeing nothing but the sky-line of the roofs. But I grew to love it, hearing from René and from Lili of all the poetry and gladness that Paris made possible in their young and burdened lives, and which could have been thus possible in no other city of the earth.

City of Pleasure you have called her, and with truth; but why not also City of the Poor? For what city, like herself, has remembered the poor in her pleasure, and given to them, no less than to the richest, the treasure of her laughing sunlight, of her melodious music, of her gracious hues, of her million flowers, of her shady leaves, of her divine ideals?

WILLIAM MAKEPEACE THACKERAY
(1811–1863)

Best known today as the author of *Vanity Fair* (1848), a satirical classic of English fiction, Thackeray was widely admired in his own time for his acerbic wit and talent for caricature. Born in British India, he returned to England before inheriting his father's fortune, which he promptly squandered. After trying his hand at art in Paris, he fell into journalism in London, where he eventually made a name for himself thanks to his sharp, humorous prose and his popular, serialized novels. In this extract, Thackeray writes about Parisian artists with an intriguing mixture of cynicism and respect.

ON THE FRENCH SCHOOL OF PAINTING:

WITH APPROPRIATE ANECDOTES, ILLUSTRATIONS,
AND PHILOSOPHICAL DISQUISITIONS.

IN A LETTER TO MR. MACGILP, OF LONDON.

The three collections of pictures at the Louvre, the Luxembourg, and the Ecole des Beaux Arts, contain a number of specimens of French art, since its commencement almost, and give the stranger a pretty fair opportunity to study and appreciate the school. The French list of painters contains some very good names—no very great ones, except Poussin (unless the admirers of Claude choose to rank him among great painters),—and I think the school was never in so flourishing a condition as it is at the present day. They say there are three thousand artists in this town alone: of these a handsome minority paint not merely tolerably, but well understand their business; draw the figure accurately; sketch with cleverness; and paint portraits, churches, or restaurateurs' shops, in a decent manner.

To account for a superiority over England—which, I think, as regards art, is incontestable—it must be remembered that the painter's trade, in France, is a very good one; better appreciated, better understood, and, generally, far better paid than with us. There are a dozen excellent schools in which a lad may enter here, and, under the eye of a practised master, learn the apprenticeship of his art at an expense of about ten pounds a year. In England there is no school except the Academy, unless the student can afford to pay a very large sum, and place himself under the tuition of some particular artist. Here, a young man, for his ten pounds, has all sorts of accessory instruction, models, &c.; and has further, and for nothing, numberless incitements to study his profession which are not to be found in England:— the streets are filled with picture-shops, the people themselves are pictures walking about; the churches, theatres, eating-houses, concert-rooms are covered with pictures: Nature itself is inclined more kindly to him, for the sky is a thousand times more bright and beautiful, and the sun shines for the greater part of the year. Add to this, incitements more selfish, but quite as powerful: a French artist is paid very handsomely; for five hundred a year is much where all are poor; and has a rank in society rather above his merits than below them, being caressed by hosts and hostesses in places where titles are laughed at and a baron is thought of no more account than a banker's clerk.

The life of the young artist here is the easiest, merriest, dirtiest existence possible. He comes to Paris, probably at sixteen, from his province; his parents settle forty pounds a year on him, and pay his master; he establishes himself in the Pays Latin, or in the new quarter of Notre Dame de Lorette (which is quite peopled with painters); he arrives at his atelier at a tolerably early hour, and labours among a score of companions as merry and poor as himself. Each gentleman has his favourite tobacco-pipe; and the pictures are painted in the midst of a cloud of smoke, and a din of puns and choice French slang, and a roar of choruses, of which no one can form an idea who has not been present at such an assembly.

You see here every variety of *coiffure* that has ever been known. Some young men of genius have ringlets hanging over their shoulders—you may smell the tobacco with which they are scented across the street; some have straight locks, black, oily, and redundant; some have *toupets* in the famous Louis-Philippe fashion; some are cropped close; some have adopted the present mode—which he who would follow must, in order to do so, part his hair in the middle, grease it with grease, and gum it with gum, and iron it flat down over his ears; when arrived at the ears, you take the tongs and make a couple of ranges of curls close round the whole head,—such curls as you may see under a gilt three-cornered hat, and in her Britannic Majesty's coachman's state wig.

This is the last fashion. As for the beards, there is no end to them; all my friends, the artists, have beards who can raise them; and Nature, though she has rather stinted the bodies and limbs of the French nation, has been very liberal to them of hair, as you may see by the following specimen. Fancy these heads and beards under all sorts of caps—Chinese caps, mandarin caps, Greek skull-caps, English jockey caps, Russian or Kuzzilbash caps, middle-age caps (such as are called, in heraldry, caps of maintenance), Spanish nets, and striped worsted nightcaps. Fancy all the jackets you have ever seen, and you have before you, as well as the pen can describe, the costumes of these indescribable Frenchmen.

In this company and costume the French student of art passes his days and acquires knowledge; how he passes his evenings, at what theatres, at what *guinguettes*, in company with what seducing little milliner, there is no need to say; but I knew one who pawned his coat to go to a carnival ball, and walked abroad very cheerfully in his *blouse*, for six weeks, until he could redeem the absent garment.

These young men (together with the students of sciences) comport themselves towards the sober citizen pretty much as the German *bursch* towards the *philister*, or as the military man, during the empire, did to the *pékin:*—from the height of their poverty they look down upon him with the greatest imaginable scorn—a scorn, I think, by which the citizen seems dazzled, for his respect for the arts is intense. The case is very different in England, where a grocer's daughter would think she made a misalliance by marrying a painter, and where a literary man (in spite of all we can say against it) ranks below that class of gentry composed of the apothecary, the attorney, the wine-merchant, whose positions, in country towns at least, are so equivocal. As for instance, my friend, the Rev. James Asterisk, who has an undeniable pedigree, a paternal estate, and a living to boot, once dined in Warwickshire, in company with several squires and parsons of that enlightened county. Asterisk, as usual, made himself extraordinarily agreeable at dinner, and delighted all present with his learning and wit. "Who is that monstrous pleasant fellow?" said one of the squires. "Don't you know?" replied another. "It's Asterisk, the author of so-and-so, and a famous contributor to such-and-such a magazine. "Good heavens!" said the squire, quite horrified; "a literary man! I thought he had been a gentleman!"

Another instance. M. Guizot, when he was minister here, had the grand hotel of the ministry, and gave entertainments to all the great *de par le monde*, as Brantôme says, and entertained them in a proper ministerial magnificence. The splendid and beautiful Duchess of Dash was at one of his ministerial parties; and went, a fortnight afterwards, as in duty bound, to pay her respects to M.

GERTRUDE STEIN
(1874–1946)

Famous for her magnificent art collection and intense social life in Paris, Gertrude Stein's legendary salon welcomed painters and writers such as Pablo Picasso and Ernest Hemingway long before they were stars. Her fabled art collection, meanwhile, gathered outstanding works of experimental painting by artists like Matisse at a time when buyers were few and far between. But Stein was much more than a gifted host and canny collector, or the author of the phrase 'a lost generation'. She was also a literary pioneer. Her distinctive style had an undeniable impact on Hemingway's seminal prose, and her fizzing inventive books relentlessly challenged literary conventions. Stein was also devoted to her life partner, Alice Toklas, from whose perspective she wrote a beguilingly eccentric 'autobiography', excerpted here.

from The Autobiography of Alice B. Toklas

Before I tell about the guests I must tell what I saw. As I said being invited to dinner I rang the bell of the little pavilion and was taken into the tiny hall and then into the small dining room lined with books. On the only free space, the doors, were tacked up a few drawings by Picasso and Matisse. As the other guests had not yet come Miss Stein took me into the atelier. It often rained in Paris and it was always difficult to go from the little pavilion to the atelier door in the rain in evening clothes, but you were not to mind such things as the hosts and most of the guests did not. We went into the atelier which opened with a yale key the only yale key in the quarter at that time, and this was not so much for safety, because in those days the pictures had no value, but because the key was small and could go into a purse instead of being enormous as French keys were. Against the walls were several pieces of large Italian renaissance furniture and in the middle of the room was a big renaissance table, on it a lovely inkstand, and at one end of it note-books neatly arranged, the kind of note-books French children use, with pictures of earthquakes and explorations on the outside of them. And on all the walls right up to the ceiling were pictures. At one end of the room was a big cast iron stove that Hélène came in and filled with a rattle, and in one corner of the room was a large table on which were horseshoe nails and pebbles and little pipe cigarette holders which one looked at curiously but did not touch, but which turned out later to be accumulations from the pockets of Picasso and Gertrude Stein. But to return to the pictures. The pictures were so strange that one quite instinctively looked at anything rather than at them just at first. I have refreshed my memory by looking at some snap shots taken inside the atelier at that time. The chairs in the room were also all Italian renaissance, not very comfortable for short-legged people and one got the habit of sitting on one's legs. Miss Stein sat near the stove in a lovely high-backed one and she peacefully let her legs hang, which was a matter of habit, and when any one of the many visitors came to ask her a question she lifted herself up out of this chair and usually replied in French, not just now. This usually referred to something they wished to see, drawings which were put away, some German had once spilled ink on one, or some other not to be fulfilled desire. But to return to the pictures. As I say they completely covered the white-washed walls right up to the top of the very high ceiling. The room was lit at this time by high gas fixtures. This was the second stage. They had just been put in. Before that there had only been lamps, and a stalwart guest held up the lamp while the others looked. But gas had just been put in and an ingenious American painter named Sayen, to divert his mind from the birth of his first child, was arranging some mechanical contrivance that would light the high fixtures by themselves. The old landlady extremely conservative did not allow electricity in her houses and electricity was not put in until 1914, the old landlady by that time too old to know the difference, her house agent gave permission. But this time I am really going to tell about the pictures.

It is very difficult now that everybody is accustomed to everything to give some idea of the kind of uneasiness one felt when one first looked at all these pictures on these walls. In those days there were pictures of all kinds there, the time had not yet come when there were only Cézannes, Renoirs, Matisses and Picassos, nor as it was even later only Cézannes and Picassos. At that time there was a great deal of Matisse, Picasso, Renoir, Cézanne but there were also a great many other things. There were two Gauguins, there were Manguins, there was a big nude by Valloton that felt like only it was not like the Odalisque of Manet, there was a Toulouse–Lautrec. Once about this time Picasso looking at this and greatly daring said, but all the same I do paint better than he did. Toulouse–Lautrec had been the most important of his early influences. I later bought a little tiny picture by Picasso of that epoch. There was a portrait of Gertrude Stein by Valloton that might have been a David but was not, there was a Maurice Denis, a little Daumier, many Cézanne water colours, there was in short everything, there was even a little Delacroix and a moderate sized Greco. There were enormous Picassos of the Harlequin period, there were two rows of Matisses, there was a big portrait of a woman by Cézanne and some little Cézannes, all these pictures had a history and I will soon tell them. Now I was confused and I looked and I looked and I was confused. Gertrude Stein and her brother were so accustomed to this state of mind in a guest that they paid no attention to it. Then there was a sharp tap at the atelier door. Gertrude Stein opened it and a little dark dapper man came in with hair, eyes, face, hands and feet all very much alive. Hullo Alfy, she said, this is Miss Toklas. How do you do Miss Toklas, he said very solemnly. This was Alfy Maurer an old habitué of the house. He had been there before there were these pictures, when there were only Japanese prints, and he was among those who used to light matches to light up a little piece of the Cézanne portrait. Of course you can tell it is a finished picture, he used to explain to the other American painters who came and looked dubiously, you can tell because it has a frame, now whoever heard of anybody framing a canvas if the picture isn't finished. He had followed, followed, followed always humbly always sincerely. A few minutes after Alfy came in there was a violent knock at the door and, dinner is ready, from Hélène. It's funny the Picassos have not come, said they all, however we won't wait at least Hélène won't wait. So we went into the court and into the pavilion, and dining room and began dinner. It's funny, said Miss Stein, Pablo is always promptness itself, he is never early and he is never late, it is his pride that punctuality is the politeness of kings, he even makes Fernande punctual. Of course he often says yes when he has no intention of doing what he says yes to, he can't say no, no is not in his vocabulary and you have to know whether his yes means yes or means no, but when he says a yes that means yes and he did about tonight he is always punctual. These were the days before automobiles and nobody worried about accidents. We had just finished the first course when there was a quick patter of footsteps in the court and Hélène opened the door before the bell rang. Pablo and Fernande as everybody called them at that time walked in. He, small, quick moving but not restless, his eyes having a strange faculty of opening wide and drinking in what he wished to see. He had the isolation and movement of the head of a bull-fighter at the head of their procession. Fernande was a tall beautiful woman with a wonderful big hat and a very evidently new dress, they were both very fussed. I am very upset, said Pablo, but you know very well Gertrude I am never late but Fernande had ordered a dress for the vernissage tomorrow and it didn't come. Well here you are anyway, said Miss Stein, since it's you Hélène won't mind. And we all sat down. I was next to Picasso who was silent and then gradually became peaceful. Alfy paid compliments to Fernande and she was soon calm and placid. After a little while I murmured to Picasso that I liked his portrait of Gertrude Stein. Yes, he said, everybody says that she does not look like it but that does not make any difference, she will, he said. The conversation soon became lively it was all about the opening day of the salon indépendant which was the great event of the year. Everybody was interested in all the scandals that would or would not break out. Picasso never exhibited but as his followers did and there were a great many stories connected with each follower the hopes and fears were vivacious.

While we were having coffee, footsteps were heard in the court quite a number of footsteps and Miss Stein rose and said, don't hurry, I have to let them in. And she left.

When we went into the atelier there were already quite a number of people in the room, scattered groups, single and couples all looking and looking. Gertrude Stein sat by the stove talking and listening and getting up to open the door and go up to various people talking and listening. She usually opened the door to the knock and the usual formula was, de la part de qui venez-vous, who is your introducer. The idea was that anybody could come but for form's sake and in Paris you have to have a formula, everybody was supposed to be able to mention the name of somebody who had told them about it. It was a mere form, really everybody could come in and as at that time these pictures had no value and there was no social privilege attached to knowing any one there, only those came who really were interested. So as I say anybody could come in, however, there was the formula. Miss Stein once in opening the door said as she usually did by whose invitation do you come and we heard an aggrieved voice reply, but by yours, madame. He was a young man Gertrude Stein had met somewhere and with whom she had had a long conversation and to whom she had given a cordial invitation and then had as promptly forgotten.

The room was soon very very full and who were they all. Groups of Hungarian painters and writers, it happened that some Hungarian had once been brought and the word had spread from him throughout all Hungary, any village where there was a young man who had ambitions heard of 27 rue de Fleurus and then he lived but to get there and a great many did get there. They were always there, all sizes and shapes, all degrees of wealth and poverty, some very charming, some simply rough and every now and then a very beautiful young peasant. Then there were quantities of Germans, not too popular because they tended always to want to see anything that was put away and they tended to break things and Gertrude Stein has a weakness for breakable objects, she has a horror of people who collect only the unbreakable. Then there was a fair sprinkling of Americans, Mildred Aldrich would bring a group or Sayen, the electrician, or some painter and occasionally an architectural student would accidentally get there and then there were the habitués, among them Miss Mars and Miss Squires whom Gertrude Stein afterwards immortalised in her story of Miss Furr and Miss Skeene. On that first night Miss Mars and I talked of a subject then entirely new, how to make up your face. She was interested in types, she knew that there were femme decorative, femme d'intérieur and femme intrigante; there was no doubt that Fernande Picasso was a femme decorative, but what was Madame Matisse, femme d'intérieur, I said, and she was very pleased. From time to time one heard the high Spanish whinnying laugh of Picasso and gay contralto outbreak of Gertrude Stein, people came and went, in and out. Miss Stein told me to sit with Fernande. Fernande was always beautiful but heavy in hand. I sat, it was my first sitting with a wife of a genius.

Before I decided to write this book my twenty-five years with Gertrude Stein, I had often said that I would write, The wives of geniuses I have sat with. I have sat with so many. I have sat with wives who were not wives, of geniuses who were real geniuses. I have sat with real wives of geniuses who were not real geniuses. I have sat with wives of geniuses, of near geniuses, of would be geniuses, in short I have sat very often and very long with many wives and wives of many geniuses.

As I was saying Fernande, who was then living with Picasso and had been with him a long time that is to say they were all twenty-four years old at that time but they had been together a long time, Fernande was the first wife of a genius I sat with and she was not the least amusing. We talked hats. Fernande had two subjects hats and perfumes. This first day we talked hats. She liked hats, she had the true French feeling about a hat, if a hat did not provoke some witticism from a man on the street the hat was not a success. Later on, once in Montmartre she and I were walking together. She had on a large yellow hat and I had on a much smaller blue one. As we were walking along a workman stopped and called out, there go the sun and the moon shining together. Ah, said Fernande to me with a radiant smile, you see our hats are a success.

Miss Stein called me and said she wanted to have me

meet Matisse. She was talking to a medium sized man with a reddish beard and glasses. He had a very alert although slightly heavy presence and Miss Stein and he seemed to be full of hidden meanings. As I came up I heard her say, Oh yes but it would be more difficult now. We were talking, she said, of a lunch party we had in here last year. We had just hung all the pictures and we asked all the painters. You know how painters are, I wanted to make them happy so I placed each one opposite his own picture, and they were happy so happy that we had to send out twice for more bread, when you know France you will know that that means that they were happy, because they cannot eat and drink without bread and we had to send out twice for bread so they were happy. Nobody noticed my little arrangement except Matisse and he did not until just as he left, and now he says it is a proof that I am very wicked, Matisse laughed and said, yes I know Mademoiselle Gertrude, the world is a theatre for you, but there are theatres and theatres, and when you listen so carefully to me and so attentively and do not hear a word I say then I do say that you are very wicked. Then they both began talking about the vernissage of the independent as every one else was doing and of course I did not know what it was all about. But gradually I knew and later on I will tell the story of the pictures, their painters and their followers and what this conversation meant.

Later I was near Picasso, he was standing meditatively. Do you think, he said, that I really do look like your president Lincoln. I had thought a good many things that evening but I had not thought that. You see, he went on, Gertrude, (I wish I could convey something of the simple affection and confidence with which he always pronounced her name and with which she always said, Pablo. In all their long friendship with all its sometimes troubled moments and its complications this has never changed.) Gertrude showed me a photograph of him and I have been trying to arrange my hair to look like his, I think my forehead does. I did not know whether he meant it or not but I was sympathetic. I did not realise then how completely and entirely American was Gertrude Stein. Later I often teased her, calling her a general, a civil war general of either or both sides. She had a series of photographs of the civil war, rather wonderful photographs and she and Picasso used to pore over them. Then he would suddenly remember the Spanish war and he became very Spanish and very bitter and Spain and America in their persons could say very bitter things about each other's country. But at this my first evening I knew nothing of all this and so I was polite and that was all.

And now the evening was drawing to a close. Everybody was leaving and everybody was still talking about the vernissage of the independent. I too left carrying with me a card of invitation for the vernissage. And so this, one of the most important evenings of my life, came to an end.

ERNEST HEMINGWAY
(1899–1961)

The Hemingway myth describes a daring adventurer and hard-drinking man's man who married four times, survived two plane crashes, adored bullfighting and boxing, and wrote with scrupulous force about love, death and war. After his suicide, revelations of his long private suffering and poor personal behaviour, along with changing social attitudes, have troubled this view. For many, though, key aspects of the myth survive: Hemingway remains the inimitable, if much imitated, father of modern writing, whose fondness for parsimony was codified in his famous 'iceberg theory' of literary style. And he continues to be closely associated with Paris in the 1920s. In this extract, drawn from his posthumously published memoir about the period, Hemingway evokes one of his first ever visits to the iconic bookshop Shakespeare and Company, whose owner, Sylvia Beach, had let the young, cash-strapped writer borrow books without charge.

from A Moveable Feast

Home in the rue du Cardinal Lemoine was a two-room flat that had no hot water and no inside toilet facilities except an antiseptic container, not uncomfortable to anyone who was used to a Michigan outhouse. With a fine view and a good mattress and springs for a comfortable bed on the floor, and pictures we liked on the walls, it was a cheerful, gay flat. When I got there with the books I told my wife about the wonderful place I had found.

'But Tatie, you must go by this afternoon and pay,' she said.

'Sure I will,' I said. 'We'll both go. And then we'll walk down by the river and along the quais.'

'Let's walk down the rue de Seine and look in all the galleries and in the windows of the shops.'

'Sure. We can walk anywhere and we can stop at some new café where we don't know anyone and nobody knows us and have a drink.'

'We can have two drinks.'

'Then we can eat somewhere.'

'No. Don't forget we have to pay the library.'

'We'll come home and eat here and we'll have a lovely meal and drink Beaune from the co-operative you can see right out of the window there with the price of the Beaune on the window. And afterwards we'll read and then go to bed and make love.'

'And we'll never love anyone else but each other.'

'No. Never.'

'What a lovely afternoon and evening. Now we'd better have lunch.'

'I'm very hungry,' I said. 'I worked at the café on a café crème.'

'How did it go, Tatie?'

'I think all right. I hope so. What do we have for lunch?'

'Little radishes, and good *foie de veau* with mashed potatoes and an endive salad. Apple tart.'

'And we're going to have all the books in the world to read and when we go on trips we can take them.'

'Would that be honest?'

'Sure.'

'Does she have Henry James too?'

'Sure.'

'My,' she said. 'We're lucky that you found the place.'

'We're always lucky,' I said, and like a fool I did not knock on wood. There was wood everywhere in that apartment to knock on, too.

Permissions Acknowledgements

MACMILLAN COLLECTOR'S LIBRARY

**Own the world's great works of literature in
one beautiful collectible library**

Designed and curated to appeal to book lovers everywhere,
Macmillan Collector's Library editions are small enough to
travel with you and striking enough to take pride of place
on your bookshelf. These much-loved literary classics
also make the perfect gift.

Beautifully produced with gilt edges, a ribbon marker,
bespoke illustrated cover and real cloth binding, every
Macmillan Collector's Library hardback adheres to the
same high production values.

Discover something new or cherish your favourite
stories with this elegant collection.

**Macmillan Collector's Library:
own, collect, and treasure**

Discover the full range at
macmillancollectorslibrary.com